WATERLOO

THE CAMPAIGN OF 1815

I am delighted that Monsieur Jacques Logie's
excellent book has been translated for an English
version. I am happy to commend it to anyone
who is interested in this most important period in
European History.

His Grace the Duke of Wellington
KG., LVO., OBE., MC., DL

BY THE SAME AUTHOR:

1830. De la Régionalisation à l'Indépendence, Duculot, 1980
Waterloo. L'évitable défaite, Duculot, 1984
Waterloo, 1815. L'Europe face à Napoléon (sous la direction de Jacques LOGIE), Crédit Communal, 1990
Napoléon. La dernière bataille, Racine, 1998
Les magistrats des Cours et Tribunaux de Belgique, 1795-1814, Droz, 1998

THIS WORK HAS BEEN WRITTEN WITH THE SUPPORT
OF THE COMMISSIARIAT GÉNÉRAL AU TOURISM OF
THE REGION OF WALLONIA AND OF THE 'BATAILLE DE
WATERLOO 1815' INTERCOMMUNAL ASSOCIATION

JACQUES LOGIE

WATERLOO
THE CAMPAIGN OF 1815

SPELLMOUNT

Note concerning the titles of works:
The titles of all paintings, engravings, etc illustrating the text have
been rendered into English.
The titles of the books, papers, articles, etc used as references have, on the
other hand, been left in their original tongue, since it is, of course, under
those titles that the researcher would locate them in libraries or archives.

First published by Éditions Racines, 2003
Rue du Chatelain, 49, B-1050 Bruxelles
www.racine.be

Copyright © Éditions Racines, 2003

British Library Cataloguing in Publication Data:
A catalogue record for this book is available
from the British Library

ISBN 1-86227-328-6

This Edition published in the UK in 2006
by
Spellmount Limited
The Mill, Brimscombe Port
Stroud, Gloucestershire, GL5 2QG

Tel: 01453 883300
Fax: 01453 883233
E-mail: enquiries@spellmount.com
Website: www.spellmount.com

1 3 5 7 9 8 6 4 2

Printed in Great Britain

CONTENTS

PREFACE

It is one of life's paradoxes that the most significant dates to be found in the histories are those of battles, while so many events marking progress and humanity are often forgotten. This is not to say that it is in these latter events only that the evolution of peoples has been forged.

In this context, it cannot be denied that the clash at Waterloo stands as a date of major importance.

Today, it has become the scene of a surprising confrontation, that of the imaginary and the real.

It is doubtless associated with the ending of an epic. An epic which concerns not only a man out of the common mould who imposed himself on history, with all his excesses, his qualities and his defects, but also a coalition which defended its ideals with honesty and sincerity.

But the 'myth' of Waterloo also seems to have arisen out of its outcome, which took so long to decide, and out of the many testimonies of which it has been the subject. The battle has spawned not only numerous strategic, political – and even philosophical – analyses, but also fictional works. All equally underline the importance of 18 June 1815.

I congratulate M Jacques Logie for his courage and ambition in producing another contribution to our understanding of the battle and its effects, in the form of a wide-ranging book which truly meets our expectations, while also introducing aspects hitherto unpublished.

It also comes at a time when the site itself is the subject of major projects designed to enhance it and to increase the information presented to the hundreds of thousands of tourists (or pilgrims) who visit it each year.

This work has succeeded if it enables all who read it to immerse themselves once more in this titanic combat, to acquire a better understanding of the stakes involved and to measure Waterloo's importance in the origins of the construction of modern Europe.

SERGE KUBLA
Minister of Tourism
Burgomaster of Waterloo

To Professor Jean Tulard,
who encouraged the renewal of interest in Napoléonic studies

FOREWORD

Every day, hundreds of visitors from the four corners of the world come to Waterloo for the first time.

Has the glory of the vanquished been eclipsed by the fame of the conquerers? Or is it simply an intuitive belief that the battle on 18 June 1815 marked the end of an epoch and the beginning of a new era in European history?

The controversies about the causes of the defeat or the reasons for the victory have been the source of those intellectual and emotional games which take the form of imagining the different courses history might have taken.

The melancholy evocation of a vanished world, the fascination for an already distant past, but one which seems to be brought closer by the legend of gleaming military glory than by the desolate present-day images of the reality of war; are these perhaps the reasons for a persistent interest in this great battle of the early nineteenth century?

Behind these parade ground formalities, these preconceptions, lies hidden a very different historical and human reality, the discovery of which forms the purpose of this book.

Jacques Logie, Plancenoit

PART ONE

THE 1815 CAMPAIGN

Napoléon addresses his troops before the battle, a scene from Sergei Bondarchuk's film *Waterloo* (1970)

1. THE HISTORICAL BACKGROUND TO THE 1815 CAMPAIGN

The battle of Waterloo marks the end of the Wars of Revolution and of the Empire.

From 1789 onwards, two notions took root in France which were to result in the overthrow of the international order. The right of peoples to decide their own fate, based on the principle of national sovereignty, constituted a new element in European human rights and would serve as a justification for the seizure of territory by France. The doctrine of natural frontiers was also advanced in support of French expansionism. It was expressed by Danton, speaking to the Convention on 21 January 1793: 'The borders of France are determined by nature; we shall advance to the four corners of the horizon, to the Rhine, to the sea, to the Alps and to the Pyrenees. It is there that the boundaries of our Republic must be set.'

Such were the grounds for the annexation of the Austrian Netherlands and the left bank of the Rhine, and for the creation of the sister republics in Holland, Switzerland and Italy.

This expansionist policy ran up against the determined opposition of Great Britain: 'England will never agree that France is entitled to assume the right, whenever it wishes and under the pretext of natural law – of which it is to be the sole judge – to set aside the political system of Europe, which has been established by solemn treaties. Furthermore, the British government [...] will never view with indifference a circumstance where France poses as the ruler of the Netherlands, directly or indirectly, or as the general arbitrator of European rights and liberties. If France truly wishes to live in peace and friendship with England, she must show herself to be willing to renounce her ideas of aggression and aggrandisement and to remain within her own borders, without insulting other governments, without disturbing their peace and without violating their rights[1].'

These principles never ceased to guide the British government throughout the next twenty years and show why Great Britain was the instigator of every coalition which was formed for the containment of French expansion.

After his overthrow of the *Directoire* on 18 Brumaire year VIII, (9 November 1799) Napoléon Bonaparte continued to pursue the same foreign policy.

The period introduced by the Peace of Lunéville with Austria (9 February 1801) and the Peace of Amiens with Great Britain (25 March 1802) enabled him to consolidate his power internally, but peace with Britain was frail and was denounced a year later. The French refusal to sign a trading agreement with London and the refusal of the British to give up the island of Malta led to the breakdown, in which Great Britain took the initiative.

Napoléon responded by occupying the Electorate of Hanover, which was the British king's personal fief and by preparing, at Boulogne, for the invasion of the British Isles. This latter project was brought to an end by the destruction of the French fleet by Nelson at Trafalgar (21 October 1805).

The annexation of Piedmont (September 1802), the occupation of the Swiss Republic, on which Bonaparte proceeded to impose the Act of Mediation (February 1803), the growing French influence within the German Diet and, above all, the abduction and execution of the Duc d'Enghien (March 1804) drove Austria, Russia and Great Britain into the formation of the Third Coalition.

On 2 December 1805, the victory of Austerlitz over the combined Austrian and Russian armies opened the door for Napoléonic imperialism in Europe. Bonaparte, who had had himself anointed emperor a year earlier, imposed on Austria the Treaty of Pressburg, depriving it of three million people and obliging it to cede not only Venice, Istria and Dalmatia, but also Swabia and the Tyrol.

In the first six months of 1806, Napoléon transformed the Electorates of Wurtemburg and Bavaria into kingdoms, toppled the Bourbons of Naples from their throne, conferring it on his brother Joseph, and transformed the Dutch Republic into the Kingdom of Holland for his brother Louis. At the same time, he replaced the thousand-year-old Holy Roman Empire by a Confederation of the Rhine, in which French influence predominated.

In 1806, Prussia, which Napoléon had for a time considered as an ally, joined with Great Britain, Saxony, Russia and Sweden to form the Fourth Coalition. The Prussian defeats at Jena and Auerstadt (14 October 1806) set off a debacle. The Polish campaign against the Russians, half-checked at Eylau (8 February 1807), then followed by victory against the Russians at Friedland (14 June 1807) resulted in the Treaty of Tilsit.

Draconian conditions were imposed on Prussia: she was henceforth to be confined to four provinces, Brandenburg, Pomerania, Prussia and Silesia, as well as suffering the imposition of a considerable war indemnity. The vanquished Russia now became France's ally, while forced to accept the radical changes which Napoléon was still to apply in Germany.

From the territories seized from Prussia between the Elbe and the Rhine, together with a part of Hanover, he created the kingdom of Westphalia, which he gave to his younger brother, Jérôme. The Elector of Saxony, elevated to the status of king, reigned over the Grand Duchy of Warsaw, comprising those parts of Poland taken from Prussia. The Confederation of the Rhine now stretched as far as the Vistula. Napoléon had thus re-established the German empire for his own benefit, since the Confederation, composed of client states, was from now on obliged to supply him with both subsidies and fighting troops.

Great Britain constituted Napoléon's remaining foe. Having failed to vanquish her in the field, he embarked on economic strangulation by prohibiting the sale on the Continent of British-manufactured products – the Continental Blockade. In this respect, Napoléon pursued the policy of the *Directoire*, but extended it to the whole of the continent.

The Emperor had laid the foundations for this on 21 November 1806, with the Decree of Berlin. Its provisions were strengthened by the further Decree of Milan (17 December 1807), which henceforth proposed to treat any vessel sailing to or from Great Britain as a prize of war. In order to ensure compliance with these draconian measures, which could be effective only if they were strictly applied, Napoléon was drawn into a new policy of expansion.

In 1810, he annexed Holland, where his brother Louis was refusing to bring ruin on his subjects by observing the blockade. At the same time, all the towns along the German coast, from the mouth of the Ems to the Elbe estuary, and including the free ports of Bremen and Hamburg, became French *départements*. With the Pope continuing to adopt a neutral stance, the Papal states had suffered the same fate in 1809.

The kingdom of Portugal, a traditional market for British goods since the beginning of the eighteenth century, was occupied by a French army at the end of 1807. A few months later, at Bayonne, Napoléon, by questionable means, obtained the abdication of the Spanish king, Charles IV, and installed on the throne in Madrid his brother Joseph, who was replaced in Naples by his brother-in-law Murat, in the manner of a game of dominoes.

This *coup de force* provoked a general uprising in the country, supported by British troops, under the command of first Sir John Moore and later Sir Arthur Wellesley. There followed a war which endured for five years, which ended with the evacuation of the Peninsular by the French and in which they had expended some of their best troops.

Taking advantage of Napoléon's absence in Spain, whence he had gone in the autumn of 1808 to bring succour to his brother Joseph, Austria entered the war, supported by British subsidies, but was defeated at Wagram in July 1809. The peace signed in Vienna on 14 October 1809 was catastrophic for the Emperor Francis I, who lost four million subjects, with Galacia being added to the Grand Duchy of Warsaw; Salzburg and the upper valley of the Inn being ceded to Bavaria; and Carinthia, Carniola, civil Croatia and military Croatia, with Dalmatia, Dubrovnik (Kotor) and Istria (Trieste), now comprising the seven Illyrian provinces of the French Empire.

Napoléon was at the pinnacle of his power. Never since the days of Charlemagne had a nation so dominated Europe. The French Empire covered one hundred and thirty *départements*; it included a third of Italy, a part of Switzerland, the Low Countries, Holland, Rhenish Prussia and the entire

German coastal fringe. Napoléon was king of Italy, the mediator of the Swiss Confederation and the protector of the Confederation of the Rhine. The kingdoms of Naples, Westphalia and Spain, governed by blood relations, were dependent states. Sweden, long a faithful ally of Great Britain, submitted in its turn to the blockade, while a French Marshal, Bernadotte, was chosen as his heir by the ageing king (August 1810).

That same year Napoléon, having discarded his first wife, Joséphine de Beauharnais, obtained the hand of the Archduchess Marie-Louise, daughter of the Emperor of Austria, Francis I, and niece of the last Queen of France, Marie-Antoinette. Now master of Europe, he saw himself through this union as taking his place within the circle of the ancient monarchies.

The continent now enjoyed two years of peace. He whom the British called 'the Corsican Ogre' seemed to be replete and relishing his power. With the birth of a son, on whom was conferred the title of King of Rome (20 March 1811), the future of the 'fourth dynasty' seemed assured.

The break with Russia, where the application of the continental blockade had aroused deep discontent, decided Napoléon on the invasion of that country, with the object of imposing his will on Alexander I. The Emperor's objective was a major victory, followed by negotiation. However, despite the victory of Borodino (7 September 1812) and the entry of the French army into Moscow, the Tsar rejected all negotiation. The Imperial army was obliged to mount a retreat through the bitter conditions of an earlier-than-usual winter. The losses were enormous: of the 600,000 men, including the allied contingents, who entered Russia in July, scarcely 70,000 recrossed the Niemen. The Grand Army had lost its reputation of invincibility and it was never to be able to recover its former power.

This imperial defeat persuaded Prussia to rejoin the victorious troops of Alexander I and Austria to propose an armistice. Napoléon, turning to conscription, built a new army, but left his seasoned troops in Spain. In the spring of 1813 he gained the victories of Bautzen and Lützen. The Congress of Prague (5 July – 10 August) followed, at which the Allies offered peace, with France retaining its natural boundaries, but with its rejection by Napoléon hostilities were resumed and Austria joined the coalition.

The battle of Leipzig, which the Germans dubbed the Battle of the Nations, sealed the fate of the Napoléonic Empire. The defeated French armies were forced to retire across the Rhine, while Spain was abandoned, following defeat at Vittoria. France was exhausted; its arsenals were empty, as were the coffers of the *Trésor Impérial*, hitherto replenished by the war indemnities imposed on the vanquished.

At the start of 1814 the Allies crossed the Rhine, while Wellington gave battle before Toulouse. Despite an heroic campaign in France, conducted with derisory resources, Napoléon was unable to prevent the coalition forces from marching on Paris, which capitulated on 30 March. On 2 April 1814, the Imperial Senate, casting its sycophancy to one side, voted for the Emperor's downfall, his abdication following on 6 April. On the same day the Senate recalled to the throne of France the younger brother of Louis XVI, who assumed the title of Louis XVIII.

The Treaty of Paris, signed on 30 May 1814, returned France to its boundaries of 1791. The Convention of Fontainbleau (11 April) granted Napoléon I dominion over the Island of Elba – an operetta kingdom for the former master of Europe – an annual pension of two million francs and a small bodyguard.

In France, the blunders committed by Louis XVIII's entourage became the cause of increasing discontent and led to plotting by both the Bonapartists and the liberals.

Napoléon on his island grieved for the absence of the Empress Marie-Louise and even more that of his son, while assailed by a hazy sense of danger, real or imagined, from assassination or deportation to a more distant island. In the end, rumours concerning disagreements between the former coalition partners persuaded the Emperor to attempt the recovery of his throne.

On 1 March 1815, having slipped past the British navy, Napoléon landed at Golfe Juan at the head of a thousand men. Without firing a shot, he rallied to his side the soldiers sent to intercept him and roused the enthusiasm of the people all along his route from Grenoble to Auxerre, so that 'the Eagle flew from steeple to steeple as far as the very towers of Notre-Dame itself'. On 20 March the Emperor entered Paris, whence Louis XVIII had just hastily fled, taking refuge at Ghent and protected by British troops stationed in the new kingdom of the Netherlands.

Restored to power by the popular discontent against the Bourbons, Napoléon's very nature would not allow him to govern by relying upon the support of people who, in many regions, had rediscovered the revolutionary and patriotic fervour of 1792. Once installed in the Tuileries, he determined that he alone should hold the reins of power. But the intention of the opposition, which had forced his abdication in 1814, was to use the situation to establish a liberal Empire in the place of the absolute authority wielded by Napoléon during the years of victory.

He was therefore obliged to make concessions to the bourgeoisie. These were embodied in the supplementary Act to the Constitutions of the Empire, drafted by Benjamin Constant. This liberal text provided in particular for ministerial responsibility, the publication of parliamentary debates, the suppression of censorship and judgment with respect to the press and freedom of worship, but created a chamber of hereditary peers. The plebiscite by which the limited and property-owning electorate was invited to approve this text constituted something of a check. No-votes were rare, but there were many abstentions.

The results of the elections to the Chamber of Deputies gave further evidence of this difficulty. The bourgeoisie, in whose hands alone political power rested, revealed its lack of warmth for the regime. Of the six hundred and twenty-nine deputies, there were scarcely a hundred Bonapartists, lost among a crushing majority of 'liberals' of many origins, who were determined to clip the Eagle's wings. The election of Lanjuinais to the presidency of the Chamber of Deputies exemplified this unspoken disapproval, which was ready to change to open hostility. The scarcely veiled threat of a revolt by the political class when the Emperor was absent had an inevitable influence on his decisions in the course of his last brief campaign.

Bonaparte had seized power by a military *coup d'état* fifteen years earlier; it would have to be on the field of battle that his destiny would be decided.

The news that Napoléon had left Elba shot through the Congress of Vienna like a bolt of lightning. On 13 March, the Powers signed a declaration which affirmed their view that, by his escape, 'Napoléon Buonaparte has placed himself outside civil and human relationships; and that, as the enemy and disturber of world peace, he has rendered himself open to public justice²'.

This was an out and out declaration of war. In the course of the next few weeks, Napoléon occupied himself in trying to defuse this new and threatening coalition. By turns, he attempted to isolate the Tsar, by revealing a secret treaty signed between Louis XVIII, Austria and Great Britain against Russia, then to woo Austria by holding up the prospect of his abdication in favour of the young King of Rome, and finally to convince everyone of his acceptance of France's new frontiers.

But the Powers did not allow themselves to be moved by these overtures, whose sincerity was of a wholly tactical nature. A Council of War held at Vienna on 19 April and presided over by the Tsar fixed 1 June for the start of the campaign, later to be postponed until early July.

Napoléon, recognising the inevitability of conflict, had, even while attempting to negotiate, begun to return to a war footing an army which had been cut by half under Louis XVIII. After the recall of soldiers from leave, the embodiment of volunteers and the levying of the class of 1815, Napoléon had at his disposal about 178,000 regular troops.

With the mobilisation of the National Guard and veterans and the embodiment of 'federated' workers from Paris and Lyons, he was able to provide about 435,000 men for the garrisoning of fortresses – less well equipped but generally imbued with a certain spirit of patriotism. The measures he had taken gave him to hope that, by the autumn, something approaching 800,000 would be available.

However, the coalition had also mustered considerable forces, with a plan for the coordinated invasion of France. In the north, the Anglo-Dutch army (99,000 men under Wellington) and the Prussian army of the Lower Rhine (117,000 men under Blücher) were to march on Laon and Paris. In the east, a Russian army (150,000 men), commanded by Barclay de Tolly and Winzingerode, and an Austrian army (210,000 men) under the orders of Schwarzenberg, attacking through Sarrebrück and Basle respectively, would converge on the capital via Nancy and Langres. On the Lombardy plain, 50,000 Austro-Piedmontais were preparing to march on Lyon, while 25,000 Neapolitans were making for the Var. Beyond the Pyrenees, a Hispano-Portuguese army was threatening the Bayonne region. In all, nearly 650,000 men were completing their preparations for invasion. When he compared the forces in the field, Napoléon must have been minded to temporise and adopt a defensive stance, since time was on his side.

Since the investment of the fortresses to the north and east was tying down a significant proportion of the opposing forces, the Emperor was entitled to hope, with a larger and more coherent army than that of 1814, for a repeat of the exploits of the campaign in France. Paris, transformed into a fortified camp, should hold firm this time, under the personal command of the Minister for War, Marshal Davout, a fine soldier who made no bones about his support for this plan. Nevertheless, at the end of May Napoléon chose to strike the first blow, with a surprise attack on the Anglo-Dutch and Prussian forces lying in the Netherlands.

The motives which drove the Emperor to this course seem to have been political. The defensive plan implied the abandonment of the regions where patriotism was highest: Alsace, Lorraine and Champagne. From a psychological standpoint, the advance of the enemy armies could only re-ignite royalist sedition in the Midi and the West, dampen patriotic enthusiasm and strengthen the latent opposition of the deputies.

The Emperor also cherished the illusion of separating Great Britain from the coalition by destroying the British army in the Netherlands. Such a victory, he reasoned, would bring down the Tory government of Castlereagh and return the Whigs to power. The latter, with little taste for imposing the Bourbons on France, would be satisfied with the acceptance by Napoléon of the Treaty of Paris. However, the passing by the House of Commons on 25 May of the supply vote requested by Castlereagh for the new campaign should have shown Napoléon the solidity and the resolution of the Conservative majority, which remained inflexibly hostile.

Deployment of the British troops in squares, a scene from the Sergei Bondarchuk film *Waterloo* (1970)

In order to understand a battle fought in the year 1815, in which the methods used were those pertaining at the end of the eighteenth century, it is necessary to be familiar with the types of weapon available and their employment by the three traditional arms: infantry, cavalry and artillery.

THE INFANTRY AND ITS WEAPONS

The musket

The chief weapon of the infantry in the field was the flintlock rifle, or musket, which was loaded through the muzzle and which fired spherical lead balls of large calibre.

These projectiles had a low muzzle velocity (320 metres per second for the French musket of 1777). Their killing power was achieved by the fact that the man hit absorbed the whole of the kinetic energy available at the moment of impact. The ball often remained in the body.

The muskets were very crude weapons so far as sighting was concerned. Though the weapon might be fitted with a foresight, there was no corresponding backsight, and the firer had to be content with running his eye along the barrel.

This was reflected in the firing effectiveness. According to a British colonel of that time, Hanger: 'A soldier's musket, if not exceedingly ill-bored [as many of them were] will strike the figure of a man at 80 yards; it may even at a 100; but a soldier must be very unfortunate indeed who shall be wounded by a common musket at 150 yards, provided his antagonist aims at him; and as to firing at a man at 200 yards with a common musket, you may just as well fire at the moon and have the same hopes of hitting your object.[3]'

To the inherent inaccuracy of the weapon must be added the random firing conditions: there were many misfires,

The French musket was first introduced in 1777 and slightly changed in 1801. It weighed 4.65 kg and was 1.53 m long. Its bore was 17.78 mm and it fired a ball weighing 21 grams. On account of its size, it was colloquially known as 'the five foot six inch clarinet'.

The British musket was officially called the British Land Pattern but was familiarly known as the 'Brown Bess'. It was in service from 1750 to 1850, had a bore of 19.3 mm and fired a ball weighing 32 grams. It was less accurate than the French weapon, since the windage of its barrel (i.e. the clearance between the wall and the shot) was greater. This was done deliberately to facilitate loading, thus tending to increase the rate of fire, although at the expense of range and accuracy.

The carbine was shorter than the musket, had a bore of 16 mm and fired a ball weighing 23 grams. The ball was forced into the barrel with a mallet, its diameter being the same as, or slightly greater than the bore of the rifled barrel. Much more accurate than the musket, the carbine was effective up to 180 metres and still formidable up to 270 metres, but its low rate of fire made it above all a skirmisher's weapon.

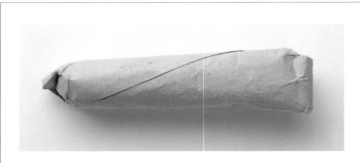

Reproduction cartridge

The rate of fire varied from army to army. While the French foot-soldier fired one round per minute, his British counterpart, better trained and wielding a weapon which was easier to reload, fired two and the Prussian (who cut his cartridge open with a blade pressed against the breech) fired three.

In addition, on account of imperfections in the lock, misfires were four times more frequent with the French musket than with the British one.

between 15 and 20 % in wet weather, while the contours of the ground and the smoke which spread very rapidly across the battlefield also had to be contended with. In combat, the firing effectiveness at 90 metres lay between 6 and 15%, which led seasoned troops to hold their fire until their opponents were no more than 40 or 50 metres away.

The black powder used for firing produced clouds of smoke, as this re-enactment of musket firing shows. The same effect was caused by artillery.

The rate of fire was low. The infantryman had to tear open the cartridge, made of stout paper, with his teeth, then pour the powder into the barrel, tamp it down with an iron rammer, spit the ball into the barrel, push it against the plug, pour more powder into the pan and close the latter, finally bringing the weapon up the shoulder and firing. In the French army the individual soldier was issued with 50 cartridges, this figure being 60 in the British army, except for the rifle battalions where the men were given 80.

The carbine

The Baker carbine was the only weapon with a rifled barrel used during the campaign and was to be found only in the British army, its issue being restricted to the British 95th Regiment of Foot (Riflemen) and to a few light companies of the King's German Legion (KGL)[4].

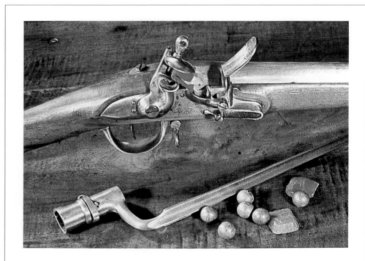

A 1777 model musket, with bayonet, balls and gun-flints.

The bayonet

All muskets were equipped with a bayonet, 40 cm long, triangular in section, which was fixed to the end of the musket by means of a socket. It provided the infantryman with a means for hand-to-hand fighting, either during the final phase of an attack or defensively against cavalry or infantry attacks. The Baker carbine was equipped with a long sword-bayonet, fixed to the barrel in a way which allowed it to be easily detached and used alone.

Fighting with the bayonet was rare since, as was noted by General Hughes, '… it was often the fear inspired by the bayonet, rather than its actual use, which decided the outcome of the engagement'. The army surgeon George J Guthrie asserted that '… regiments charging with the bayonet never met face-to-face, for the excellent reason that as soon as one of the two adversaries was sufficiently close to cause any damage the other would turn about and retreat'.

The partiality for bayonet charges attributed to the French dated from the early years of the Revolution, when the enthusiasm of the volunteers made up for their deficiencies in the use of firearms.

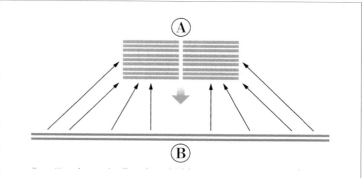

A. French battalion of approximately 850 men, comprising 6 companies formed in columns by divisions, with a front of 2 companies, 45 men in each. In the front line: 180 muskets.

B. British battalion of 500 men in 2 ranks, front rank kneeling, second rank standing. Fire power: 500 muskets.

The 28th at Quatre-Bras, after Captain Jones (Philip J Haythornthwaite, *Wellington's Military Machine*, p.91).

The fighting techniques of the infantry

Except for the skirmishers, who fought individually, musket firing was carried out in volleys. The first volley was generally fired by battalions, which in the British army were drawn up in two ranks, and in three ranks in the French and Prussian armies. After that, firing was by companies or half-companies, on account of the smoke.

The formation in two ranks used by the British allowed each soldier to use his musket, which was not the case for the French infantrymen, where the third rank was unable to take part in the firing. Drawn up in this way, a British battalion of 500 men, deployed over a front of 150 metres,

fired 1,000 to 1,500 shots per minute, while an advancing French column comprising, as at Waterloo, 180 men in line, could fire a volley of only 360 rounds while halted 50 metres from the enemy. This superiority in firepower played an essential role during the campaign in the Peninsular and at Waterloo.

The redoubtable effectiveness of the British foot was very well described by the future Marshal Bugeaud, who fought in the Spanish campaign: 'The British generally took up good defensive positions, which were carefully selected and as a rule on sloping ground, behind whose crest a large proportion of their men would find cover. The bombardment, as was usual, opened the proceedings. Then without further delay, with no proper reconnaissance of the position and without checking whether the terrain offered any possibility for sideways or turning movements, we advanced straight to our front, taking the bull by the horns.

'When we got up to about a thousand metres from the British lines, the men started to become anxious and excited; their pace began to change and become a shade hastier and more disorderly. The British on the other hand, stood silent and impassive with weapons grounded, like a long red wall, daunting in appearance and making no little impression on the new recruits. With the gap closing rapidly, cries of *"Vive l'Empereur"* and *"En avant, à la baïonnette!"* arose from our midst. Some men hung their shakos on the ends of their muskets and the pace quickened to a run; the ranks began to intermingle and many soldiers started to open fire as they ran. And all the while, the British red line, ever silent and unmoving, even when we were no more than three hundred metres away, seemed quite unaware of the storm which was about to break upon it.

'The contrast was striking; more than one of us began to reflect that the enemy's fire, so long withheld, was going to be extremely unpleasant when it did finally break out. Our ardour began to cool: the moral effect, so irresistible in action, of this seemingly unshakeable composure in the face of the disorder which sought to replace by noise that which it lacked in steadiness, weighed heavily on our hearts. At that moment of agonized expectation, the British line made a quarter of a turn and raised their muskets to the fir-

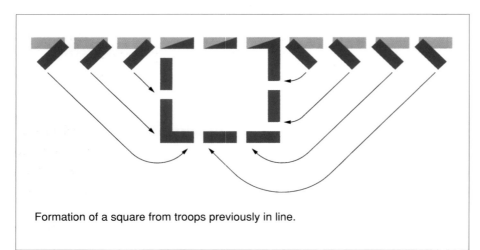

Formation of a square from troops previously in line.

ing position. Many of our men found themselves nailed to the spot by some indefinable reaction, while they opened fire in a hesitant manner. The enemy's reply, a simultaneous and precise volley, burst upon us like a thunderbolt, with deadly effect. Decimated, we wavered, reeling under the blow and trying to regain our equilibrium. As we tried to do so, the enemy's silence was broken by three fearsome Hurrahs. As the third rang out, they were upon us, driving us before them in disorder. Yet, to our great astonishment, they did not pursue their advantage beyond a few hundred metres, but calmly returned and reformed their line, to await the next attack[6].'

In both defence and attack, the armies deployed skirmishers to their front. They fought in line, but spaced several metres apart, using the ground for cover and taking one another's place after firing. These fighting methods were those used by the Colonists in the American War of Independence and it was only after that time that they made their appearance in the armies of Europe. Sometimes amounting to as much as 25 % of the strength of the French army, but fewer amongst the other belligerents, their fire was both deadly and demoralising to the troops in the line who were exposed to their shooting, while they themselves, mobile and isolated, were in little danger from the inaccurate weapons of their opponents.

On the defensive, the infantry generally deployed in line, in order to achieve the maximum firepower against the attacker. But faced with a cavalry attack, they formed a square, a difficult manoeuvre requiring intense training[7]. A battalion of 500 men formed up in a square presented a hedge of bayonets 20 metres square against which no more than fifteen horsemen could deliver a frontal assault. The centre of the square was occupied by the officers and the musicians grouped around the colours. Although this formation was extremely effective against a cavalry attack, it became perilous if the latter was accompanied by horse artillery and supported by the infantry. The majority of squares were of battalion strength, with the men in two or three ranks. They were disposed in a chequerboard pattern or in an oblique line, to provide each other with supporting fire.

When attacking, the infantry marched in battle, or open order. This type of formation, which demanded strict alignment, was slow and not very practicable on broken ground, while it required troops who were well-trained. This was the arrangement used for the attack by the British brigades led by Adam and Mitchell in the evening at Waterloo.

In the French army, deployment in columns came to be used more and more during the Imperial wars, since it was most suited for unseasoned conscripts.

Once it had come within range of the enemy – fifty metres away – the infantry spread out, the first few ranks discharged their weapons, and then charged with the bayonet. The effect of these columns arriving with the shock of a battering ram was considerable, most often accentuated by being supported by the fire of the horse artillery, which opened fire on the enemy line from close range.

If the infantry was threatened by a cavalry attack on the open plain, it either formed a square or close columns, the outer files of which faced outwards on all sides.

CAVALRY

In those days the cavalry comprised two broad classes: the first consisted of the hussars, the light cavalry and the lancers[8] (found only in the French or Prussian army, in the latter being known as Uhlans), whose principal functions were reconnaissance and pursuit; the second was represented by the heavy cavalry, usually composed of dragoons, which were used as shock troops against the infantry. The French army also included regiments of *cuirassiers* and *carabiniers*, who wore breast-plates, which did not provide complete protection against musket balls.

The horseman's principal weapon was the sabre, either curved or straight, but all of them also carried a pistol and a *mousqueton*, or carbine. This latter was a shortened musket, which enabled a rider either to take part in skirmishes on foot or to fire on infantry which had formed square.

On the battlefield, the cavalry coordinated its activities with those of the infantry. If the infantry opened the attack, the cavalry stationed itself several hundred feet to the rear, on the flank of the attacking columns, poised to charge the enemy forces, falling on them in an oblique approach. If the foot was repulsed, the cavalry charged to their rescue.

If, however, it was the cavalry which began the attack, the infantry followed some way behind the squadrons, using them as protection and providing a shield behind which they could reform should they meet with a reverse.

The cavalry's principal manoeuvre was the charge, this movement starting at the trot, with only the last two hundred metres covered at the gallop. 'As they neared the enemy', wrote General Brialmont, 'if the charge was against the infantry, the riders uttered loud shouts, to encourage their horses, to frighten the enemy and to drive the whistling of shot from their own minds[9].'

Confrontations between two bodies of cavalry, on the other hand, while spectacular, were not very deadly. According to a witness of one episode in the battle: 'There was no hesitation shown on either side; each fell upon the other with furious determination and while we all expected a horrible clash, yet we saw nothing. As if by mutual agreement, each side opened its ranks to allow its adversary to pass through at the charge, rather like the fingers of the left hand might allow those of the right to pass. Very few were unhorsed. After that the two bodies reformed[10].'

If the cavalry found it difficult to move on a wide front, as was the case at Waterloo, it charged in echelon.

The tactical unit was the regiment, comprising three squadrons, each of which was a hundred riders strong. Three or four regiments made up a brigade in the Anglo-Dutch army, or a division in the French army.

While, in both these armies, the cavalry was assembled in large units, in the Prussian army it was split up amongst the brigades, although a reserve was included in each army corps.

ARTILLERY

All the fighting nations used cannon and howitzers with smooth bores and various types of projectile.

The cannon

In France in 1767, General Gribeauval introduced a series of reforms for lightening and rationalising the artillery, to make it an instrument of the first order. In Great Britain, it was to be the end of the century before similar improvements were introduced, by General Congreve.

The cannon were of bronze and measured 1.60 m for the six-pounder guns and up to 2.30 m for the twelve-pounders.

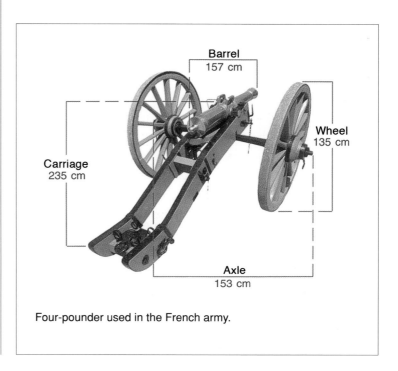

Four-pounder used in the French army.

Sketch by Captain Cavalié Mercer showing the disarray into which the guns of his battery had fallen at the end of the battle of Waterloo.

They weighed between 300 kg and one ton and were supported on wooden carriages running on two wheels, 1.30 to 1.50 m in diameter.

The howitzers, also of bronze, were mounted on carriages of the same type, with a maximum length of 70 cm and a weight of 300 kg.

The cannon were hauled by teams of six to eight horses. For firing, the guns were turned about and their trails supported on a limber.

Positioning of a battery was a long and complex operation. The ideal location was forward of the line, but hidden from the enemy's sight, so as to prevent its presence being revealed until it opened fire. It needed a wide open space in front of it and it could not be positioned on ground which was too sloping. Preferably, the cannon would be placed on a crest in such a way that the ammunition waggons about 50 metres to the rear were shielded from the enemy's fire. The guns were spaced some twenty metres apart and arranged in an irregular line, to avoid being enfiladed.

A cannon was usually served by five men, apart from the ammunition-carriers, the drivers and auxiliary personnel.

The training of the cannon, by the gun captain, required it to be moved by hand; the elevation was then adjusted with the aid of a sighting screw, a notch and a foresight. Firing caused the gun to recoil one or two metres and manhandling it back in position, perhaps a hundred times in the course of a day, was an exhausting task; in hot weather the gunners might be found working in their shirtsleeves.

After each firing the barrel had to be swabbed out with a sponge staff, after which the powder charge, packed in a cloth bag, was introduced, followed by the projectile, each of them being pushed into the barrel by means of the rammer attached to the other end of the sponge staff. Two men were allotted to this task.

A fourth man was responsible for maintaining the cannon's vent and for priming the charge by forcing a pin into the hole to puncture the powder bag. The firer applied the linstock, a type of torch trimmed with a slow match, against the vent to ignite the charge.

As well as the horse artillery, whose teams were mounted, there was the foot artillery, whose guns were of the larger bores. A company or battery of foot artillery was generally composed of six or eight guns, six cannon and two howitzers. Each battery possessed a large number of personnel: a British foot battery, or 'brigade', had 5 officers and 97 gunners, not counting 88 men for driving the teams pulling both cannon and ammunition waggons. Cavalié Mercer's horse troop had, for six guns, 226 horses together with 104 officers, NCOs, gunners and drivers.

Artillery sizes

At Waterloo, the British army used nine-pounder guns in the foot artillery and six-pounders in the horse artillery. Both arms used 5½-inch howitzers. In the Prussian army, the foot artillery was equipped with six- and twelve-pounder cannon and seven- and twelve-pounder howitzers. The horse artillery used six-pounder cannon and 5½-pounder howitzers.

In the French army, the foot artillery in the regiments used six- and eight-pounder cannon, while the twelve-pounders were embodied in a general reserve formation. The horse artillery employed four- and six-pounder cannon and six-pounder howitzers. It should be mentioned that the term pound derived from the weight of the ball and not the size of the bore. The destructive force was determined by the kinetic energy, which is proportional to the weight and the square of the velocity. The effectiveness of a twelve-pounder was therefore greater than that of a six-pounder, irrespective of the range.

During the Peninsular campaign the British artillery, which was largely provided with six-pounders, was obliged to equip itself with nine-pounders, to counter the French twelve-pounders.

Ammunition

The **round cannon ball** was of wrought iron and accounted for 80 % of the projectiles used. Its destructive effect was directly dependent on its trajectory. After touching the ground once, it usually rebounded a second time. Flying on this trajectory, at heights of less than 1.80 m, it would hit any soldier or horse in its path.

At Waterloo, the state of the ground, sodden by the night's heavy rain, reduced the effectiveness of the ricochets, with balls tending to bury themselves in soft or sloping soil.

The rate of fire usually amounted to two shots per minute, it being necessary to avoid overheating of the gun, which would have induced the premature ignition of the powder charge while the gun was being readied for firing.

A sufficient supply of ammunition was immediately available to allow each gun to fire for an hour to an hour and a half (about 180 shots per gun, including case shot). This stock was replenished by the waggons in the first echelon.

The effectiveness of the firing is difficult to determine, it being necessary to distinguish between the results of range firing, for which there are precise figures, and the more problematical results obtained from use in the field. On exercise, it can be said that at 550 metres a six-pounder placed 50 % of its shots on the target, but at 800 metres no more than 20 %. These figures must be halved for combat conditions, when the smoke, the misfires, the periods when the cannon's field of fire was masked by friendly troops, the time needed to train the gun and the mobility of the targets all conspired to reduce the rate of firing and its effectiveness.

If it is estimated that one shot on target would put one or two men out of action, a gun, well tended and accurately trained, could thus hit between 60 and 120 of the enemy in one hour's firing at an effective range, i.e. less than 550 m.

At Waterloo, the average number of rounds fired by the British artillery reached 129 per gun, the record being held by the Sandham battery, which fired 183 rounds for each gun.

1. The four-pounder cannon ball was a solid sphere of forged iron, with a diameter of 8.2 cm and a weight of 1.960 kg (4 pounds). Each charge of black powder weighed one third that of the ball, i.e. 0.650 kg for a four-pounder cannon. The powder charge was contained in a cylindrical bag of the same diameter as the barrel and made of stout cloth. The ball was secured by means of two thin strips of tin-plate, placed cross-wise over a wooden *sabot* of slightly smaller diameter, hollowed out to receive it.

2. Table of sizes and ranges.

Size	Ball		Charge	Range (m)	
	weight (kg)	diameter (cm)	(kg)	maximum	effective
Four-pounder cannon	1.96	8.2	0.65	1,200	800
Eight-pounder cannon	3.92	10.4	1.30	2,400	1,500
Twelve-pounder cannon	5.88	11.9	1.99	2,600	1,800
Six-inch howitzer	16.17	16.2	1.80	1,200	750
Eight-inch howitzer	21.56	21.8	2.00	1,400	900

The **howitzer shell** was a hollow iron sphere containing a powder charge which was exploded by means of a fuse consisting of a small amount of powder, which was ignited by the combustion of the projectile's propulsive charge. As a rule, each battery possessed two howitzers.

The fuse was normally set to explode on impact. The destructive power of the shell resided in the shower of splinters which it threw horizontally, while its curved trajectory allowed it to be fired over the heads of friendly troops. At Waterloo, the Bull battery bombarded

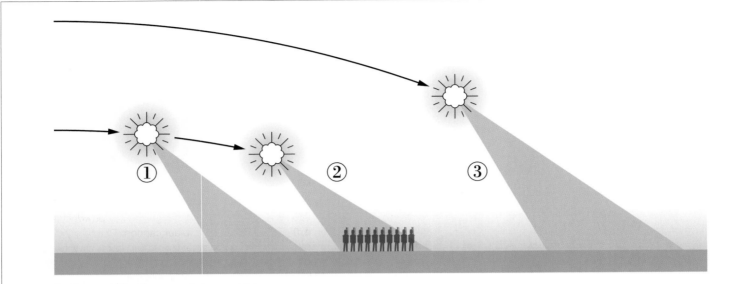

Setting and effectiveness of shrapnel firing.
1. Correct trajectory, fuse set too short. 2. Correct trajectory, fuse set correctly. 3. Incorrect trajectory, fuse set correctly.

Goumont Wood in this way, over the heads of the defenders of this strongpoint.

Shrapnel, invented by the Englishman Henry Shrapnel in 1784, also known as case or canister shot, was used exclusively by the British troops. It consisted of a hollow metal sphere containing an explosive charge together with a certain number of balls (from 27 to 65 depending on the calibre). Explosion took place while the shell was still in the air, the precise moment being determined by a fuse. The effectiveness of shrapnel, which could be fired by both cannon and howitzers, depended on the accurate setting of the fuse.

Properly used, it was a deadly weapon and projectiles fired from a distance of 900 m would be spread across a stretch of ground 90 m in depth.

Canister consisted of a light metal container holding a mixed collection of balls, which spread out as they left the cannon, rather like a very large shotgun cartridge.

The useful range of the balls varied between 250 and 500 m. Canister was principally used defensively against infantry or cavalry. At 90 m, the diameter of the scatter was nearly 10 metres. At 180 m, a salvo from a battery of 6 six-pounders could put between 100 and 150 men out of action, equivalent to a volley from a battalion at 90 metres.

Congreve rockets were perfected in 1805 by Sir William Congreve, who got the idea from the rockets used by Tippoo Sahib at Seringapatam in 1779.

This weapon, which was very advanced for its day, was in three parts: the tube containing the rocket mixture, a shell filled with an incendiary charge, and the launching tube.

Launching took place with the aid of a trestle supporting a U-shaped wooden bracket, which acted as the guide for the rocket stick, the inclination of which could be altered at will. At the time of the Napoleonic Wars, the range of Congreve rockets was of the order of two km, greater than the radius of action of a twelve-pounder cannon.

Shrapnel shell.

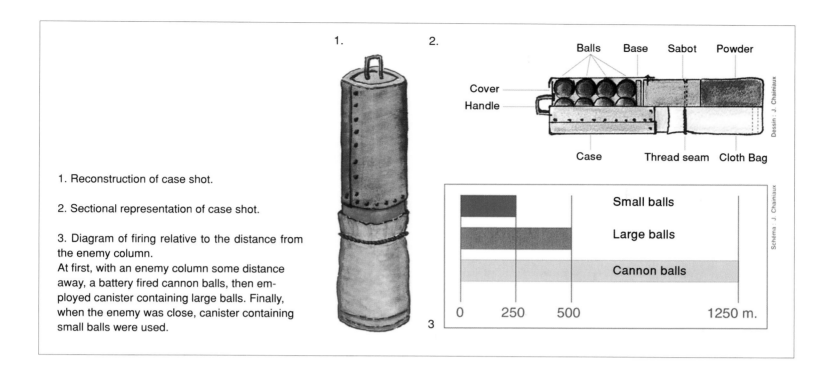

1. Reconstruction of case shot.

2. Sectional representation of case shot.

3. Diagram of firing relative to the distance from the enemy column.
At first, with an enemy column some distance away, a battery fired cannon balls, then employed canister containing large balls. Finally, when the enemy was close, canister containing small balls were used.

This new weapon saw service only in the British army. It was used with success in the bombardment of Boulogne in 1806 and, in particular, of Copenhagen in 1807, causing severe fires. A corps of rocket troops served in the Peninsular and at Leipzig. The effectiveness of rockets against troops in open country proved to be disappointing, but psychologically, the use of such unusual weapons induced a certain panic in the opposing ranks when they were first encountered.

During the Waterloo campaign, the only unit to be so equipped was Whinyate's horse troop. It went into action during the clash at Genappe on 17 June.

Firing a Congreve rocket. English engraving c.1820.

The employment of the artillery

The role of the artillery was essentially that of support for the infantry. At Waterloo, Wellington expressly prohibited his gunners from engaging in artillery duels, that is to say, from directing their fire against opposing batteries.

At the time of the Napoleonic Wars, 'softening-up' barrages do not seem to have had much effect. At ranges above 700 metres, the very rudimentary optical sighting devices were not conducive of good results. Nevertheless, although casualties scarcely amounted to more than two or three per cent, the psychological importance of having to suffer fire without being able to reply could be unsettling to troops who were inexperienced or over-exposed, as was the case for the Bijlandt brigade at Waterloo.

The horse artillery moved forward with the assault columns and the cavalry and halted when it was considered to be within a satisfactory range. While an attack was being launched, or during cavalry charges, frontal firing was not possible, since the field of fire was masked by the deployment of the troops the guns were supporting. In those circumstances the gunners were wont to move to one side of the attacking column, to take the defenders in the flank.

Unlike Blücher, who tended to distribute his batteries at regular intervals along his front, Napoléon often carried the day by concentrating the fire of several dozen cannon, which could unnerve or even break the opposing infantry.

FLAGS AND ENSIGNS

To the military mind of those days, the flag had its own innate value. From a practical aspect, it served as a rallying point on the battlefield; but more, in terms of morale, it formed a mystic link between the regiment and the sovereign. The extent of the victory was measured by the number of flags captured and the loss of a unit's colours was felt as the worst dishonour that it could suffer, which accounts for the furious and mortal single combats which took place around them. They were symbols demanding particular protection and it was an honour for those to whom they were entrusted[11].

In Napoléon's armies there were Eagle Bearers after 1808 and standard bearers in the British army after 1813, this duty being generally allotted to the veteran senior NCOs. In the French army, each regiment had its flag, a double thickness of silk fringed with gold, 80 cm square, comprising three vertical panels coloured blue, white and red and surmounted by a gilded bronze eagle.

In the British army, each regiment possessed two emblems, a Union Jack representing the King's authority and another in the regimental colours. They were very large, about 2 square metres, and demanded great physical strength when flourished in any wind. They were carried by the two youngest officers in the battalion, escorted by two experienced sergeants. These were dangerous duties and Sergeant Lawrence of the 40th, entrusted with the care of the colours at four o'clock in the afternoon of 18 June 1815, approached his new duty with misgivings: 'That was a job which I had no liking for at all, but I did my best. Fourteen sergeants had already fallen, dead or wounded, defending the colours, not to mention the associated officers, and both the staffs and the standards were nearly in shreds[12].'

The Prussian flags were of the same size as the British and were decorated in their centres with an eagle with two wings, on a coloured background. Each battalion possessed two flags[13].

THE MUSICIANS

The armies' music may be considered separately as drums, fifes and cornets in the infantry, trumpets and drums in the cavalry and, thirdly, the regimental bands.

The first two formed part of the regiments and took part in the fighting. They moved with the troops in action, placed on the flanks of the columns and not in front of them, as shown in the majority of films. Their role was essentially the transmission of orders in the field, where the din of battle and the dispersion of the skirmishers rendered commands by voice or gesture ineffective.

Thus, at the battle of Dresden, when the drummers of the *3rd tirailleurs* of the Guard were killed by a hail of shrapnel, the Old Guard halted, wondering who had given the order to do so[14]. But trumpet calls and drums also governed the daily life of the soldier, for reveille, meals, marching, halts and training.

The role of the regimental bands was very different. They marched at the head of parades and reviews, marking the step, as well as encouraging the men before battle and even,

The Captive Eagle. Taken by the Royal Dragoons from the 105ᵗʰ French Regiment at Waterloo.
Coloured etching from a painting by J P Beadle. Wellington Museum, Waterloo.

during it, playing martial airs from further to the rear of the front line. These musicians were not professional soldiers.

Sometimes the infantry sang as they formed up in the front line, like the Prussian troops who, as they entered the deadly furnace of Plancenoit, chanted one of Luther's chorales.

In the Scottish regiments of the British army, the troops were roused by the pipers. These men, who were not a part of the army but symbolised the honour of the clan, often demonstrated unbelievable bravery, exemplified by the bag piper of the 79th Regiment at Waterloo, who positioned himself outside the square, between two cavalry charges, in defiance of the enemy.

MOBILITY

Since the armies moved essentially on foot, any progress was very slow. The men bore heavy loads – pack, rifle and cartridge pouch – and their paths frequently lay across the fields, since the roads were reserved for the artillery and the transport.

While the cavalry could cover about five kilometres in an hour, the infantry, artillery and supply columns had difficulty in achieving an average of more than three. A French army corps, consisting of three divisions of infantry, one of cavalry and a unit of artillery, formed a column fourteen kilometres long.

Communications on the battlefield, between the units engaged in the action and with the army corps on campaign, were maintained by means of mounted messengers – staff officers who carried orders from the commanding general. Most frequently these instructions were verbal if given at the place of action, or written if they were intended for troops at a more distant location.

The messengers needed to proceed with care, often using guesswork to find their way to the intended recipient and making wide detours to find a route where they would not run into the enemy's own couriers. The transmission of messages under such conditions was slow and problematical. On 18 June, the bearers of orders from Napoléon to Grouchy first followed the road to Quatre-Bras, then passed through Sombreffe, finally reaching Wavre by the route taken by the columns.

THE COMMISSARIAT

The Anglo-Dutch and Prussian armies stationed in Belgium were billeted on the locals. Billeting orders were passed to the troops and the feeding of the soldiers fell on the shoulders of the host families.

In the field, improvisation was the order of the day. In principle, the feeding of both men and horses was accomplished from the baggage train. The reality was altogether different. The baggage train would fall well behind the troops as they marched and more often than not the soldiers were obliged to provide for themselves.

At the start of the campaign, a bread ration was distributed to the French army, sufficient for three days. By 17 June, the majority of the men had used up all their supplies, a state of affairs illustrated by this account from a senior officer attached to the headquarters of Foy's division: 'In the evening of Waterloo, in the pack of a dead soldier, I caught sight of half a loaf, which I devoured – there is no other word for it – having for the previous two days existed on nothing but beer[15].'

The French and Prussian armies had a reputation for living off the country, subsisting by looting, pillaging or commandeering whatever they needed. A French officer recalled: 'Everywhere, the passage of the army was marked by devastation and robbery. As soon as the troops had come to a halt, however brief, in the vicinity of some village, they poured like a torrent on to the unhappy dwellings exposed to their voracity: drink, victuals, furniture, linen, clothing, all disappeared in a moment. When we left it the next morning, a village where we had camped now consisted of nothing but a vast pile of ruins – one might even say debris – around which was scattered all of the houses' former furnishings. The neighbourhood, normally covered with abundant crops, appeared to have been destroyed by a storm of hailstones, while the spots where bivouac fires had been, blackened and barren in the midst of these crops and meadows reduced to rubbish dumps, seemed like places which had been struck by lightning[16].'

Where a town was occupied, this was done by means of requisitions which were raised to cover the needs of the troops. Thus, when Grouchy's retreating corps entered Namur on 20 June, it demanded the immediate provision of 3,000 *setiers* (about 8 pints) of oats, 2,400 litres of *eau-de-vie*, 5,716 pounds of meat, 15,000 *rations* of biscuits and

14,000 loaves. In the event, the brevity of the Frenchmen's stay rendered this impossible, but instead the town found itself on the following day having to satisfy the requirements of the Prussians, which amounted to iron for the farriers, medicines for both men and horses and boots for soldiers who lacked them, facing pillage as the only alternative.

In principle, the commissariat of the British army was better organised. Instead of requisitions, the commodities demanded for provisioning the troops were paid for, though this was not always the case in the field.

Wellington condemned pillaging, which he considered to be not only detrimental to discipline but inefficient. On 27 June, he complained to a Dutch general: 'The troops of His Majesty the King of Holland pillage and steal everywhere they go; even the headquarters, the house where I myself am staying, is not excluded. The consequence of this is that the troops of His Majesty the King of Holland are starving, while the other troops in the army are well fed. Your troops enter a village and destroy and pillage everything; the population flees and the resources which could be got there, for yourself and for everyone, are lost[17].'

Alcohol was essential for raising the courage of the combatants. Before or during a battle, the soldiers were given a measure of spirits. Thus, in the middle of the fighting on 18 June, a British commissary delivered to one of the battalions for which he was responsible a cask of rum, which was immediately distributed to the soldiers manning the square. Some British witnesses reported that the cavalry regiments in the line at the conclusion of the battle, having been quartered the whole day at Braine-l'Alleud, were in a state of advanced drunkenness.

While turning the horses out to graze made up for the dearth in the supply of oats, it was not easy to feed and water the mounts of thousands of horsemen: it was necessary to find water supplies, while often, in bivouac, fatigue parties had to be sent out to search for forage, to the detriment of the crops. The brief 1815 campaign was particularly hard on the horses, which could sometimes remain two or three days without having their harness or saddles removed, in sweltering temperatures.

WOMEN IN THE ARMIES

Some women following the armies enjoyed a wholly official standing, while others, such as the wives or mistresses of the officers, the soldiers' wenches or the prostitutes, were much less accepted.

In the French army, military regulations provided in each regiment for *vivandières*, or canteen-keepers, from whom the soldiers could procure items which met their immediate needs. These persons were attached to the battalions or squadrons, possessed a horse or a handcart and sold victuals and small items of daily use, such as writing paper, laces, buttons, spirits and the vinegar which was added to the water in flasks and bottles.

In addition, each unit was accompanied by from two to four laundresses, who washed the soldiers' shirts, drawers, handkerchiefs and gaiters[18]. These women formed part of the army, but did not wear uniform.

In the British army, soldier's wives, not more than six per company, were allowed to accompany the troops, to carry out the same tasks.

Napoléon. Oil on canvas by Louis David. Musée Royal de l'Armée, Brussels.

3. THE ARMIES IN THE FIELD AND THEIR COMMANDERS

In supreme command of the French army was the Emperor Napoléon, whose personality has fascinated generations. Scion of a minor noble family in Corsica, Napoléon Bonaparte became an officer of artillery under the *ancien régime*. It was the Revolution which provided him with the opportunity to express his powerful personality and to provide the outlet for his ambition. By turns partisan of Corsican independence and Jacobin protégé of the Younger Robespierre, he distinguished himself at the siege of Toulon in 1793 and was promoted general.

In disgrace after *Thermidor*, he sided with Barras, becoming his adviser during the Parisian insurrection of *Vendémiaire* (1795). As a reward he was given command of the army in Italy. By the end of the 1796-97 campaign he had acquired the military glory and the political influence which enabled him, in the name of the *Directoire*, to negotiate the Treaty of Campo Formio.

He had now become a nuisance and was sent to Egypt (1798), tasked with cutting one of Great Britain's routes to India, but with the secret hope that this would result in the reversal of his burgeoning fortunes. After various successes, though none of them decisive, Bonaparte abandoned his army and returned to France. There, on 18 *Brumaire* year VIII (9 November 1799), he overthrew the *Directoire* by a military coup d'état.

He introduced the office of Consul, which was changed to Consul for life after the Peace of Amiens (1802). In 1804, the Corsican general proclaimed himself Emperor of the French with the title of Napoléon I. Henceforth, the story of his personal adventures was to become part of the fabric of the history of France.

Although put together in haste, the Army of the North was composed exclusively of veterans, all of whom had fought in at least one campaign.

They were a mixture of patriot and bonapartist and their morale was of the highest. 'Today, it is no longer merely enthusiasm, but a frenzy which reigns amongst the troops', reported a British spy from Paris at the end of May[19]. However, the reverse face of this degree of adulation was a deep distrust of their senior officers, who, having served Louis XVIII during the imperial interregnum, were suspected, rightly or wrongly, of being royalists.

In any event, uneasiness reigned amongst the senior officers, who were for the most part privately sceptical about the ultimate outcome of the campaign. As General Delort wrote: 'A large number of officers and generals, who very recently had not only taken the oath of allegiance to the King, but who had demonstrated their great devotion to his person and to the princes of the blood, found themselves, by the whim of fortune, placed in a most difficult position between honour and love of their country, and the duty which demands loyalty and the necessity to fight to maintain the dignity and the independence of France. These motivations, exerting equal power on noble hearts, cast them into irresolution and discouragement[20].'

The attitudes of the marshals upon the Emperor's return is illustrative of this state of mind. Some of them, such as Marmont, Augereau and Victor, had followed Louis XVIII to Ghent, while others, such as Oudinot, Macdonald and Massena, had, though avowing their loyalty, voluntarily stood aside or had declined to accept any command. Few of the marshals were to serve during the Hundred Days.

Order of battle

Headquarters:
Commander-in-chief: Napoléon Bonaparte
Chief of Staff: Marshal Soult, Duke of Dalmatia

Imperial Guard:

Old Guard of Foot: 1st, 2nd, 3rd and 4th grenadiers (7 battalions)	3,800 men
1st, 2nd, 3rd and 4th *chasseurs* (8 battalions)	4,600 men
Young Guard: Comte Duhesme (8 battalions)	4,200 men
Light cavalry: Comte Lefèbvre-Desnouettes (10 squadrons)	2,000 men
Heavy cavalry: Baron Guyot (8 squadrons)	2,000 men
Artillery:	
Old Guard: 6 foot batteries (48 guns)	
4 horse batteries (24 guns)	2,000 men
Young Guard: 5 foot batteries (40 guns)	
1 horse battery (6 guns)	1,000 men
Total	**19,600 men**

I corps: Drouet, Comte d'Erlon

4 divisions of infantry: Quiot, Donzelot, Marcognet, Durutte (33 battalions)	17,700 men
1 division of cavalry: Jacquinot (12 squadrons)	1,800 men
6 batteries (46 guns)	1,100 men
5 companies of engineers	350 men
Total	**20,950 men**

II corps: Comte Reille

4 divisions of infantry: Bachelu, Jerôme Bonaparte, Girard, Foy (41 battalions)	21,800 men
1 division of cavalry: Piré (12 squadrons)	1,800 men
6 batteries (46 guns)	1,000 men
5 companies of engineers	400 men
Total	**25,000 men**

III corps: Comte Vandamme

3 divisions: Lefol, Habert, Berthezène (31 battalions)	15,000 men
1 division of cavalry: Domon (9 squadrons)	1,000 men
5 batteries (38 guns)	,000 men
2 companies of engineers	150 men
Total	**17,150 men**

IV corps: Comte Gérard

3 divisions of infantry: Pécheux, Vichery, Hulot (replacing de Bourmont, defected to the enemy 15 June (26 battalions)	12,900 men
1 division of cavalry: Maurin (14 squadrons)	1,600 men
5 batteries (38 guns)	1,000 men
3 companies of engineers	200 men
Total	**15,700 men**

VI corps: Mouton, Comte Lobau

3 divisions of infantry: Simmer, Jannin, Teste (20 battalions)	9,400 men
4 batteries (32 guns)	700 men
2 companies of engineers	200 men
Total	**10,300 men**

Cavalry Reserve

I corps: Comte Pajol

2 divisions: Soult, Subervie (24 squadrons)	2,500 men
2 horse batteries (12 guns)	300 men
Total	**2,800 men**

II corps: Comte Exelmans

2 divisions: Strolz, Chastel (31 squadrons)	3,000 men
2 batteries (12 guns)	290 men
Total	**3,290 men**

III corps: Kellermann, Comte de Valmy

2 divisions: Lhéritier, Roussel (25 squadrons)	3,400 men
2 batteries (12 guns)	300 men
Total	**3,700 men**

IV corps: Comte Milhaud

2 divisions: Wathier, Delort (24 squadrons)	2,700 men
2 batteries (12 guns)	300 men
Total	**3,000 men**

Total strength of the Army of the North: 90,000 infantrymen, 22,000 cavalrymen and 366 guns.

Marshal Soult. Oil on canvas by G P A Healy. The Victoria & Albert Museum, London.

The Minister for War, Davout, perhaps the most remarkable soldier of the Empire, took on the immense task of reorganising the army and, as Governor of Paris, that of maintaining calm in the capital during Napoléon's absence.

The choice of Soult as major-general and chief of staff was maladroit. His sycophancy to gain the favour of Louis XVIII, his severity towards his former comrades when he was Minister for War, his outspokenly royalist declarations following the return from Elba, followed by his bonapartist retractions, had the effect of depriving this excellent soldier, with his glorious past, of all prestige. In addition, between Soult and the commanders of the major units, such as Drouet d'Erlon and Exelmans, there existed personal animosity which did nothing to ease his task.

The reasons for the employment of Ney can only be wondered at. The marshal, whose role was pivotal during the fall of the Empire in 1814, was compromised in the course of the first Restoration. With the return from Elba he became the author of several declarations of a partisan nature: 'That

madman will never forgive me for his abdication, he could well have my head within six months' or: 'Leave Bonaparte to me. We shall go after that wild beast[21].' On 7 March, Ney assured the King: 'Sire, I trust we shall contrive to bring him back in an iron cage[22].'

But these resolutions melted away like snow in the summer sun; at Auxerre he returned to the fold, alerted by the enthusiasm of his soldiers and outwitted by the Emperor's emissaries. After Waterloo, he would pay for this defection with his life. Despite his adhesion to the cause, Ney found himself offered no post and was left in the background. Bitter and disillusioned, he withdrew to his estates; it was not until 11 June that Napoléon wrote to Davout: 'Send for Ney. If he wishes to be in the first battle, let him be at Avesnes on the 13th[23].'

Grouchy, newly promoted to marshal after his short campaign against the Duke d'Angoulême, was given command of the reserve cavalry; Mortier was given the Guard, but at the start of hostilities was detained at Avesnes by an attack of the gout.

Although it consisted of veterans, the Army of the North betrayed certain defects at command level. As a result of the purges and reinstatements during the Hundred Days, many officers had only recently received their appointments and had not had the chance to build the bonds of confidence essential for exerting their authority.

The basic formation was the division, composed of two brigades, each comprising two regiments, which generally consisted of two battalions of 550 to 600 men, divided into six companies. A division was thus approximately 5,000 infantrymen strong with, in addition, an artillery battery of six cannon and two howitzers, a company of engineers and a supply train squadron.

The cavalry division closely followed the pattern of the infantry, each regiment consisting of three squadrons of approximately 120 men, the strength of a division thus being about 1,500. The divisional artillery was mounted, each battery having four cannon and two howitzers. An army corps was made up of three or four infantry divisions, one cavalry division and one artillery reserve.

The British army was under Wellington's overall command.

Arthur Wellesley was born into a titled British family, which had been established in Ireland for several centuries. After Eton, he continued his studies in Brussels and Angers.

Wellington. Oil on canvas by Sir Thomas Lawrence, 1814. Apsley House, The Wellington Museum, London.

In 1787 he purchased an ensign's commission and, rising rapidly through the junior ranks, he obtained his lieutenant-colonelcy in 1793. He faced the revolutionary armies of France for the first time during the Flanders campaign of 1794-1795, which ended with the withdrawal of the small British expeditionary force.

Dispatched to India (1796), he took part in the fighting against Tippoo Sahib and in the victory at Seringapatam (1799). Promoted major general in 1803, he distinguished himself against the Mahrattas before returning to England in 1805.

In 1808 his victory at Vimeiro in Portugal forced the French troops who had invaded that kingdom to retreat, but adverse criticism brought about his temporary disgrace and he was brought home. The following year he returned to the Peninsula at the head of a small army of 25,000 men. In the course of five years, one after the other, he vanquished Napoléon's marshals who, rent by quarrels and jealousies, were fighting a confused war in an insurgent Spain.

His successes, against Soult at Porto and against Victor at Talavera, earned Wellesley elevation to the peerage and the titles of Viscount Wellington and Baron Douro. Following an inconclusive result at Bussaco, he halted Masséna at the Lines of Torres Vedras (1810) and then forced him to retreat after Fuentes de Oñoro (1811).

Passing to the offensive during the winter of 1812, he took possession of Ciudad Rodrigo and Badajoz. Victory over Marmont at Salamanca in July opened the gates of Madrid. He was brought to a halt before Burgos and fell back on Portugal, but in the following spring the decisive victory at Vittoria forced all French troops to abandon Spain and King Joseph to vacate his erstwhile throne. Wellesley, Marquis of Wellington since 1812, assumed the rank of field marshal.

In 1814 he invaded France; there the battle of Orthez brought about the fall of Bordeaux and Toulouse, but the campaign was brought to an end by the abdication of Napoléon. Wellington was created a duke and Marquis of Douro, as well as being appointed ambassador in Paris to the court of Louis XVIII.

The landing from Elba found Wellington caught by surprise in Vienna, where he had replaced the Foreign Secretary, Castlereagh, in the sittings of the Congress. Appointed commander-in-chief of the British forces on the Continent, the Duke arrived in Brussels on 4 April and assumed command of the Anglo-Hanoverian and Belgian-Dutch armies stationed in the Netherlands.

Successful commander, cautious with his men's lives, he owed his success in Spain to his tactical skills and to the optimum use he made of the firepower of his small army. At that point, Wellington had never faced his contemporary, Napoléon.

The British army was a disparate assembly in which Britons represented only half the total strength. All were professional soldiers, although, out of 30,000 men, only 7,000 were veterans. The other units from the Spanish campaign had been sent across the Atlantic, where since 1812 the United States had once more been at war with Britain. The contingents of Wellington's army began to disembark at Ostend and Antwerp in April 1815. Not without some difficulty, Wellington managed to get the majority of his generals from Spain appointed to lead the main units: Hill, Alten, Ponsonby, Picton, Maitland…

The British rank and file had been recruited from among the unemployed, hit by the first industrial crisis. High enlistment bounties and pay greater than the wages of an unskilled worker made a twenty-year engagement an attractive prospect. Well-trained, particularly in musketry, and led by excellent NCOs, this infantry had proved itself in Spain, even if Wellington viewed it with disdain: 'They are the scum of the earth, who joined for the drink[24].' Discipline was very hard, based on corporal punishment, namely the lash.

The officer corps was recruited in accordance with a system reminiscent of former times. Ranks between ensign and lieutenant colonel were obtained by purchase; above that, they depended on social rank and seniority. The British officer was also a man of the world, who treated war as a sport. Very brave in battle, but without any contact with his men, he had received no military training and was more often than not completely lacking in ability. Concerning this aspect, Wellington wrote: 'No one ever reads a regulation or an order as if they required his conduct to comply with them and that with no more attention than he would give to an amusing novel. This is why, when complex schemes need to be executed […] each gentleman proceeds according to his personal whim, so that the scheme ends in failure. They then come to me and ask me to retrieve the situation, and thus my troubles are multiplied[25].'

The cavalry, excellently mounted, was commanded by officers who were full of fire and dash.

The remainder of Wellington's army was composed of German mercenaries. The King's German Legion (KGL)

Order of battle

Headquarters: Commander-in-chief, Field Marshal the Duke of Wellington
Chief of staff (quarter-master general): Colonel Sir William Howe Delancey
Foreign liaison officers: Prussia: Carl von Müffling; Spain: Miguel de Alava

I army corps: The Prince of Orange	
Chief of staff: Baron Jean-Victor de Constant Rebecque	
1st British division: Cooke	
Maitland and Byng brigades (4 battalions)	4,061 men
Sandham and Kuhlmann batteries (12 guns)	610 men
Total	**4,671 men**

3rd British division: Alten	
Colin, Halkett, Ompteda and Kielmansegge brigades (14 battalions)	6,970 men
Lloyd and Cleeves batteries (12 guns)	476 men
Total	**7,446 men**

2nd Dutch division: Perponcher	
Bijlandt and Saxe-Weimar brigades (11 battalions)	7,951 men
Bijleveld and Stevenart batteries (16 guns)	270 men
Total	**8,221 men**

3rd Dutch division: Chassé	
Detmers and Aubremé brigades (12 battalions)	6,902 men
Krahmer de Bichin and Lux batteries (16 guns)	297 men
Total	**7,199 men**

Dutch cavalry division	
Trip, Ghigny and van Merlen brigades (24 squadrons)	3,405 men
Petter and Gey van Pittius 2 half-batteries (12 guns)	241 men
Total	**3,646 men**
Artillery reserve (16 guns)	554 men

II army corps: Lord Hill	
2nd British division: Clinton	
Adam, du Plat and William (Hew) Halkett brigades (12 battalions)	6,833 men
Bolton and Sympher batteries (12 guns)	610 men
Total	**7,443 men**

4th British division: Colville	
Mitchell, Johnstone and Lyon brigades (12 battalions)	7,212 men
Brome and von Rettberg batteries (12 guns)	492 men
Total	**7,704 men**

Dutch troops: Prince Frederick of the Netherlands	
Anthing Indian brigade (5 battalions)	
1 battery (8 guns)	3,729 men

1st Dutch division: Stedman	
Hauw and de Eerens brigades (11 battalions)	6,543 men
1 battery (8 guns)	119 men
Total	**6,662 men**

General reserve: Duke of Wellington	
5th British infantry division: Picton	
Kempt, Pack and Vincke brigades (12 battalions)	7,158 men
Rogers and Braun batteries (12 guns)	493 men
Total	**7,651 men**

6th British division: Cole	
Lambert and Best brigades (8 battalions)	5,149 men
Unett and Sinclair batteries (12 guns)	650 men
Total	**5,799 men**

7th British division in garrisons	11,545 men
General artillery reserve (26 guns)	1,260 men

Brunswick contingent: Duke William Frederick of Brunswick	
8 battalions	5,376 men
4 squadrons	933 men
2 batteries (16 guns)	510 men
Total	**6,808 men**

Nassau contingent: von Kruse	
3 battalions	2,900 men

British and Hanoverian cavalry: Lord Uxbridge	
Somerset, Ponsonby, Dörnberg, Vandeleur, Grant, Vivian, Arenschildt and von Estorff brigades (81 squadrons)	10,155 men
Horse artillery, 6 batteries (36 guns)	1,050 men
Total	**11,205 men**

Total strength of the Anglo-Dutch army: 86,000 infantrymen, 13,500 cavalrymen and 222 guns.

had been formed in 1803 from the wreckage of the army of the Grand Elector of Hanover and furnished 7,500 soldiers of excellent quality.

The Brunswick corps, 6,500 strong, was commanded by Duke William Frederick of Brunswick in person, who was driven by a fierce desire for revenge against Napoléon who, by the Treaty of Tilsit, had robbed him of his estates. Filled with volunteers possessed of the highest patriotic emotions, this corps was composed of very young soldiers who had never been under fire. Their morale was deeply affected by the death of the Duke at Quatre-Bras.

Wellington's army was completed by a large contingent of Hanoverians (24,000 men), whose official title was 'Royal British Troops of the Electoral Principality of Brunswick-Luneburg'. Less reliable than those of the German Legion, these troops were nevertheless of good quality.

The Dutch army was included in the total strength placed under Wellington's orders. It was of recent creation, as was the Kingdom of the Netherlands itself, created by the treaty of XXXVIII articles included in the final text issued by the Congress of Vienna on 9 June 1815.

Since the end of 1813, the ruling prince of the Netherlands, the future William I, had undertaken to raise a military force in the northern provinces, based on the British model. With the return of peace, Belgian and Dutch soldiers who had served under the Empire were incorporated into it and short-service engagements were resorted to in order to swell the ranks. Recruitment was difficult, for enthusiasm was in short supply and desertion took its toll. Some of the Dutch units had acquired a certain military experience during the campaign in Holland in 1813-1814, but the majority had never seen a shot fired in anger. In particular was this the case with the militia battalions.

Amongst those raised in the northern provinces, there was a strong patriotic spirit, but in the Belgian battalions a certain indifference reigned, for any nationalist feelings were yet to be aroused in the southern provinces of the new-born Kingdom of the Netherlands[26].

Of the regular troops there were some 15 to 20 % who had formerly served in the armies of the Empire, sometimes having been forcibly recruited from prisoners freed after the Treaty of Paris, together with a certain number of German mercenaries.

The officer corps was of high quality and wide experience, the majority of the unit commanders having fought

Jean-Victor de Constant Rebecque.
Oil on canvas by J B Van Der Hulst.
Koninklijk Nederlands Leger-en Wapenmuseum, Delft.

many campaigns with the Imperial armies or having served the former Kingdom of Holland. The chief of staff, General Jean-Victor de Constant Rebecque, was a remarkable personality who had served under Wellington in Spain and possessed his full confidence.

An Orange Nassau regiment, raised in William I's German possessions, and a regiment recruited in the Duchy of Nassau completed this Dutch army, which had a strength of 26,000 men, including 4,300 cavalrymen.

Rightly or wrongly, neither the Duke of Wellington nor the Prussian commanders evinced much confidence in this Belgian-Dutch army, whose loyalty and firmness appeared doubtful.

After the campaign, Fitzroy Somerset, the Duke of Wellington's military secretary, confided to a relative his opinion of the troops in the army: 'Of these troops the German Legion and the British were the only part on whom complete reliance could be placed. The Hanoverians fine men, but undisciplined and unaccustomed to service and badly officered. The Dutch and Belgians very bad. The Brunswickers tolerably good while they had their Prince at their head. The New Nassauers showed no qualities but speed in retreat and great respect for cannon balls[27].'

In the Anglo-Dutch army, the basic infantry unit was the brigade, which generally comprised four battalions, whose average strength was 600 men. Two or three brigades, together with two artillery batteries, each with six to eight guns, made up a division, six to seven thousand strong. In addition, Wellington's army possessed a large cavalry force, formed of brigades or divisions.

The Prussian Army of the Lower Rhine was commanded by Gebhard Leberecht von Blücher. The son of an aristocratic Mecklenburg family, he was involved, as a very young man, in the Seven Years War (1756-1763). With the return of peace, his taste for women, the tables, drink and duelling saw him cast out of the army by Frederick II. After the latter's death, he resumed his military career and, reaching the rank of general, saw service with the Prussian armies in their campaigns against Revolutionary France in 1793 and 1794.

Following a second period out of the army, he commanded a Prussian corps at Auerstadt (1806) and, despite a skilful withdrawal, he capitulated at Schwartau. Refusing to accept defeat after the Treaty of Tilsit, he was banished to his estates by King Frederick William III, who disapproved of his militancy. Around 1811 he suffered from a severe mental disorder in the form of obsessional neurosis.

Won over to the cause of Tugenbund, a fanatical patriot and popular figure, he was given command of the Prussian right wing during the German campaign of 1813. Notwithstanding his defeats at Lutzen and Bautzen, he was appointed commander in chief of the army, being in that post when he invaded France in 1814. Despite his numerical superiority, his strategic errors during that campaign resulted in numerous reverses, notably at Montmirail and Vauchamps.

Furious that the convention of 23 August 1814 concerning the capitulation of Paris decided upon its preservation, he resigned his command. This did not dissuade him from frequenting the Parisian gaming houses, dressed in ordinary civilian clothes, declaring that France ought to be dismembered.

On the return of Napoléon, Blücher, who had vowed that he would capture him and have him shot, was recalled to command the Prussian army stationed in the Netherlands. Though a mediocre strategist, he was a remarkable leader of men and was dubbed by his troops 'General Vorwärts' (General Forward).

The Army of the Lower Rhine was the main force which Prussia was able to contribute to the campaign. After the Treaty of Paris, a large number of the troops had been disbanded and at the beginning of 1815 the country had no more than fifty thousand men under arms, guarding the Rhine. Napoléon's return concentrated minds and led to the recall of the *Landwehr* (the militia) to the colours. From April, the army, under Blücher's command, gradually took up its quarters in the Liège and Namur areas.

The quality of the Prussian troops was very uneven; compared to the battalions of the line, battle-hardened in the campaigns of 1813 and 1814, most of the *Landwehr* regiments were weaker metal.

General Müffling, the Prussian liaison officer with Wellington, wrote: 'Our infantry does not possess the physical strength nor the endurance of the British infantry. The great majority of our troops are too young and too inexperienced. We cannot count on them being able to fight for a whole day. We shall have to find our strength in a short offensive combined with the defensive: attack late on in the afternoon, so that the fighting reaches its peak as night approaches. Our men do not know how to husband their strength; under our officers' lead, they give in one hour that which ought to last for four[28].'

The cavalry was frankly mediocre. It was split up amongst the army corps in a support role, was unable to operate in a body and was obliged to restrict itself to reconnaissance tasks and to direct support. Of the *Landwehr* cavalrymen, 60 squadrons out of 135, it could just about be said that they were schooled in horsemanship, but, barely trained, they were of no use in combat. Blücher himself recognised that they were more of an impediment.

The artillery, although their teams were only mediocre, were many in number and well trained. But the army's major trump cards were the quality of its general staff and the patriotism of the troops.

The chief of the general staff, General Count von Gneisenau, was a wise and prudent soldier. He enjoyed the trust of Blücher, who went so far as to call him 'his own mind'. The chief of staff of III corps – von Thielmann's

Marshal Blücher. Oil on canvas by George Dawe. The Victoria and Albert Museum, London.

Gneisenau. Oil on canvas by George Dawe.
The Victoria and Albert Museum, London.

– was none other than Colonel von Clausewitz, the future eminent military writer.

The Prussian troops evinced a wild patriotism, born of the memory of the humiliations suffered by their country and of the extortions wrung by the French army.

By contrast, the same state of mind was not to be found in the Saxon and Westphalian contingents in Blücher's army. On 2 May at Liège, several Saxon battalions mutinied, to cries of 'Long live the King of Saxony, long live Napoléon!'. These men, 14,000 in number, were disarmed and sent back to Germany, several of their ringleaders being shot. The majority of the troops disbanded on the day before Ligny were from the 18,000 Westphalians serving in the Army of the Lower Rhine.

The basic unit was the brigade, generally composed of three regiments of infantry and one battery of 6 cannon and 2 howitzers, reinforced by one or two squadrons of cavalry, amounting to approximately 200 horsemen. The average strength of an infantry brigade was 6,500 men, making it equivalent to a French division. The four army corps each comprised four infantry brigades, one relatively small cavalry reserve (on average 2,000 horses) and an artillery reserve consisting of 20 to 40 cannon and the same number of howitzers.

Order of battle

Headquarters:

Commander-in-chief: Field Marshal von Blücher,
    Prince of Wahlstatt
Chief of staff: Lieutenant General Count von Gneisenau
Foreign liaison officers: Great Britain: Col. Sir H Hardinge;
Holland: Major General van Panhuys

I corps: von Zieten

4 brigades: von Steinmetz, von Pirch II, von Jagow, Henckel von Donnersmarck (34 battalions)	27,817 men
Cavalry reserve: von Röder (32 squadrons)	1,925 men
12 batteries (96 guns)	1,019 men
Total	**30,761 men**

II corps: von Pirch I

4 brigades: von Tippleskirch, von Kraft, von Brause, Langen (36 battalions)	25,836 men
Cavalry reserve: von Wahlen-Jürgass (36 squadrons)	4,468 men
10 batteries (80 guns)	1,454 men
Total	**30,761 men**

III corps: von Thielmann

4 brigades: von Borcke, von Kemphen, von Luck, von Stülpnagel (30 battalions)	20,611 men
Cavalry reserve: von Hobe (25 squadrons)	2,405 men
6 batteries (48 guns)	964 men
Total	**23,980 men**

IV corps: von Bülow

4 brigades: von Hake, von Rijssel, von Losthin, von Hiller (36 battalions)	25,381 men
Cavalry reserve: Prince William of Prussia (43 squadrons)	3,081 men
11 batteries (88 guns)	1,866 men
Total	**30,328 men**

Total strength of the Army of the Lower Rhine: 116,827 men
    and 312 guns.

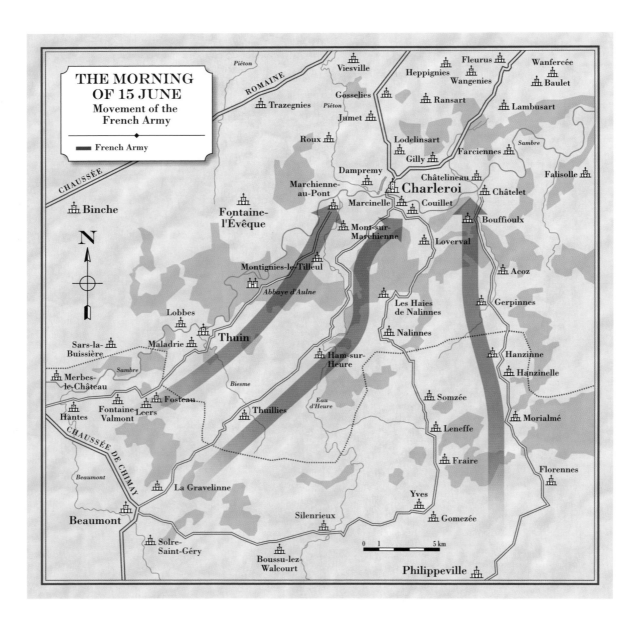

THE MORNING
OF 15 JUNE
Movement of the
French Army

━━━ French Army

Piéton
ROMAINE
Trazegnies
Piéton
Gosselies
Jumet
Roux
Dampremy
Marchienne-
au-Pont
Marcinelle
Mont-sur-
Marchienne
Montignies-le-Tilleul
Abbaye d'Aulne
Viesville
Heppignies
Fleurus
Wangenies
Wanfercée
Baulet
Ransart
Lambusart
Lodelinsart
Sambre
Gilly
Farciennes
Châtelineau
Falisolle
Charleroi
Châtelet
Couillet
Bouffioulx
Loverval
Acoz
CHAUSSÉE
Binche
Fontaine-
l'Évêque
N
Les Haies
de Nalinnes
Gerpinnes
Lobbes
Nalinnes
Sars-la-
Buissière
Maladrie
Thuin
Hanzinne
Hanzinelle
Sambre
Merbes-
le-Château
Ham-sur-
Heure
Biesme
Somzée
*Eau
d'Heure*
Fosteau
Hantes
Fontaine-
Valmont
Leers
Thuillies
Leneffe
Morialmé
CHAUSSÉE DE CHIMAY
Beaumont
La Gravelinne
Fraire
Florennes
Yves
Beaumont
Silenrieux
Gomezée
Solre-
Saint-Géry
Boussu-lez-
Walcourt
Philippeville

0 1   5 km

4. THE OPENING OF THE CAMPAIGN: 15 JUNE 1815

NAPOLEON'S STRATEGIC PLAN

Wellington's army was deployed in depth facing the French frontier, from Menin to Morlanwelz, so that it covered Brussels, Ghent and Antwerp. The object was to protect the little court of Louis XVIII, which had found refuge at Ghent, and above all the British communications with the coast at Ostend and Antwerp.

In his confidential instructions at the end of April, Wellington had envisaged a French attack only in a westerly direction, between the Lys and the Scheldt, between the Scheldt and the Sambre, or along both banks of the Scheldt. This assumption required the Anglo-Dutch army to concentrate on Enghien, Hal, Braine-le-Comte and Nivelles.

On 3 May Wellington and Blücher met at Tirlemont to confer, when it appears to have been agreed that, in the event of a French offensive, the Prussians would assemble around Sombreffe within two days, in order to come to the aid of the Anglo-Dutch by means of a flank attack[29].

The quarters occupied by Blücher's army covered a very wide area: Bülow's IV Corps was lying between Liège and Waremme, Thielmann's III Corps between Dinant and Huy, II Corps under Pirch I between Namur, Hannut and Wavre and I Corps under Zieten between Charleroi and the frontier. Blücher himself had his headquarters at Namur, while Wellington's was at Brussels.

From mid-May onwards, erroneous or inaccurate intelligence gathered by the Allies concerning Napoléon's intentions was to have the effect of lulling them into a false sense of security. They no longer expected the French to launch an offensive; on 3 June Blücher wrote to his wife: 'We shall soon be entering France (the invasion had been planned to begin on 1 July). We could easily be here for another year, for Bonaparte will not attack us[30].' On 13 June, Wellington wrote to one of his correspondents: 'I think we are now too strong for him here[31].'

Napoléon, for his part, had made his decision at the end of May and orders for the concentration of the troops at his disposal were issued during the first days of June.

The Emperor had decided to attack at the junction point of the two allied armies, with the aim of splitting them apart from the beginning. Some uncertainty surrounds Napoléon's strategic plan if one examines the subsequent version to be found in the Saint Helena papers. According to the latter, on assembling his army between Beaumont and Philippeville, Napoléon proposed to march on Charleroi and to force von Zieten's corps, which was occupying the frontier zone, back on to the main body of the Prussian forces.

The Emperor was then to bring Blücher to battle, if the latter, quickly concentrating his troops, accepted the challenge. His next move was to press on towards Brussels, either confronting Wellington, if the latter came to the aid of his Prussian ally, or forcing him to re-embark his forces, if he chose to retreat on Ghent or Antwerp.

The attack was timed for dawn on 15 June.

THE ADVANCE OF THE FRENCH TROOPS

Napoléon's plan provided for a concentric advance on Charleroi in three columns, each deployed in two echelons.

The lefthand column, consisting of Reille's II Corps, followed by d'Erlon's I Corps, was to advance from Solre-sur-Sambre via Thuin to Marchienne-au-Pont.

The centre column was to have as its advance guard Pujol's cavalry, followed by Vandamme's III Corps. Following them would be the Guard, Lobau's VI Corps and the cavalry reserve under Grouchy. This column was to advance to Charleroi from Beaumont, via Jamioulx and Marcinelle.

The righthand column, consisting of Gérard's IV Corps, reinforced in echelon by Delort's cavalry division, was to advance from Philippeville to Châtelet via Florennes and Gerpinnes.

Each column had some thirty kilometres to cover and Napoléon anticipated, if tents were struck at three in the morning, that he would have a mass of 60,000 men before Charleroi by the time midday was approaching. His plan was not to be accomplished without difficulty, nor without encountering very significant delays.

II Corps, which comprised the lefthand column, left at dawn and occupied Thuin, Lobbes and Montignies-le-Tilleul, brushing aside the Prussian outposts which opposed them. However, it was nearly eleven o'clock by the time its leading regiments reached Marchienne and one o'clock was approaching when, having seized the bridge, the French troops crossed the Sambre to establish themselves a league beyond it, on the Brussels road near Jumet. By then it was three o'clock in the afternoon.

I Corps, which was required to follow up these movements, was due to suffer considerable delay; by nightfall only two of its divisions had crossed the Sambre, with the third still at Marchienne and the last at Thuin.

The movement of the central column, which comprised the bulk of the French troops, was reconnoitred by Pajol's light cavalry corps. The latter, in the saddle at daybreak, was by half-past eight approaching Marcinelle, having along the way sabred all the Prussian outposts, but, in order to force the barricaded bridge over the Sambre which barred the way to Charleroi, infantry was required. The arrival towards midday of sappers and sailors of the Guard, supported by elements of the Young Guard which had taken short cuts, enabled the obstacle to be overcome and Charleroi to be entered which, faced with the numerical superiority of the French, the Prussians had just abandoned.

Vandamme's corps, which should have set off in the wake of the advance guard, had remained in its bivouac until seven a.m., its marching orders having failed to arrive, and it was three in the afternoon before it reached Charleroi. VI Corps remained in the rear and did not cross the Sambre.

The righthand column (Gérard's corps) left its bivouacs at Philippeville two hours late and had its advance further upset by the defection of General Bourmont, commanding his division in the advance guard. On arrival at Florennes this royalist officer abandoned his troops and went over to the enemy, together with the officers on his staff. By nightfall IV Corps had got no further than Châtelet, where it bivouacked without having fired a single shot the entire day.

THE ALLIES' REACTIONS

The intelligence concerning the deployment of the French forces, which had been obtained by Gneisenau despite the precautions taken by Napoléon, decided the former to order Pirch I's corps to assemble at Mazy and Thielmann's at Namur[32]. In the event of an attack, Zieten was to carry out a fighting withdrawal on Fleurus, where the whole army was to regroup. These arrangements were communicated to Wellington's headquarters, which however convinced him that no action need be taken.

By eight o'clock in the morning of the 15th, Zieten was no longer under any illusions about the seriousness of the French attack. He ordered his troops, who were quartered to the west of the Charleroi-Brussels road (von Steinmetz' brigade), to retreat. To allow this operation to take place, he fought delaying actions on the bridges at Marchienne, Charleroi and Châtelet. To cover the movement, the majority of Pirch II's brigade took up positions on the heights above Gilly.

At the same time, Zieten sent messengers to inform Blücher at Namur and Wellington at Brussels of the French offensive. The Prussian field marshal's reaction was immediate. At nine o'clock he ordered his army to concentrate on Sombreffe, where in the afternoon he set up his headquarters, at the same time advising Wellington of the steps he had taken.

There was some delay before this crucial information reached Brussels. Zieten's message was delivered to Wellington only at three that afternoon, while that from Blücher arrived at six o'clock[33].

The headquarters of the Prince of Orange remained in ignorance of the events all morning, although Prince William himself had learnt of the attacks on the Prussians while visiting the outposts of General van Merlen, in the direction of Saint-Symphorien. The Prince, after ordering Chassé to concentrate his division on Haine-Saint-Paul, then set off to rejoin Wellington at Brussels, where that same evening they were due to attend the ball to be given in their honour by the Duchess of Richmond.

At about midday, General de Constant Rebecque received from Mons a letter informing him of a French attack on Charleroi. He at once transmitted this news to Brussels, where at about three o'clock it was brought to Wellington, as he was lunching with the Prince of Orange.

Concluding that the Prussians were strong enough to counter what could only be a diversion by Napoléon, the Duke took the view that there was no particular action for him to take[34]. Constant Rebecque, on the other hand, showed initiative; at midday he ordered Perponcher's division to send his 1st Brigade (Bijlandt) to Nivelles and his 2nd (Saxe-Weimar) to the strategically important crossroads at Quatre-Bras, which commanded the road from Charleroi to Brussels.

OPERATIONS OF THE FRENCH ARMY DURING THE AFTERNOON OF 15 JUNE

At about two o'clock, after a hasty lunch in the house of an ironmaster of Charleroi, Napoléon positioned himself on the outskirts of the town, a few hundred metres from the junction of the Fleurus and Brussels roads, near a little estaminet called 'Belle-Vue'.

After ordering reconnaissances to the north (Jumet) and to the east (Gilly), he dismounted from his horse and called for a chair, in which he took a short nap, while the Young Guard marched past, to the sound of cheers from their ranks.

At about three o'clock, advised of the presence of Prussian troops at Gosselies – it was the Steinmetz brigade of Zieten's Corps, which had been retreating in disorder from Fontaine-l'Eveque – he ordered Reille's and d'Erlon's Corps to march to that village and drive the enemy away. At the same time, a strong advance guard of cavalry was sent to Gilly, where another of Zieten's brigades was assembled.

It was at that moment that Marshal Ney arrived in the Emperor's presence. Ney, 'bravest of the brave', without

retinue, without staff, had made haste to rejoin the army as soon as the invitation to do so reached him. Napoléon received him benevolently: 'Good day to you Ney, I am very glad to see you. You are to assume command of I and II Infantry Corps. I shall also give you the two regiments of light cavalry and lancers in my Guard, but do not use them. Tomorrow you will be joined by the heavy cavalry reserves under Kellermann. Get going, harass the enemy[35].'

With this cavalry, the Marshal came up to Gosselies at about half-past four, but the Prussians fell back towards Heppignies, avoiding combat. The cavalry of Piré and Lefèbvre-Desnouettes continued their advance northwards, followed a good way to their rear by small parties of infantry from Bachelu's division (II Corps).

At Frasnes-lez-Gosselies, they ran up against a battalion of the Nassau regiment and a Dutch artillery battery. The French commenced an encircling manoeuvre, forcing the Allied detachment to retire towards the main force of the Saxe-Weimar brigade. The latter was occupying Quatre-Bras, with its forward posts at Bossut Wood (non-existent today), to the west of the road, and at Gémioncourt Farm to the east.

Lefèbvre-Desnouettes' cavalry and a battalion of infantry arrived at nine p.m. and bivouacked at Frasnes. Reille's closest division (Bachelu) was at Mellet, with another (Foy) at Gosselies, while Girard's and Jérôme's divisions were in contact with the Prussian rearguards at Wangenies and Ransart.

At nine o'clock that evening the Duke of Saxe-Weimar dispatched a request for help to the headquarters at Braine-le-Comte, emphasising the precariousness of his position and his shortage of ammunition. General de Constant Rebecque ordered Perponcher to send reinforcements to Quatre-Bras, but without evacuating Nivelles, which remained an essential piece on Wellington's strategic chessboard should the French launch an attack in the Mons direction.

At four o'clock, as Ney left Napoléon, Marshal Grouchy, in command of the army's cavalry reserve, arrived to seek instructions. Before coming to any decision, Napoléon went off to the right wing to size up the situation. The Pirch II brigade was occupying the Gilly position with no more than 6,000 men, but was slowly being reinforced with elements of von Jagow's 3rd brigade. Pajol's cavalry, in contact since the early afternoon, had been unable to dislodge the

Prussian infantry, which was established in the houses of the village.

By verbal order, Napoléon entrusted command of the right wing to Grouchy. With Vandamme's III Infantry Corps, one division of which was beginning to emerge from Charleroi, attacking their front and Exelmans' corps of dragoons taking them in the flank, the marshal was able to rout the Prussians and drive them back towards Sombreffe.

Vandamme hesitated, overestimating the strength of his adversary, so much so that it was six o'clock before the French columns began to move off. Zieten did not wait for the clash, but pulled his troops back towards Lambusart and Fleurus.

Grouchy, impatient to push on to Sombreffe, wanted Vandamme to forge ahead, but the latter, pleading the fatigue of troops who had been marching throughout the day in great heat and claiming '… not to have received any order from the cavalry commander[36]', declined to take further action and gave the order to bivouac.

WELLINGTON'S RESPONSE

At ten o'clock, Lieutenant Webster was ordered by General de Constant Rebecque to convey the news of the attack at Quatre-Bras to the Prince of Orange. Galloping at full tilt through the summer night, he covered the thirty-two kilometres from Braine-le-Comte to Brussels in record time and at half-past eleven placed the message in the Prince's hands.

From the early evening various confirmations of the French attack towards Charleroi had been arriving at the Allied general headquarters. Nevertheless, Wellington remained puzzled about Napoléon's intentions: 'If everything is as General Zieten thinks', he explained to the Prussian liaison officer, General Müffling, 'I shall concentrate my forces on my left wing, so as to concert my actions with those of the Prussian army, but if a part of the enemy forces were to march on Mons, I would be obliged to concentrate in the centre. Before coming to a decision therefore, I must await news from my outposts at Mons. However, while the destination of my troops is uncertain, that they are to move is certain; I shall issue orders to ensure that they are ready to march[37].'

These orders to muster at their billeting points were transmitted to the Anglo-Dutch divisions at about seven p.m. Further instructions to speed up the movements and to edge the assembly points eastwards, in the direction of Braine-le-Comte, Enghien and Nivelles were dispatched at ten o'clock.

Despite the situation, the Duke did not deem it necessary to abandon his intention of attending the Duchess of Richmond's ball in the rue de la Blanchisserie. The leaders of Belgian nobility, the general officers of the Anglo-Dutch armies and the most prominent members of the British community in Brussels were expected to be at this fashionable event. When, towards eleven o'clock, he called at Müffling's quarters to invite him to accompany him to the event, he explained his position by saying: 'The numerous friends of Napoleon who are here, will be on tiptoe; the well intentioned be pacified; let us therefore go all the same to the Duchess of Richmond's ball[38].'

Supper had just been served when Webster handed the Prince of Orange General de Constant's dispatch: '… this love letter is scented with powder[39]' laughed the Prince, as he was opening it. Prince William then sought the Duke and, whispering in his ear, gave him the news of the attack at Quatre-Bras.

Wellington, sceptical at first, refused to believe in this direct threat to Brussels and, at the risk of seeing Napoléon succeed at the first attempt, was not prepared to separate the Allied armies. Finally, he rose from the table, called over one of his staff officers and ordered him to bear an order to the troops forming the general reserve for them to leave Brussels two hours later. The Duke then calmly resumed his seat and said, to no one in particular: 'I have no further orders to give[40].'

One of the guests, Lieutenant William Verner of the 7th Hussars, recalled: 'Just as we entered the state room and before we had time to go into the Ball room, we were met by Ld. Lord George Lennox [who] said "Verner, the Prussians have been attacked and defeated, and I am going to order the Duke's horses, who is going off immediately." I observed to Captain O'Grady, "Let us go into the room that we may say we were in the Ball room." It is scarcely necessary to say that the room was in the greatest confusion and had the appearance of anything but a Ball room. The officers were hurrying away as fast as possible in order that nothing might prevent their joining their Regiments. At this

Delivery of de Constant's dispatch to the Prince of Orange at the Duchess of Richmond's ball.
Engraving taken from the painting by W Heath, *Intelligence of the Battle of Ligny.*
Victoria and Albert Museum, London.

moment, Lord Uxbridge came to the door. He said, "You gentlemen who have engaged partners, had better finish your dance and get to your quarters as soon as you can." I observed to O'Grady, "Standish, this is no time for dancing, let us try and secure a Cabriolet without loss of time, and be off as soon as we can."[41].'

The dinner party drew to a close; Wellington did not leave the ball until three in the morning. As he took leave of his host, the Duke of Richmond, he confided to him, 'Napoléon has humbugged me, by God! He has gained twenty-four hours march on me[42].'

Quatre-Bras. Oil on canvas by Lady Butler. E Brassine Collection.

THE MORNING OF 16 JUNE

As dawn broke, the Duke was still not convinced that the French offensive had Brussels as its objective. He had gone to the length of ordering the concentration of his troops and had moved their mustering areas somewhat to the west, but the strategic significance of the Quatre-Bras position was still to assume a paramount importance in his mind. After leaving the Duchess of Richmond's ball, Wellington snatched a few hour's sleep before leaving at six for Quatre-Bras, which he did not reach until nine thirty, where the Prince of Orange awaited him.

Meanwhile, de Constant Rebecque had not remained inactive during the night, but had taken some vital steps. At half-past eleven he had suggested to General Perponcher that he should concentrate his entire division on Quatre-Bras and had recalled Chassé to Nivelles, with Collaert's cavalry in support at Arquennes.

Although it was still early in the morning, the heat was already intense; the French infantry found shelter amid the fully-grown crops in the wheatfields, beneath the leafy branches of La Hutte Wood and inside the houses of Frasnes village.

The only contacts were with strong parties of cavalry, which were exchanging shots with the outposts, but Wellington was under no illusions about this apparent calm and ordered the bulk of his army forward to Quatre-Bras, which both guarded the road to Brussels and formed the indispensable hinge of the link with the Prussian army mustered around Sombreffe.

The Naveau Mill at Fleurus. Pencil sketch, unsigned, *c*.1820. Musée Wellington, Waterloo.

The Prussian army was occupied with its redeployment. I Corps, which had borne the brunt of the French attack on the previous day, had established itself for the night between Saint-Armand and Fleurus. II Corps had bivouacked at Mazy and III Corps at Namur and it was nearing midday before they arrived at Sombreffe. Blücher had no more than 83,000 men at his disposal, since IV Corps, still gathering itself together in the Hannut area, would be unable to rejoin the main army before the morrow. The field marshal was nevertheless resolved to join battle with Napoléon at the Ligny position, which had been identified by his staff two months earlier.

At about one o'clock, Wellington and Müffling, taking advantage of the calm still reigning at Quatre-Bras, met Blücher and his staff at Bussy Mill, on the Brye heights. The Duke was insistent on knowing his ally's intentions and he urged him to stand and fight, lest the former find himself having to face the entire French army alone, were the Prussians to retreat.

Blücher, and more especially his chief of staff Gneisenau, had wanted to compensate for the absence of Bülow by the collaboration of the Anglo-Dutch army[43]. For Gneisenau, the main point was to secure the assistance of one of Wellington's army corps, to act as a tactical reserve for the Army of the Lower Rhine. The Duke rejected this request, but remained evasive: 'Well! I will come, provided I am not attacked myself[44].' At two o'clock the cannon began to boom at Quatre-Bras, to which Wellington immediately returned.

The psychological importance of the meeting at Bussy Mill cannot be too greatly emphasised. The ambiguity of Wellington's words were to plant distrust in Gneisenau's mind for the remainder of the campaign, concluding as he did that the Duke was not to be relied upon, having failed to honour what he believed to be a promise of assistance on 16 June.

On the evening of 15th, the Emperor congratulated himself on the day's results. Without too much difficulty, he had advanced deep into enemy territory, with his army gathered around Charleroi, driving before it foes who retired rather than accept combat.

Napoléon persuaded himself that the Allies, disconcerted by his unexpected offensive, were falling back upon their operating bases, the Prussians to Liège and Maastricht and the Anglo-Dutch to Ostend and Antwerp. The direction of the Prussians' retreat tended to confirm this theory: had they moved with the purpose of joining up with the British, they would have withdrawn northwards and not towards the north-east, thus exposing the road to Brussels.

On the morning of the 16th therefore, the Emperor decided on his plan of action. Together with Grouchy and the right wing, he would make for Sombreffe and Gembloux. If there was a Prussian corps still sitting in one or other of these positions, he would attack it. With the ground to the east thus explored and cleared, he would rejoin Marshal Ney and the left wing at Quatre-Bras, together with his reserve waiting at Fleurus, in order to march on Brussels, at night if necessary. At about eight a.m., the orders for the execution of these movements were dispatched.

Grouchy having reported that Prussian columns, which appeared to be coming from Namur, were moving towards Saint-Amand, Napoléon reached Fleurus at about eleven o'clock. There, he had an observation post set up on the roof of Naveau Mill overlooking the plain.

Marshal Ney. Oil on canvas by François Gérard. Musée de l'Armée, Paris.

THE BATTLE OF QUATRE-BRAS

Ney, convinced that he was facing only a weak rearguard, passed the morning awaiting Napoléon's orders. These he received at eleven o'clock and immediately he ordered Reille's Corps to seize the crossroads and establish themselves there, pushing the leading division towards Genappe. But the bulk of II Corps had remained in the Gosselies area and a delay ensued while Foy's division joined up with that of Bachelu, before combat was joined at about two o'clock.

At that point, the Prince of Orange had 8,000 men and 16 cannon to oppose Ney's 9,600 infantry, 4,600 cavalry and 34 cannon.

Attacking on the right of the road, Bachelu's thrust took him as far as Pireaumont. Foy's 1st brigade advanced along the high road, seizing Lairalle and Gémioncourt Farms, while his 2nd brigade advanced through Bossut Wood.

The Anglo-Dutch position was on the point of being taken by storm when Wellington appeared, having returned from Brye. He was preparing to give the signal to retreat when Picton's division and the Brunswick Corps made their providential appearance on the road from Brussels.

These troops, drums beating and pipes sounding, had left Brussels at about two in the morning, as the first colours of dawn were painting the sky. At eight they were at Waterloo, awaiting the order to march to either Nivelles or Quatre-Bras. When, at ten o'clock, Wellington came to his decision, they were sent on their way southwards, but were halted at Genappe, where soup was to be prepared. Alerted by the sound of the gunfire, they emptied out the contents of their cooking pots and hastened towards the battle. Their arrival,

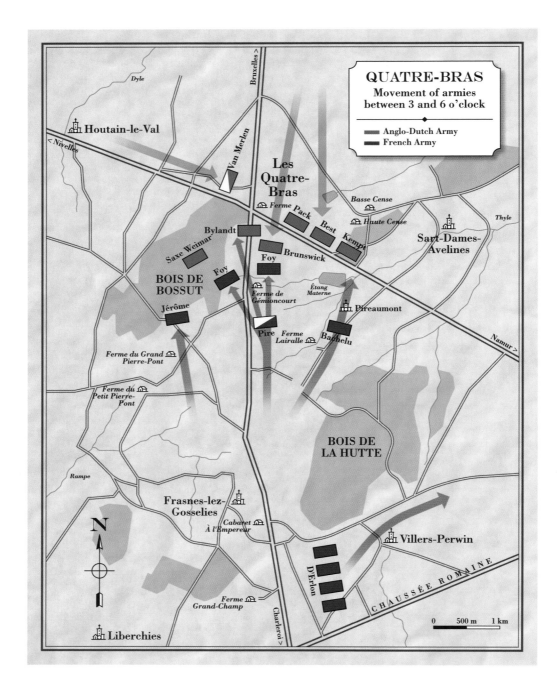

combined with that of van Merlen's Belgian-Dutch cavalry brigade, which had hastened from Nivelles, restored the situation. The time was now nearing four o'clock.

Reille's last division, that of Jérôme Bonaparte, arrived on the field of battle in its turn, reinforcing the French left. It seized Pierrepont Farm and then plunged into Bossut Wood.

In order to enable the Picton and Brunswick infantry to deploy, the Prince of Orange called on van Merlen's brigade to charge the enemy immediately. The latter cavalry, greatly tested by a nine-hour march in overpowering heat, was thrown back in disorder by Piré's squadrons. The Prince of Orange, who had moved forward towards Gémioncourt, owed his safety solely to the speed of his horse.

At that moment Ney received a dispatch from Soult, written at two o'clock, informing him that, given the Prussian dispositions, Napoléon had changed his mind. Instead of a demonstration to force the Prussian rearguards to retreat, a pitched battle was now the plan, in which Ney was assigned a leading role.

QUATRE-BRAS
Movement of armies between 6 and 8 o'clock

Anglo-Dutch Army
French Army

Dyle

Houtain-le-Val

< *Nivelles*

Les Quatre-Bras

Basse Cense

Ferme

Kruse

Haute Cense

Thyle

Perponcher

Best

Kielmansegge

Sart-Dames-Avelines

C. Halkett

Pack

Kempt

BOIS DE BOSSUT

N

Maitland

Ferme de Gémioncour

Étang Materne

Pireaumont

Byng

Foy

Ferme Lairalle

Bachelu

Ferme du Grand Pierre-Pont

Jérôme

Kellermann

Namur >

Pire

Ferme du Petit Pierre-Pont

0   500 m   1 km

BOIS DE LA HUTTE

Bruxelles >

Charleroi >

Rampe

Quatre-Bras looking towards Waterloo.
Coloured aquatint. Illustration taken from
the book, *The Campaign of Waterloo,* by
Robert Bowyer, London, T Bensley &
Son, 1816. Private collection.

While the Emperor assailed Blücher's troops by a frontal attack, Ney was to deploy to his right and, after sweeping up what lay before him, encircle the Prussian army. On receipt of this message, Ney determined on a general attack to take possession of the crossroads.

On the right, Bachelu, having mastered Pireaumont, pushed on towards the Namur road, but his impetus was halted by Picton's battalions, which had meanwhile deployed on the left of the Allied line. Subjected to close-range fire from six battalions, ambushed in standing corn and then charged with the bayonet, the French fell back to their start line, where they reformed.

In the centre, Foy formed his men up in two columns, one on either side of the road, and advanced towards the crossroads. Five hundred metres from his goal, he collided with several battalions of Brunswickers commanded by Duke Frederick William. A charge, by Uhlans and Hussars, was easily repulsed by the French infantry, while the Brunswicker battalions between the road and Bossut Wood fled before reaching the enemy. Attempting to rally them, the Duke of Brunswick fell mortally wounded.

Piré's cavalry, supporting the attack, pursued the fugitives. Seeing the enemy in full flight, the lancers and light cavalry galloped up to the crossroads, where Wellington very nearly fell into their hands, making his escape thanks to the speed of his horse Copenhagen. They charged Picton's regiments vigorously, while the latter hastily formed up in squares which, though sustaining heavy losses, were not broken. Lacking infantry support, Piré's squadrons were unable to achieve any significant success and were obliged to retire exhausted.

It was now six o'clock and Wellington's situation was scarcely more favourable than it had been an hour and a half earlier, despite his numbers being for the present the equal of Ney's. The Marshal had just received a new order, which Soult had dispatched at a quarter past three: 'You are to deploy on the field so as to encircle the enemy's right and strike him hard in the rear. His army is lost if you act vigorously. The fate of France is in your hands – do not hesitate for an instant to carry out the movement which the Emperor has ordered and then make for the high ground at Brye and Saint-Amand[45].'

At the same time, the Marshal learnt that d'Erlon's corps, which constituted his reserve, had been summoned by Napoléon to the battlefield at Ligny. Furious to find himself

The Battle of Quatre-Bras. Unsigned watercolour by Jean-Baptiste Madou. Private collection.

assigned a task whose importance he well understood, while deprived of the means to accomplish it, Ney, disdaining the Imperial instructions, sent d'Erlon a categorical order, commanding him to return his troops to the left wing without delay. For the immediate moment, however, he proposed to profit from his present advantage. He had his artillery increase the rate of its accurate and effective fire and ordered the general movement of his columns, under cover of a wide deployment of his skirmishers.

Once more, Wellington, at a moment of great danger, received an opportune reinforcement of fresh troops. This time, it was Lieutenant General Count Alten who arrived from Nivelles with two brigades of infantry, one British led by Colin Halkett, the other Hanoverian under Kielmansegge, amounting to 5,400 men and 12 cannon. To enable them to be deployed, the 92nd Gordon Highlanders put in a charge along the road and, at the cost of heavy casualties, drove back the French who had advanced to within three hundred metres of the crossroads.

To make his thrust, Ney's reserve now consisted solely of a brigade of *cuirassiers* – 600 sabres. He called on Kellermann: 'My dear general', he said in an abrupt tone, 'the safety of France is at stake, an exceptional effort is required. Take your cavalry and throw yourselves into the midst of the English. Fall on them full tilt!' The Comte de Valmy pointed out to the Marshal how limited were his resources: 'Never mind,' cried Ney, 'charge with what you have. Fall on them full tilt. I will send all the cavalry we have after you…Go…Go at once!'

Kellermann obeyed and formed his two regiments into columns by squadrons. Once within the enemy's range, he lost no time in giving the order to charge, as he recounted, '…in order to give my men no time to think about things or to imagine the full degree of the danger'.

The clash was terrible. 'The first regiment encountered was the 69th, composed of Scotsmen, which discharged its weapons at a range of twenty paces, but the *cuirassiers*, far from being stopped, fell on them full tilt, destroyed them completely and bowled over all who were in their way. Some even got as far as the Quatre-Bras Farm, where they were slain[46].'

The *cuirassiers*, caught in the crossfire from the Allied infantry and supported too belatedly by Piré, were unable to impose themselves and had to fall back. Kellermann, his horse killed by a musket ball, regained the French lines on foot.

That was the end of the French attacks. Ney, with no further reserves to hand, was obliged to abandon his attempts to seize the crossroads. Worse, following Alten, more British reinforcements came on the scene; Cooke and the second echelon of the Brunswicker Corps arrived and compelled him to go on to the defensive. As night fell, Wellington was able to retake Pireaumont and Gémioncourt Farms and Bossut Wood, although he could not manage to break out from them.

At nine o'clock that evening, the two armies were pretty well back in the positions they had been occupying in the morning; by then Wellington had 35,000 men, which were further reinforced during the night. At dusk, Ney was finally joined by d'Erlon's 20,000 men. Each side had lost approximately 5,000 men, dead or wounded. The next day would decide the issue.

THE BATTLE OF LIGNY

The battlefield of Ligny occupied a vast plain, through whose gentle undulations the River Ligne flowed from Saint-Amand to Sombreffe and Balâtre. The valley was marshy and the stream, its banks steep in places, was difficult to cross. The disposition of the two armies was somewhat unusual. Blücher's troops were formed in a kind of inverted right angle, with the point at Sombreffe and the two arms extending as far as Boignée to the right and Saint-Amand to the left.

The Prussian right was very strong: in the first line, Zieten's corps occupied Wagnelée, Saint-Amand and Ligny with three brigades (Steinmetz, Jagow and Henckel), while Pirch II's brigade and Röder's cavalry were in reserve near Brye. In the second line, deployed along the road to Nivelles, from the Roman road as far as Sombreffe, were the four infantry brigades (Tippelskirsch, Krafft, Brause and Langen) and Jürgass' cavalry from Pirch I's corps.

The left, resting on Tongrinne and Boignée, consisted of Thielmann's corps, with the brigades of Borcke, Kemphen, Luck and Stülpnagel, and Hobe's cavalry.

On his left, Napoléon had deployed Vandamme's three divisions (Habert, Berthezène and Lefol), reinforced by Girard's division.

In the centre, between the two arms of the right angle, was Gérard's corps, two divisions of which (Pécheux and

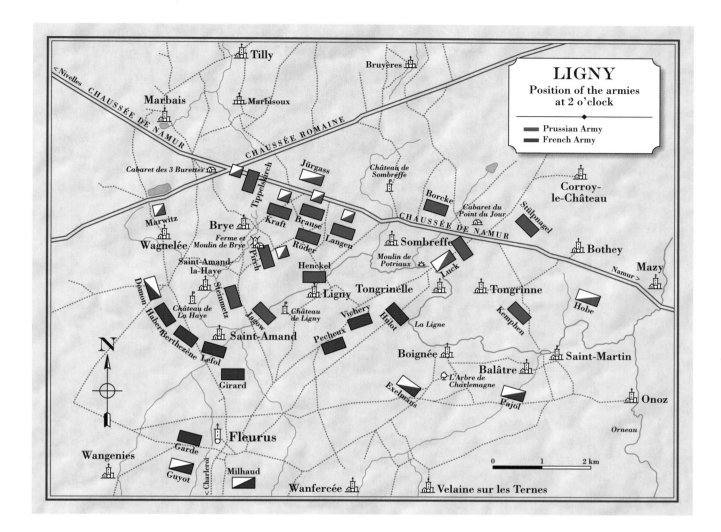

LIGNY
Position of the armies
at 2 o'clock

Prussian Army
French Army

Vichery) faced Zieten, while Hulot's single division and Exelmans' and Pujol's cavalry corps stretched out facing Thielmann's corps.

The Guard, Lobau's corps and Milhaud's heavy cavalry, stationed at Fleurus, constituted the reserve.

In all, Napoléon had 71,000 men and 242 cannon, against Blücher's 83,000 men and 224 cannon.

Napoléon's original plan had been simply to drive the Prussians from what he presumed was a rearguard position and to accelerate their retreat towards Namur or Liège. But at two p.m., seeing the enemy columns assembling between Sombreffe and Brye, he decided to take advantage of Blücher's apparent readiness to stand and fight and engage him in a decisive battle.

Following the most classical of military traditions, he proposed to launch a frontal attack and then, by a turning movement from the left, crush him between the jaws of his pincers. While III and IV Corps thus attacked the enemy in the direction of Saint-Amand and Ligny, Ney, after trampling down the minor elements which might be standing in his way, was to push down the Namur road and encircle the Prussian army.

The marshal was informed of the Emperor's changed intentions in two dispatches from Soult, received at four o'clock and half-past five respectively, which charged him at all costs to capture Quatre-Bras. To achieve this objective, he would be reinforced by I Corps, marching to him from Gosselies and whose arrival was imminent. However, Ney had learnt that d'Erlon had been sent, by the direct orders of the Emperor, to march towards the Prussian rear and that he could therefore no longer count on him. What had led to these changes?

At about three thirty, as the battle of Ligny was in progress, the Emperor, who attached the greatest importance to the encircling manoeuvre which he had entrusted to Ney, sent to him an aide-de-camp bearing a pencil-written note, asking Ney to lend him support in the form, at the very least, of I Corps. 'You are to say to Ney', Napoléon had stressed, 'that no matter what situation he is in, this order must be complied with absolutely; that I do not attach great importance to what happens today where he is and that all that matters is taking place here with me, for I want to have done with the Prussian army. For his part, he must, if he cannot do better, content himself with the containment of the British army[47].'

This officer, meeting the head of I Corps column at Frasnes, took it upon himself to divert it in the Ligny direc-tion, even before he had passed the Emperor's orders on to Ney and without the knowledge of d'Erlon. The latter was the first to hear of the business, as he recounted: 'I went on ahead to see what was happening at Quatre-Bras ... Beyond Frasnes I was joined by General Labédoyère, who showed me a pencil-written note which he was taking to Marshal Ney and which instructed him to send my army corps to Ligny. General Labédoyère told me that he had already given the order for this movement and had redirected my column, pointing out where I could rejoin it. Immediately I set off in that direction and sent my chief of staff, General Delcambre, to Marshal Ney to advise him of my new desti-nation. Marshal Ney sent him back to me, stipulating that I must without fail return to Quatre-Bras[48].'

Blücher's heroic fight of 16 June 1815.
Coloured etching, attributed to G Böttger Senior, published by Camp, 1816. Musée Royal de l'Armée, Brussels.

At about six o'clock, the order reached Durutte's division, which was marching at the head of I Corps, in the direction of Wagnelée and Brye. Comte d'Erlon prevaricated, losing time in doing so, but finally ordered the column to turn around, though leaving Durutte outside Wagnelée. By the time I Corps returned to Frasnes, night was approaching.

It was three o'clock when, in overpowering heat, three cannon shots, fired by the Guard's battery, gave the signal for the French attack to be launched against the Prussian centre and right wing at Ligny and Saint-Amand.

Vandamme's Corps opened the action at Saint-Amand; General Lefol, having harangued his division, launched it against the village in three columns, to the sound of drums and bands playing the *Chant du Départ*. Despite the absence of any preparatory artillery barrage and strong resistance from Jagow's battalions, the French dislodged them, but a counter-attack by Steinmetz prevented them from breaking out of the village. While Berthezène's division deployed to the left of Lefol, Girard, without great loss, took possession of Le Hameau and La Haye.

In the centre, the attack on Ligny launched by Gérard's corps met with serious difficulties. Three times Pécheux' division was thrown back by Henckel's infantrymen occupying the village, who were well supported by the cannon, which swept the approaches with their fire. Relentlessly, Gérard brought up 12-pounder batteries from the Guard to reinforce his artillery. A hail of bullets and shells fell upon the village, in which fires were started.

Pécheux, with a brigade from Vichery's division in support, began a violent assault, which was characterised by extremely ferocious fighting. Every house was contested, in the narrow streets the soldiers fired at one another at point-blank range and the fighting became hand-to-hand.

'The men slaughtered one another', said a Prussian officer, 'as if driven by a personal hatred. It seemed as if each of them saw in his opponent a mortal enemy on whom he rejoiced to find a chance to be revenged. No one thought to flee or to plead for quarter[49].' Blücher, to resist the fury of the French attacks, was obliged to throw in, one by one, the reserves of Henckel's and Jagow's brigades, as well as Kram's brigade and part of Langen's brigade from Pirch I's corps.

The French, who had also had to introduce Vichery's second brigade, succeeded, at the cost of two and a half hours of merciless fighting, in taking possession of the eastern half of the village, without managing to cross the Ligne, the left bank of which, together with the church and the château, remained in Prussian hands.

Meanwhile, Grouchy, on the right, confined himself, without much difficulty or loss, to a demonstration which held down Thielmann's Corps.

From the top of Bussy Mill, Blücher had been watching anxiously the progress of Vandamme's corps which, after an hour's fighting, was in a position to threaten his communications with Wellington along the Nivelles-Namur road, or to initiate a manoeuvre to encircle the defenders of Ligny.

In order to ward off the dangers threatening his right wing, he ordered Pirch II's brigade to counter-attack against La Haye, while Tippelskirch's brigade, supported by Jürgass' cavalry, attacked Vandamme's troops on their flank.

After two unsuccessful attacks, the Pirch II soldiers became discouraged. Old Blücher made for them and, living up to his nickname of 'General Vorwärts', urged them: 'Hold fast lads! Don't let those fellows tell you what to do! Forward, for God's sake, forward![50]'

A third attack yielded them possession of the Château of La Haye, key to the position. General Girard was mortally wounded and his men were forced back towards Le Hameau.

Tippelkirch's actions were not crowned with the same success. Vandamme, forewarned by the enemy's preparations, dispatched one brigade of Habert's division and Domon's cavalry towards Wagnelée. Two battalions deployed as skirmishers, hidden in the tall wheat and supported by a battery of eight cannon loaded with case-shot, surprised the Prussians, who had emerged from Wagnelée without having taken the precaution of reconnoitring their line of advance. The head of the column, overwhelmed by fire which was as brisk as it was unexpected, broke up in disorder, while the rest of the brigade beat a retreat. Inexplicably, Jürgass' cavalry remained inactive.

It was then nearly half-past five. Despite the bitterness of the fighting and the tenaciousness of the combatants, neither Napoléon nor Blücher had achieved any significant success. However, each of them believed that he could win the day, by throwing his reserves into a decisive manoeuvre. In this respect, the Emperor wielded a clear advantage, in the shape of more than 30,000 fresh troops (the Guard, Lobau's VI Corps and Milhaud's cavalry), while Blücher, in the attritional fighting of the afternoon, had used up nearly all his resources.

Napoléon's plan envisaged the puncturing of the enemy centre at Ligny, so as to take his right wing in the rear, massed at Saint-Amand. In the Emperor's mind, this attack should coincide with the arrival of Ney, or at the least d'Erlon, at Brye. Three quarters of the Prussian army, caught between two fires, would be destroyed. This scheme was all the more remarkable in that he used to his advantage Blücher's own intentions, which were to encircle the French left, for which the latter had massed the bulk of his forces before Saint-Amand.

Lacking any news of Ney, Napoléon made his arrangements for the final attack. To provide for all eventualities, he sent the Young Guard and six battalions of the Old Guard to reinforce his position at Saint-Amand, while he himself marched on Ligny with three battalions of the Old Guard, Lobau's Corps, the heavy cavalry of the Guard and Milhaud's *cuirassiers*.

These movements were in the course of execution when Napoléon received from Vandamme a report of the presence on the left of an unidentified column, which was probably hostile. The Emperor, uneasy, caused the preparations for the attack to be halted and sent an aide-de-camp to the spot, to check the truth of matters. The news of the threat by an enemy column had spread amongst Vandamme's troops and had caused '…a kind of panic', said General Lefol[51].

This wavering coincided with a new attack on Saint-Amand by the brigades of Tippelskirch, Pirch II and Krafft. Outflanked, the French gave way. Le Hameau was retaken, La Haye reoccupied and a part of Saint-Amand lost. Four regiments of the Young Guard were brought into the line, which was stabilised and enabled the French to recover the ground lost at Saint-Amand and Le Hameau.

At Ligny, the Prussians had also renewed their attacks and it was with the greatest of difficulty that IV Corps, wholly taken up with the defence of the village, succeeded in holding on.

By this time, on the other side of the battlefield, Thielmann had abandoned the hopes he had nurtured since the early afternoon and, weakened by the involvement of his Langen and Stülpnagel brigades, he confined himself to the occupation of Potriaux.

It was then nearly half-past seven. Blücher, satisfied with his troops' success, decided to concentrate his last efforts on Vandamme's corps and then to fall back on the road to Fleurus. Placing himself at the head of Langen's last battalions, he renewed the assault on Saint-Amand with the remains of the Steinmetz, Brause, Pirch II and Tippelskirch brigades – all that remained of 41 battalions.

'My men have fired all their cartridges as well as emptying the pouches of the dead – they have no more bullets to fire', Pirch II objected. 'Fix bayonets then!' cried Blücher, flinging himself forward at the head of his troops[52].

The weather all day had been heavy and stifling, but the sun was now hidden behind large black storm clouds which covered the sky; the rain began to fall and the rumble of thunder added its sound to that of the artillery. Habert's, Duhesme's and Girard's divisions fell back, but the Prussian attack was broken by the three light cavalry regiments of the Guard deployed before La Haye.

While Blücher staked everything at Saint-Amand, Napoléon, relieved to find that the column which had appeared beyond Wagnelée was the leading division of I Corps, struck at Ligny. Preceded by a considerable cannonade, three regiments of grenadiers and a regiment of light cavalry of the Old Guard attacked Ligny, followed by all of VI Corps' infantry, flattening everything in their path. The Prussians, exhausted, overwhelmed and discouraged, offered only feeble resistance. The attack was accompanied by the regimental bands playing 'Victory is ours', while Guyot's and Milhaud's squadrons covered either flank. Röder's cavalry was hastily summoned, to try and halt the breaking wave, but assailed by the fire of the infantry and a brisk charge by Milhaud's *cuirassiers*, it was thrown back with heavy losses.

Heroically, the seventy-three years-old Blücher reformed his horsemen and charged at their head, but in vain. The field marshal's horse, a superb grey which had been a gift from Britain's Prince Regent, was shot under him. Blücher escaped capture only by chance and the arrival of dusk.

The fall of Ligny, opening up the Prussian army's centre, obliged the troops engaged at Saint-Amand to retreat, falling back in haste towards the Namur road to escape encirclement. Thielmann did the same, withdrawing in good order towards Sombreffe. As darkness fell, all fighting ceased. The rain had ceased; the storm had passed on.

Ruins of Ligny. The château on the right of the engraving was situated at the western edge of Ligny, about 700 metres from the church. At that time, it was already partly in ruins. Coloured aquatint engraving and etching, published by Colburn in 1816, Musée Wellington, Waterloo.

Prince Blücher under his horse at the Battle of Waterloo. Etching and aquatint by M Dubourg, after J A Atkinson, published by E Orme on 20 August 1815. The title of the etching is incorrect – the event took place at Ligny. Musée Wellington, Waterloo.

Wellington's March from Quatre-Bras to Waterloo. Oil on canvas by Ernest Crofts. Sheffield Galleries and Museum Trust, Sheffield.

6. THE EVENTS OF 17 JUNE 1815

By the evening following the battle of Ligny, the Prussian army was beaten. It had lost 12,000 men, dead and wounded, without counting several thousand deserters and prisoners, while enemy losses did not exceed 8,500 men. However, although Blücher had given way before the thrusts of the French reserve, he had retired in good order.

Inexplicably, Napoléon, who still had fresh troops – VI Corps and abundant cavalry – to call on, took no steps to pursue the Prussian army and prevent it from reforming. He went no further than to order Exelmans' and Pajol's divisions to follow the enemy during the early hours. This inactivity saved the Army of the Lower Rhine from becoming disorganised and allowed it very swiftly to recover its operational capabilities.

Blücher, bruised by his fall, had been borne off to Mellery; at his headquarters he was thought to be either dead or a prisoner and Gneisenau therefore assumed command. An on-the-spot decision was needed to decide the direction of the retreat. A withdrawal towards Namur would bring the army closer to its lines of communication with Liège, but would widen the gap between it and its Anglo-Dutch ally. Gneisenau decided upon a retirement on Wavre, which would safeguard the links with Wellington. He sent I Corps into quarters at Tilly, II at Gentinnes and III at Sombreffe. The rearguards posted at Brye and Sombreffe remained in contact with the French pickets throughout the night.

At daybreak Zieten and Pirch broke camp, and moving via Gentinnes, Chastres and Mont-Saint-Guilbert, reached Wavre at about midday, where they took up positions on both banks of the Dyle. Thielmann proceeded to Gembloux, where his troops rested from seven until two in the after-noon. It was eight o'clock that evening when they arrived at Wavre, where they bivouacked to the north of the village.

Bülow had not taken part in the battle of Ligny and learned of the defeat as he was marching along the Roman road, in the neighbourhood of Baudeset. Moving via Walhain and Corbais, he did not reach Dion-Valmont until late in the evening.

Pajol's and Exelmans' cavalry were in the saddle at dawn. Pajol reconnoitred in the direction of Namur, gathering in stragglers such as a supply convoy and a stray battery. Arrived at Spy, he realised that there was nothing else in front of him and halted.

Exelmans' dragoons were more fortunate. Acting on information from the local inhabitants, Berton's brigade followed the trail of Thielmann's Corps, which at about nine o'clock it discovered resting on the other side of Gembloux. But Exelmans was slow in communicating this information to Grouchy. Zieten and Pirch slipped away unnoticed by the French; only two regiments of cavalry were left at Tilly, under the orders of Colonel Sohr.

Napoléon had spent the night at Fleurus; at seven that morning General Flahaut, returning from Ney's headquarters, gave him an account of the battle of Quatre-Bras. At much the same time, he received a first report from Pajol which at that time indicated that the Prussians were retiring in the direction of Namur. On the basis of this information, the Emperor dictated a long dispatch to Ney. It illustrated clearly both his illusions and his intentions on the morning of 17 June.

Napoléon believed the Prussian army to be in full flight, making for Namur and Liège. He also thought that Wellington had been obliged to fall back and ordered the

Marshal to occupy the Quatre-Bras position: '…which must now be held only by a rearguard'. If such was not the case, the Emperor would advance on it directly along the Namur road, while Ney assailed the British army with a frontal attack.

'The whole of today', he concluded, 'will be necessary to complete this operation and to restock with ammunition, collect up scattered soldiers and bring in the detachments. Give the necessary orders and make sure that the wounded are tended and carried to the rear: there have been complaints that the medical orderlies have been failing in their duties[53].'

Thus, the Emperor's plans for the morning of the 17th were limited to resupplying the army and the occupation of Quatre-Bras. When Grouchy came to him at eight o'clock, asking for his orders concerning the pursuit of Blücher, he replied testily: 'I will give you those when I think fit[54].'

At about nine o'clock, he left his headquarters at Fleurus to examine the battlefield at Ligny. Prior to this, he had sent Teste's division to support Pajol, near Namur, and had drafted a bulletin for Paris, to announce the victory. He gave orders for helping the wounded, emphasising that Prussians as well as French were to be brought in.

As the Emperor passed he was received with cheers from the men, who had been preparing their soup. He talked with them on familiar terms and congratulated the officers, then, dismounting, he chatted with his staff about the political situation in France.

DELAYED PURSUIT OF THE PRUSSIAN ARMY

It was eleven o'clock when Napoléon made his final preparations. A letter from Ney, dispatched at half-past six, but not received until ten o'clock, had informed him that the British were still at Quatre-Bras in force.

Exelmans' dispatch had reported the presence of Prussian forces at Gembloux. He sent VI Corps and the Guard to Marbais to reinforce his left and summoned Grouchy: 'Get after the Prussians – as soon as you come up with them, attack them and complete their defeat. Never let them out of your sight. I am going to rejoin Marshal Ney and join battle with the British, if they are this side of Soignes Forest. All the probabilities lead me to think that it is on the Meuse and towards Liège that Marshal Blücher is retreating, so move in that direction[55].'

To perform his mission, Grouchy was given III and IV infantry Corps, reinforced by Teste's division and Pajol's and Exelmans' cavalry corps. The marshal commented on the difficulty of his task: the enemy had eighteen hour's start and his lines of retreat were unknown. It did not seem to him very realistic to expect 32,000 soldiers to accomplish the defeat of an army of 100,000 men which had withdrawn from the battlefield neither demoralised nor disorganised. 'Do you think that you know better than I what I have to do?' was the Emperor's curt response[56].

An hour later, Napoléon confirmed his intentions with a written order: 'Proceed to Gembloux […] It is important to deduce the enemy's intentions: either he will part company with the British, or they intend to come together again to cover Brussels and Liège, trusting to the outcome of a battle[57].'

Grouchy gave the order for III Corps to march on Gembloux via Point-du-Jour, with Gérard's following. Time had already been lost, as Grouchy relates: 'As soon as the Emperor had left me […] I went to Comte Gérard's headquarters at Ligny and gave him the order for his corps to take up arms as quickly as possible […] Comte Gérard appeared very annoyed and advanced various pretexts to excuse himself from carrying it out immediately. I tried to make him understand how important it was not to delay for an instant in beginning his pursuit of the Prussians, whom the Emperor had permitted to gain fifteen or sixteen hour's start over the troops sent to pursue them, but in vain. However powerful this factor might be, it was not sufficient to overcome his surliness and, instead of calling for his horses, he ordered his people to prepare his dinner. I left him then, indignant as I pictured all the difficulties which I had met in trying to make generals such as Comte Gérard and Comte Vandamme obey me – the one exhibiting all the discontent he was feeling that his fine feats of arms of the previous day had not earned him a marshal's baton, and the other aggrieved to find himself under my command[58].'

Progress was very slow; Vandamme took three hours to reach Point-du-Jour and did not arrive at Gembloux, which had been evacuated by Thielmann's Prussians, until seven that evening, while it was past nine o'clock before Gérard appeared, even though from Saint-Amand to Gembloux it is only eleven kilometres as the crow flies.

The French troops were compressed into a single column along the road to Gembloux, which was narrow and unpaved and this, together with a violent storm which struck the

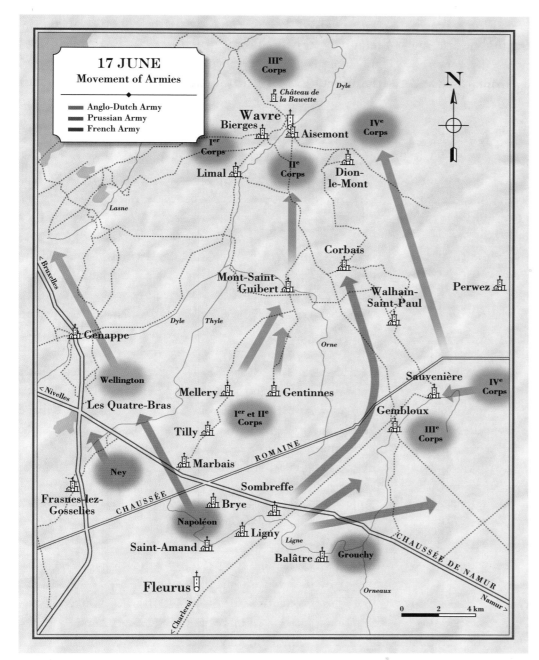

17 JUNE
Movement of Armies

◆

▬ Anglo-Dutch Army
▬ Prussian Army
▬ French Army

N

the other appears to be making for Perwez. From that, it may perhaps be inferred that one part is going to link up with Wellington and that the centre – Blücher's army – is retiring on Liège, another column with artillery having retreated through Namur...' and concluded as follows: 'If the Prussian mass retires on Wavre, I will follow it in that direction, to prevent them from reaching Brussels and enabling me to separate them from Wellington. If, on the other hand, my information proves that the main Prussian force has marched to Perwez, I will proceed to that town to pursue the enemy[59].' This dispatch reached Napoléon at his headquarters at Le Caillou at about three in the morning.

Wellington, who had spent the night at the *Roi d'Espagne* inn at Genappe, returned to Quatre-Bras at daybreak. He was in the greatest uncertainty about the outcome of the battle which his Prussian ally had fought, six kilometres away. The officer sent by Gneisenau the night before, with news of the defeat, had been wounded by a French patrol and had been unable to carry out his task. One of the Duke's aides, Alexander Gordon, was dispatched for information. At seven, he returned, reporting that the Prussians were withdrawing to Wavre.

whole area from two o'clock and turned the earthern roads into quagmires, slowed their progress.

Grouchy set up his headquarters at Gembloux. The French advance guards had lost contact and reconnoitring parties were sent in the direction of Tourinnes and Perwez to search for the enemy's trail.

At about ten that evening, Grouchy, in a message to Napoléon, summarised his information: 'According to all the reports, the Prussians are split into two columns, one seems to be on the road to Wavre via Sart-à-Walhain,

'Ma foi c'est bien loin,[60]' observed Wellington, adding: 'Old Blücher has had a damned good licking and gone back to Wavre, eighteen miles. As he has gone back, we must go too. I suppose in England, they will say we have been licked. I can't help it[61].'

He issued his orders to retreat to Waterloo and informed the field marshal of his intentions: 'I propose to take up my position at Mont-Saint-Jean. There I shall await Napoléon to join battle with him, if I can count on the support of just one Prussian corps. But if I cannot have that support, I shall be obliged to sacrifice Brussels and take up a position behind the Scheldt[62].'

Between nine and ten in the morning, the Anglo-Dutch troops set off to march down the Brussels road[63]. One column withdrew via Sart-Dames-Avelines, Baisy-Thy and Ways. The Adam, du Plat, W Halkett and Mitchell brigades, which had arrived at Nivelles during the night, moved directly to Waterloo along the Mont-Saint-Jean road.

To protect the army's possible line of retreat, Prince Frederick was ordered to assemble at Hal, Bierghes and Tubize the 1st Netherlands division (6,400 men), the Anthing brigade (3,500 men) and the Johnstone and Lyon brigades (5,000 men), which were already coming together.

This movement was accomplished with the utmost orderliness, behind a screen of cavalry and light infantry. Uxbridge was put in command of the rearguard, the Duke himself remaining at Quatre-Bras until two p.m. By one o'clock, all Allied infantry, with the exception of several Brunswicker battalions, had withdrawn and was on the way to Mont-Saint-Jean.

The manoeuvre had been perfectly executed and deceived the French. Marshal Ney had seen nothing and remained convinced that before him were at least eight regiments of infantry and two thousand horse, as he had reported to Napoléon that morning. Given the enemy's strength, he waited for the reinforcements promised by the Emperor before resuming the fight.

At midday, Lobau and the Guard were at Marbais and Napoléon sent Ney the order to attack the Allied position, while at about one o'clock he himself arrived at the head of his columns by carriage. A hussar patrol brought to him an Englishwoman who had just been taken prisoner; in confident terms, she told him that Wellington's army had escaped towards the north and that the crossroads was now occupied by cavalry alone. It was at once clear to the Emperor that he had lost the chance to catch Wellington in a trap. He leapt on his horse and, followed by his attendant squadrons, made for the advance guard at a fast trot.

As two o'clock approached, the French emerged from the Namur road on the British left. The weather, which had been very cool in the morning, had turned stormy and large black clouds were gathering above the Allied position. Captain Mercer had deployed his horse artillery troop so as to cover the road in enfilade, when General Vandeleur ordered him to move the cannon to allow his Hussars to charge: 'I was

preparing to obey, when up came Lord Uxbridge, and the scene changed in a twinkling.

"Captain Mercer, are you loaded?"

"Yes my lord."

"Then give them a round as they rise the hill, and retire as quickly as possible…They are just coming up the hill", said Lord Uxbridge. "Let them get well up before your fire. Do you think you can retire quick enough afterwards?"

"I am sure of it, my Lord."

"Very well, then, keep a good look-out and point your guns well."

'…Lord Uxbridge was yet speaking, when a single horseman, immediately followed by several others, mounted the plateau… their dark figures thrown forward in strong relief from the illuminated distance, making them appear much nearer to us than they really were. [It was the Emperor and his entourage.] For an instant they pulled up and regarded us, when several squadrons were coming rapidly on the plateau, Lord Uxbridge cried out "Fire! Fire!" And, giving them a general discharge, we quickly limbered up to retire, as they dashed forward supported by some horse-artillery guns, which opened upon us ere we could complete the manoeuvre, but without much effect. [64]'

Simultaneously, the storm broke and torrential rain deluged both armies.

The British cavalry withdrew in three columns: Vivian and Vandeleur through Baisy and Glabais, Somerset's and Ponsonby's brigades along the Brussels road and Dörnberg through Loupoigne. The 7th Hussars and the 23rd Dragoons brought up the rear on the highway.

Anxious to make up for lost time, albeit a little late, Napoléon sent the light cavalry of Jacquinot and Subervie in pursuit of the British, with a horse battery of the Guard in support. Milhaud's *cuirassiers* accompanied them in the second line, followed by I Infantry Corps.

In the midst of all this, Ney arrived, whereupon the Emperor took him to task for his inaction during the morning. The Marshal excused himself by explaining that he believed that he had had Wellington's entire army in front of him. There was a fairly brisk exchange of words, following which Napoléon galloped off to rejoin the head of the column.

The elements were at their most turbulent: torrents of water fell on the countryside, flooding the roadways and soaking the ground. At five or six paces it was impossible to distinguish the colours of the uniforms.

At first, the British rearguard was pursued by the French cavalry at a brisk pace: 'We were galloping for our lives,' said Mercer. Riding alongside his men, Uxbridge encouraged them and called: 'Make haste! Make haste! For God's sake, gallop, or you will be taken[65].'

But movement was slowed by the force of the rain. On paved surfaces the horses could maintain a trot, but the minor roads had become difficult to negotiate.

Meanwhile Uxbridge, ordering his column to remount, had deployed his two heavy cavalry brigades and two troops of horse artillery to the north of Genappe. A squadron of the 7th Hussars sniped at the enemy in the village for a while, before superior numbers forced it to retire.

The 1st Lancers under Colonel Jaquinot emerged from the village and came under fire from the British batteries.

Uxbridge sent in the 7th Hussars, who were easily repulsed, but the 1st Life Guards followed at top speed and ejected the French who were in Genappe. Now the 2nd Lancers under Sourd joined in and, after a desperate hand-to-hand fight, drove the Life Guards out again.

In the course of the mêlée, Sourd suffered several sabre slashes in the right arm, which Larrey amputated on the spot. Napoléon had been nearby and observed the engagement; as a reward for his gallantry, he made the brave colonel a general, but the latter refused his promotion: 'The greatest favour you can grant me is to allow me to remain colonel of my regiment of lancers, which I hope to lead to victory. I refuse the rank of general, if the great Napoléon will pardon me. The rank of colonel is enough for me[66].' An hour later, he remounted his horse and returned to France[67].

The eve of Waterloo, 17 June 1815. Oil on canvas by H Chartier, Musée de l'Armée, Paris.

The fight continued for nearly an hour; the cannon roared on either side and parties of horsemen sniped at the advance guards. On their side, the British deployed their rocket troop, as Mercer described: 'It was now the first time that I discovered the Major [Whinyates] and his rocket troop, who, annoyed at my having the rear, had disobeyed the order to retreat, and remained somewhere in the neighbourhood until this moment, hoping to share whatever might be going on… [As they were were leaving Genappe] in order to amuse the enemy and our own cavalry, as well as to present the former noticing the slackness of our fire, I proposed to Major MacDonald making use of the rockets, which had hitherto done nothing… at last my proposition was agreed to, and down they marched into the thick of the skirmishers in the bottom…

Whilst they prepared their machinery, I had time to notice what was going on to the right and left of us. Two double lines of skirmishers extended all along the bottom – the foremost of each line were within a few yards of each other – constantly in motion, riding backwards and forwards, firing their carbines or pistols, and then reloading, still on the move.

This fire seemed to me more dangerous for those on the hills above than for us below; for all, both French and English, generally stuck out their carbines or pistols as they continued to move backwards and forwards, and discharged them without taking any particular aim, and mostly in the air. I did not see a man fall on either side; the thing appeared quite ridiculous; and but for hearing the bullets whizzing overhead, one might have fancied it no more than a sham-fight.

Meanwhile the rocketeers had placed a little iron triangle in the road with a rocket lying on it. The order to fire is given – port-fire applied – the fidgety missile begins to sputter out sparks and wriggle its tail for a second or so, and then darts forth straight up the chaussée. A gun stands right in its way, between the wheels of which the shell in the head of the rocket bursts, the gunners fall right and left, and, those of the other guns taking to their heels, the battery is deserted in an instant. Strange; but so it was. I saw them run, and for some minutes afterwards I saw the guns standing mute and unmanned, whilst our rocketeers kept shooting off rockets, none of which followed the course of the first; most of them, on arriving about the middle of the ascent, took a vertical direction, whilst some actually turned back upon ourselves, and one of these, following me like a squib until its shell exploded, actually put me in more danger than all the fire of the enemy throughout the day. Meanwhile, the French artillerymen, seeing how the land lay, returned to their guns and opened a fire of case-shot on us, but without effect, for we retreated to our ridge without the loss of a man, or even any wounded, though the range could not have been above 200 yards[68].'

After the clash at Genappe, the pursuit of the British rearguard slowed somewhat. The weather remained appalling, with the torrential rain of a summer storm continuing to pour down on to the countryside.

At about six o'clock, the French light cavalry, in the form of Subervie's and Jaquinot's divisions, emerged on to the Brussels road near Plancenoit. Marbot's 7th Hussars pushed two squadrons and some skirmishers into La Haye Sainte. Marshal Ney, who was with the advance guard, drew up the troops, for the enemy seemed to have halted and formed his line on the other side of the valley. At this moment Napoléon arrived before La Belle Alliance, dripping wet, '…his legendary hat with its buckles torn by the rainstorm and resembling the headgear worn by Don Basilio in the Barber of Seville[69].'

He took up a position on a slight eminence to the left of the road, from where he could make out the enemy's position, and directed his telescope towards the horizon, clouded in mist and merging with the foliage of Soignes Forest.

The French advance guard had been greeted by the fire of the British cannon. Napoléon decided to discover whether a rearguard engagement, as at Genappe two hours earlier, was involved and set up a feigned charge by Milhaud's *cuirassiers*, who had just arrived. This movement, which was supported by fire from four horse batteries, earned a general response from the British line, but Wellington immediately ordered a cease-fire[70]. Several balls fell amongst the little group of officers around Napoléon.

The magnitude of the reply made it clear to the Emperor that there was no possibility of driving the enemy out that evening. He had only a small number of troops available and night would have fallen before his preparations had been completed. He ordered firing to cease.

For a long time, beneath rain which though less heavy continued to fall, he remained in the saddle outside La Belle Alliance, scanning the horizon in the failing light, trying to make out the movements of the British army. One by one, Drouet d'Erlon's divisions arrived from the road. With the sky sombre and overcast, night came on very rapidly. Napoléon gave the order to bivouac and retraced his steps to Le Caillou, where he planned to set up his headquarters.

Watercolour lithograph by Taillois after Montius. Musée Wellington, Waterloo.

La Belle Alliance

The origin of this pleasant landscape is unknown, although there is a direct link with its first occupants. In 1764, Joseph Monnoie had married a young girl, Barbe-Marie Tordeur who, like him, hailed from the Nivelles area. He built the little farm in 1766, but died shortly afterwards. His widow remarried the following year, her new husband being a farmer from Plancenoit, Jacques Dedave. This marriage was also short-lived for, in 1770, Barbe-Marie Tordeur, once more a widow, married a certain Jean-Jacques Delbauche. She died in about 1777.

According to tradition, the name Belle Alliance had been conferred on the farm, either in memory of the beauty of Marie Tordeur, or to deride her third marriage, in which her husband is supposed to have been her farmhand.
At the time of the battle, this little farm was also a tavern which served as a stopping place for the carters who transported coal from Charleroi to Brussels.

King William stopped there on 28 July 1815 when he was exploring the Waterloo plain and Tsar Alexander I did the same in October. The humble inn was visited again by the King of Prussia in 1817 and by the King of England, with the Duke of Wellington as his personal guide, in 1821.

Waterloo. The Duke of Wellington's Headquarters. Coloured aquatint engraved by Charles Turner, from a drawing done on the spot by Captain George J Jones, published in London on 20 May 1816 by Turner and Booth. Wellington Museum, Waterloo.

Wellington's Headquarters at Waterloo

The name Waterloo is very old, the first mention of it dating back to 1145. The Forest Abbey possessed considerable property in the area. The name meant a damp and marshy meadow, which described the nature of the location in which the Forest Abbey Farm was built. In 1815 Waterloo was a small village inhabited by foresters and navvies, containing a number of taverns and inns which served as stopping places for the carters who transported coal from Charleroi to Brussels. Wellington set up his headquarters in a fine building which had been built in 1705 by a road building contractor, Hubert Olivet. The widow Antoine Bodenghien was the owner and maintained it as an inn and staging post.

7. THE NIGHT OF 17 – 18 JUNE 1815

When Napoléon arrived at Le Caillou his quarters were not ready, so, while the Emperor waited for his bedroom to be made fit to receive him, he dried himself before a great fire which had been lit in the farmyard.

Once installed in the main building, he had his rain-soaked boots removed and, accompanied by Ney, sat down to supper, after which he lay on the bed. They went on talking well into the evening, until Ney finally left to return to Chantelet Farm where his own headquarters were situated. At about nine o'clock, General Milhaud arrived to report that his scouts had encountered a column of Prussian cavalry in the course of withdrawing from Tilly in the direction of Wavre.

Napoléon's sole preoccupation on that evening of 17 June was to be able to bring the Anglo-Dutch to battle on the following day. His fear was that Wellington might slip away before his eyes, whereas he was sure that the Allied troops, with their backs to Soignes Forest, would be at his mercy if they were forced to fight, since in the event of their defeat they would have but one narrow road down which to retreat to Brussels[71].

Soult did not share his optimism and pointed out to the Emperor that he was liable to find Wellington a tough opponent. Wisdom demanded that one of the infantry corps given to Grouchy be recalled since, if as Napoléon believed Blücher was in full retreat, it was pointless to waste 33,000 good troops on his pursuit. But Napoléon was convinced that he had given the Prussians such a beating that he could not imagine Blücher being able to assemble all his forces at Wavre and then join up with Wellington's army on the morrow to go on to the offensive. He therefore saw no necessity for reinforcements and dismissed Soult's suggestion.

During the night, Napoléon slept but little, disturbed by many comings and goings, some seeking orders, others reporting the results of a mission. At three o'clock, he sent General Gourgaud to check whether the British army was still in position to the south of Soignes Forest.

Napoléon thus passed the whole night in his headquarters at Le Caillou. The nocturnal escapade in which he is supposed to have gone out on foot at one in the morning, accompanied by Grand Marshal Bertrand and several officers, to inspect the picket lines, derives from a tale invented by Napoléon himself and repeated by many historians[72].

When, at Quatre-Bras on the morning of the 17 June, Wellington had learnt of Blücher's decision to withdraw on Wavre, he in turn gave the order to fall back to Mont-Saint-Jean[73], where the Allied troops began to take up their positions in the early afternoon.

The Duke had ordered that the strongpoints of Hougomont, La Haie-Sainte and Papelotte, forward of his front line, be occupied and prepared for defence. Following the artillery exchange with the French advance guard, he returned to his Waterloo headquarters, which had been set up in the Bodenghien inn, opposite the Chapelle Royale.

During the evening, Lord Uxbridge, the second-in-command of the Allied army, sought out the Duke, concerned to find out his battle plan, in case he had to take his place at the head of the army. Wellington heard him out in silence and then asked:

'Who will attack first tomorrow, I or Bonaparte?'

'Bonaparte', replied Uxbridge.

'Well, Bonaparte has not given me any idea of his projects: and as my plans will depend upon his, how can you expect me to tell you what mine are?'

The Duke rose and, placing his hand on the other's shoulder, added: 'There is one thing certain, Uxbridge, that is, that whatever happens, you and I will do our duty[74].'

These words of the Duke reveal only a part of his thoughts, for his principal preoccupation was to find out the intentions of his Prussian ally. Would Blücher be able to provide the support which the Duke had asked him for that morning, when he had decided to retreat to the Mont-Saint-Jean position? Wellington had been without news since twelve o'clock midday, yet on that news depended his decision either to accept battle the next day or to retire, not on Brussels, but to Hal, towards the Scheldt.

Weary of war, the Duke retired to bed at eleven, but rose again at three a.m. To while away the hours of waiting, he drafted various dispatches, notably to the British Ambassador in Brussels, to the Duc de Berry, who was commanding Louis XVIII's small escort at Ghent, and to one of his close friends, Lady Frances Wedderburn Webster. He urged them, while not giving way to panic, to make all necessary preparations to retreat to Antwerp, should he be defeated.

At six o'clock Wellington got on his horse to go and inspect his troops. As he was making for Mont-Saint-Jean, he was joined by a Prussian officer who brought confirmation that Blücher would, in the coming hours, provide him with the support of one or two corps[75].

The die had been cast and Wellington decided to give battle.

The armies had bivouacked under appalling conditions.

The Anglo-Dutch army was collected in an area defined by the chateau of Fichermont and the farms of Papelotte and La Haie to the east, the little village of Waterloo to the north, and the village of Braine-l'Alleud to the west.

As for the French camp, this extended along the road which ran from Quatre-Bras to Mont-Saint-Jean. Reille's and Kellermann's Corps bivouacked around Genappe; Prince Jérôme and the II Corps headquarters were installed at the *Roi d'Espagne* inn, which on the previous night had been host to the Duke of Wellington.

The light cavalry of the Guard and Milhaud's *cuirassiers*, after their clash with the Allied army, occupied the village of Plancenoit, while the infantry of d'Erlon's Corps bivouacked on either side of the road between La Belle Alliance and Rossomme. As for the Foot Guard, this had halted in the direction of Glabais, except for the 2nd battalion of light infantry of the Old Guard, which had been detailed to protect the Imperial headquarters at Le Caillou.

The night had been a very difficult one for both armies, but more so for the French troops, who had found their bivouacs only as night was falling, under driving rain, while Wellington's columns had taken up their own quarters before the storm began. Torrents of water continued to fall on both armies in their makeshift lodgings.

A British surgeon attached to the 12th Light Dragoons recounted: 'We bivouacked in open clover fields, close to, and somewhat in the rear of, the farm of Mont-Saint-Jean. When we reached our halting place, it was probably about seven in the evening and still daylight. The position of the general army was a short distance in front of us, and the red colouring of the scene, owing to the uniforms of our troops, exhibited an imposing sight… We were to pass the night on the spot we already occupied, but the officers were in want of food, drink and fuel. Of the first, our men had received a supply; the horses had also been, at least partially, cared for, – but water! There was a draw-well close to the village, or hamlet of St Jean, and that was the only resource to which thousands of thirsty ones had access. The first attack upon it was the last; for snap went the rope, and down fell the bucket, to a depth from which it could not be recovered. Disappointed in the article of water, our attention was drawn to that of fire, in procuring which we were eminently successful. The adjoining village furnished fuel in abundance. Doors, and window-shutters – furniture of every description – carts, ploughs, harrows, wheelbarrows, clock-cases, casks, tables, &c &c, were carried or trundled out to the bivouac, and being broken up, made powerful fires, in spite of the rain. Chairs were otherwise disposed of. Officers were paying two francs each for them, and the men seemed, at first, to be very well able to keep up the supply. This, at last, failed, and, for one, I was fain to buy a bundle of straw.

In front of the field which the horses occupied, ran a miry cart-road (upon which the officers' fires were kindled) and by the side of the road was a drain, or shallow ditch. Here a party of us deposited our straw and resolved to establish ourselves for the night under cover of our cloaks; but such was the clayey nature of its bottom, that the rain did not sink into the earth, but rose like a leak in a ship, among the straw, and we were in consequence, more drenched from below than from above[76].'

Watercolour lithograph by Taillois after Montius. Wellington Museum, Waterloo.

Waterloo Church

Built on the site of an old oratory dedicated to Saint Anne, the so-called royal chapel was erected at the bidding of the Governor-General of the Netherlands, the Marquis of Castañaga, and consecrated on 16 February 1690. It had been constructed in the hope of seeing the birth of an heir to Charles II, King of Spain. The original church had only a small chancel, with the dome serving as the nave. The building was enlarged in 1823 and again in 1855.

View of the hamlet of Mont-Saint-Jean. Washed aquatint. Plate VIII of the book by Robert Hill, Sketches in Flanders and Holland. London, 1816, published by J Haines & J Turner. Musée Wellington, Waterloo.

The Position of the French Army, 23rd June 1817. Watercolour attributed to James Rouse. Musée Wellington, Waterloo.

8. WATERLOO, SUNDAY 18 JUNE 1815

THE BATTLE SITE

The countryside was largely devoted to the cultivation of rye, oats, barley and clover. There were very few meadows to be seen, for stock farming, except that of sheep, was not extensive. The field boundaries were formed by hawthorn hedges and the banks along the roadsides were generally tree-lined, while dotted here and there about the countryside small clumps of trees were to be found. About a third of the land lay uncultivated and weed-infested.

In June, the rye was more forward and higher than the wheat, being over a metre high, though much less dense than the other crops, thus aiding the movements of the skirmishers, while still hiding them from the eyes of their opponents.

Outside the villages lay large farms, built on fortress lines with their buildings in the form of a square. Taking them from east to west, they were the farms of Papelotte and La Haie, near the hamlet of La Marache – marked on the maps of that time as Smohain; La Haie-Sainte and Mont-Saint-Jean, by the side of the Brussels road; and the château-farm of Goumont, near the road from Nivelles to Mont-Saint-Jean.

Along the Brussels-Charleroi road lay three hamlets: La Belle Alliance, Les Flamandes (Le Caillou) and La Maison du Roi.

In the villages of Waterloo, Mont-Saint-Jean and Plancenoit, the majority of the houses were no more than thatched cottages, sometimes of brick, but often of daub, boasting neither cellar nor upper floor and roofed with straw. The roofs overhung the walls by some distance, in order to discharge the rainwater as far away as possible, for there were no gutters. The larger farms, built of stone and brick, were roofed with slates or tiles.

The inhabitants lived in poverty, except for the big farmers, who could call on manpower which was both abundant and cheap. Everyone worked in the fields and in the winter months several who were weavers supplemented their meagre income by working at home.

In the village of Waterloo, stopping place for the carriers who transported coal from Charleroi to Brussels, there were a number of inns, while its inhabitants were variously woodcutters, foresters or roadmakers. The vigorous growth of Soignes Forest extended up to the walls of the village, with parts reaching as far as the hamlets of Le Chenois and Le Roussart. It was threaded by many avenues and traversed by the paved way which led to Brussels[77].

On the field where the French fought the British, the only trees were in Goumont Wood, which was cleared several years after the battle. To the east, where the Prussians fought, there were a number of woods – Paris, Ranson (or Hanotelet), Hubermont, Virère and Chantelet – which were all more extensive than they are today.

The fighting took place over an area of approximately fourteen square kilometres, within the boundaries of the communes of Braine-l'Alleud, Lasne and Waterloo.

In those days, the only paved roads were the Brussels-Charleroi road and the road from Mont-Saint-Jean to Nivelles. They were not mote than five to six metres in width. All the other roads were of earth. In heavy rain, such as that which fell on the night before the battle, they were rapidly churned up by the traffic, which then became bogged in the thick and heavy mud.

The following engravings show the battlefield from the Allied side.
Coloured aquatint engravings by Charles Turner, from
drawings made on the spot by Captain George J Jones,
published in London by Turner & Booth on 20 May 1816.

Waterloo. The Chemin de la Croix looking towards Ohain,
with, in the background, from left to right, Fichermont, Maransart and Plancenoit. The left wing of
Wellington's army was concentrated behind this road.

Waterloo. Wellington Tree.
The road looking in the direction of Charleroi from the ridge which marked the centre of the Allied position. In the foreground, the elm known as 'Wellington's tree', near which the Duke was stationed for part of the battle; beyond on the right, the farm of Haie-Sainte. Also in the foreground, on the left, the hedge and the tree near which General Picton was killed.

Waterloo, La Haie-Sainte *and* La Belle Alliance.
The battlefield as it appeared from the Chemin de la Croix to the east of the road.
On the left, La Haie-Sainte and its orchard; in the background, Caillois Wood.

Waterloo, Le Goumont.
Goumont château hidden in the surrounding wood, seen from the Allied
position along the Chemin des Vertes Bornes.

It was standard practice for the roads to be reserved for the waggons and artillery and for all the other troops, both infantry and cavalry, to make their way via the fields, preceded by the engineers, who opened up the way for them.

In this connection, a British staff officer described the retreat of his own division on 17 June: 'In fact, whenever the troops left the great chaussées they were placed in situations of great difficulty. This was proved on the 17th of June by the movement of the 3rd divisions through Wais la Hutte, where it crossed the Dyle, and its march was ordered to be by cross-roads parallel to the great chaussée. After crossing the Dyle the march on the cross-roads became so difficult as absolutely to make the situation of the division in some degree perilous; it did lose some of its baggage…[78].'

The lie of the land was to the defenders' advantage: in front of the ridges occupied by the Allied army stretched a kind of glacis which could be swept by the artillery from its position on the high ground, while to the rear the majority of the troops could be stationed on the reverse slope, out of sight and partially sheltered from the enemy artillery fire.

Contrary to Victor Hugo's assertion, Waterloo is not a dismal plain. Small undulations are succeeded by real valleys which, though not obvious to the casual glance, are of significance to soldiers on the march. These folds in the ground had the effect of hiding from Allied eyes some of the movements of the French columns between La Belle Alliance (hill 141) and the high points on the Vieux Chemin de Wavre[1] (hill 126). The ground occupied by the Anglo-Dutch forces had been reconnoitred by Wellington as early as 1814 as being a favourable position from which to halt a French invasion army heading for Brussels[79]. The Austrian general de Ferraris, maker in about 1777 of the first large-scale map of the Netherlands, a concise edition of which, by Captain Chanlaire, was used by the combatants in 1815, had also shown the strategic value of the position.

Twice in previous years fighting had taken place at Waterloo for control of the road to Brussels. In August 1705, the Anglo-Dutch army commanded by the Duke of Marlborough, concentrated in the area of Braine-l'Alleud, unsuccessfully thrust a party against the village, defended at the time by a native of the region, Colonel Jacques Pastur, known as Jaco.

In 1794 after the battle of Fleurus, the retreating Austrian army halted for several hours at the Mont-Saint-Jean position, before yielding to pressure from the French vanguard, commanded by the future Marshal Lefèvre.

FRENCH PREPARATIONS

The Emperor rose at an early hour. He walked up and down, hands clasped behind him and playing nervously with a pair of scissors, in the little square room which served him as bedroom, office and dining room.

Many times, going to the window, he inspected the sky, which was showing signs of clearing. The rain had ceased at dawn and a light wind had arisen. Having shaved and dressed, he received a report from General Drouot on the state of the ground, then called Gourgoud and dictated to him instructions for the army to be ready to fight by nine o'clock. At about eight, he was served with a liberal breakfast, which also took the form of a staff meeting, at which Grand Marshal Bertrand, Soult, Ney, Prince Jérôme, Reille and other generals were present.

'The enemy's army outnumbers ours by nearly a quarter', declared the Emperor, 'but the chances are at least ninety per cent in our favour and less than ten against.'

'No doubt', said Marshal Ney, 'if the Duke of Wellington had been so foolish as to await your Majesty, but I have come to inform you that his columns are already in full retreat and disappearing into the forest.'

'Your eyes have deceived you', was the reply, 'he is too late for that and would expose himself to certain defeat. He has rolled the dice and they are in our favour[80].'

Soult was far from sharing this optimism. Since the previous day he had been maintaining that Napoléon should recall to his side part of Grouchy's Corps, for he knew how difficult it would be to overthrow the British infantry, which he had himself confronted in Spain, without success.

Irritated, the Emperor replied, 'Because you have been defeated by Wellington, you consider him to be a great general. I tell you that he is a bad general, the British have bad soldiers and that it will be as easy as eating this breakfast.'

'I certainly hope so', retorted Soult[81].

Jérôme Bonaparte, the Emperor's youngest brother, joined the discussion, recalling the words of a waiter in the *Roi d'Espagne* inn at Genappe, where he had just spent the night and where Wellington had stayed on the night of the 16th/17th. These concerned the meeting of the British and Prussian armies on the Mont-Saint-Jean ridge.

Napoléon dismissed the objection with a shrug of the shoulders: 'Rubbish; the Prussian army is completely beaten. It cannot recover in a matter of two days. I shall

Watercolour lithograph by Taillois after Montius. Musée Wellington, Waterloo.

Le Caillou Farm

The farm's name of 'Caillou' (pebble) could equally be a reference to the stony nature of its soil or originate from a nearby standing stone of the neolithic era, referred to in the name of the 'Chapelle à Cayau' a short distance away. The farm was already there in 1695, at which date it was acquired by François Boucquéau. At the end of the eighteenth century it was a considerable undertaking, covering 122 bonniers. (A bonnier varied in area according to location from about 0.85 to 1.3 hectares.) In 1815 its owner was François Boucquéau's great grandson, Henri-Joseph. The farm was completely burnt down on the morning of 19 June. In 1819 the ruins were sold and the buildings were hastily rebuilt and turned into an estaminet. The provincial architect Emile Coulon purchased them in 1869 and converted them twenty years later into the buildings as they appear today. His widow sold Le Caillou to the Comtesse de Villegas, who lived there for a number of years with her husband Lucien Laudy.

Napoleon's last inspection of his army, 18th June 1815 (Morning of Waterloo).

Coloured etching after a painting by J P Beadle. Musée Wellington, Waterloo.

attack the English army and I shall defeat it. The British oligarchy will be overthrown and France will rise again, more glorious, more powerful and greater than ever.' Adjourning the meeting, he added: 'Messieurs, if my orders are properly carried out, we shall sleep tonight in Brussels[82].'

Not everyone, however, was convinced by this categoric declaration. As Napoléon was listening courteously to old Henri Boucquéau, the owner of Le Caillou, who was asking him to spare his property, the commanders of I and II Corps, Generals Drouet d'Erlon and Reille, were discussing the risks presented by a frontal attack on the British infantry. Impressed by Reille's words, Drouet urged him to go back to the Emperor and warn him. 'What's the use', was Reille's response, 'he wouldn't listen to us[83].'

At about nine o'clock Napoléon called for his horse and, accompanied by his staff, made his way towards the French outposts in the direction of Mont-Saint-Jean. Sometimes at a walking pace, sometimes at a fast trot, he rode along the columns emerging from Genappe and passed near to the troops who had bivouacked where they had halted. Despite the bad conditions in which they had spent the night, the soldiers displayed great enthusiasm and their cheers followed the Emperor as he passed.

At a point between the Decoster dwelling and La Belle Alliance, Napoléon halted his escort and conferred for a moment with the Comte d'Erlon then, accompanied only by Marshal Soult, he went on for about another two hundred paces, 'towards the right of the line, where he climbed a small hillock from where he could easily see the positions of both armies[84].'

Napoléon rejoined his staff, satisfied that the enemy army was staying put. After calling to Drouet d'Erlon: 'Tell the troops to heat their soup and put their weapons in order, then at midday we shall see', he turned about and set off back to Le Caillou with his escort[85]. He then established himself on a small mound facing Rossomme, on a bend in the road to Braine-l'Alleud.

The Morning of the Battle of Waterloo: The French await Napoleon's Orders.
Oil on canvas by Ernest Crofts, 1876. Sheffield Galleries and Museum Trust, Sheffield.

Napoléon's guide at Waterloo.
Drawing. Musée Wellington,
Waterloo.

Napoléon's Guide

Jean-Baptiste Decoster, a Fleming who hailed originally from the Louvain region, worked a small farm as well as a bar for carters along the highway to the south of La Belle Alliance. As the French army drew near, he took his wife and seven children and hid in Maransart Wood.

However, as dawn broke on the 18th, he returned to his house, whence, at about five o'clock, a French patrol took him to Le Caillou to act as a guide for Napoléon. He stayed with the Imperial headquarters for the rest of the day. As he showed little enthusiasm for the idea of following the Emperor about, to prevent him escaping his hands were tied and he was hoisted on to a horse whose saddle was attached by a halter to the saddle-bow of a cavalryman in the escort. Decoster, little used to the din of battle and overcome by panic, became agitated and turned his head away, cowering over his horse's neck. Napoléon, losing patience, rebuked him for his lack of courage: 'Come, my friend, don't fidget so much. A musket ball will kill you just as well from the rear as from the front, and will give you a much nastier wound.' He was caught up in the retreat and accompanied the Emperor as far as Charleroi. There, for his pains, General Bertrand presented him with a napoléon coin. The unfortunate farmer returned to his house on foot, to find it ransacked and half-destroyed, with his poor sticks of furniture burnt or looted. After the battle he left Plancenoit and settled at Joli-Bois, where he died in 1826. Making the best of his misfortune, he earned his living by offering his services as a tourist guide, telling of the day he spent at the Emperor's side: 'Napoléon issued his orders with much vehemence and sometimes with impatience. He sniffed continually, in an abrupt manner, apparently by habit and without being aware of it. He talked a good deal and very rapidly; he appeared animated and under pressure.'

The Emperor dismounted and ordered a table to be brought on which he could spread his maps. Having received the report of General Haxo, whom he had sent to see whether he could discern the presence of any entrenchments in the British line, he firstly dictated to Marshal Soult a dispatch informing Marshal Grouchy of his intention of meeting Wellington in a decisive engagement, then he gave his orders for the battle.

'Once the whole army has deployed in order of battle, when the Emperor passes the order to Marshal Ney, at about one o'clock in the afternoon, the attack will begin for the seizure of the village of Mont-Saint-Jean, where the roads intersect. To this end, the 12-pounder batteries of II Corps and those of the VI will join up with those of I Corps. The twenty-four artillery pieces will open fire on the troops at Mont-Saint-Jean and the Comte d'Erlon will commence the attack by sending forward his lefthand division, supporting it as necessary by the other divisions of I Corps. II Corps will advance proportionately to keep up with the Comte d'Erlon. The sapper companies of I Corps are to be ready to erect barricades on the spot at Mont-Saint-Jean.'

A pencilled note, signed by Ney, was added to this order: 'The Comte d'Erlon will appreciate that the attack is to commence on the left, rather than on the right. Communicate this new disposition to General Reille[86].'

This remark of Ney's is the only evidence of a verbal order from Napoléon, deciding on a diversion to the west of the road, towards Goumont. This was to be undertaken by II Corps, thus explaining Ney's note, aimed at Reille; the latter's forces were no longer to be coordinated with the movements of I Corps, but were to go into action on the left of the French army.

Given these new dispositions, the main action would thus no longer be hinged on either side of the road, but act solely against the centre-left of Wellington's army.

Napoléon remained at Rossomme until about four in the afternoon. An eyewitness has left the following description of the scene: 'Seated on a straw bale, the Emperor had his map spread out before him on a rough farm table. His famous spyglass frequently focussed on the various points of the battle. Between whiles, he plucked straws which he used as toothpicks. On his left, Marshal Soult awaited his orders, while the remainder of his staff stood in a group some ten paces behind. To facilitate access to the Emperor, sappers had laid out ramps around the sides of the hillock[87].'

Some time later, the Emperor moved his position further forward along the Brussels road, to the house of his guide Decoster[88].

THE DISPOSITIONS OF THE ARMIES

The French army disposed itself on either side of the road. On the eastern side, in the front line, were deployed the four divisions of d'Erlon's I Corps – Quiot, Donzelot, Marcognet and Durutte – along an earthern track which led from La Belle Alliance to the hamlet of La Marache. Behind these troops were two cavalry corps – the *cuirassiers* of Milhaud and the lancers and light cavalry of the Guard, under the orders of Lefèbvre-Desnouettes.

On the roadway, behind La Belle Alliance, was stationed Lobau's VI Corps and the Guard. To the west of the Brussels road, forward of the path leading from Plancenoit to the road from Mont-Saint-Jean to Nivelles, General Reille had positioned the three infantry divisions of his II Corps (Bachelu, Foy and Jérôme). Piré's light cavalry regiments guarded the far left of the French line, on the Nivelles road. In the second line were Kellermann's cavalry corps as well as the heavy cavalry of the Guard.

The Allied army had taken up its positions on the high ground, which ran roughly in the form of an arc, from Papelotte round to Goumont, a distance of about three and a half kilometres. From the crossroads where the highway to Brussels meets the Chemin de la Croix to the French centre at La Belle Alliance, the distance was about thirteen hundred metres. The Imperial troops were also arranged in an arc, with certain divisions at each end of the line being no more than three hundred metres from the British positions at La Marache and Goumont.

Wellington had stationed the greater part of his army to the east of the Brussels road, behind the Chemin de la Croix. The British, Hanoverian and Nassauer brigades and the German Legion were deployed in depth, from the Mont-Saint-Jean crossroads as far as Braine-l'Alleud, the latter occupied by Chassé's division of Netherlanders. By contrast, to the west of the Brussels road, along the Vieux Chemin de Wavre, there was but a single line of infantry, composed of British, Dutch and Hanoverian troops. Papelotte Farm and the hamlet of La Marache formed strongpoints at the end the British line.

This position was occupied by a part of Saxe-Weimar's Dutch brigade; a Nassauer battalion was posted in the hamlet and several companies entrenched themselves in the Château de Fichermont, a few hundred metres to the south. A brigade of British cavalry commanded by Vandeleur kept watch over the east of the Allied line.

THE FIGHT AGAINST WELLINGTON

The bloody diversion at Goumont

The manor of Goumont, nestling in its leafy grove, formed an imposing collection of buildings and outbuildings enclosed by hedges. To the south was a wood about five hectares in extent, to the east a large orchard and a formal garden, facing the rear of the château enclosed by a wall some three metres high, the whole forming an almost exact quadrilateral.

The buildings proper were arranged around a courtyard in the style of the majority of farms in the Brabant, with the farmer's house on the southern side and the château in the centre. Barns and stables formed the outer boundary. To the south a carriage gate opened on to the wood, while to the north another gateway opened on to a tree-lined avenue which led to the Nivelles road. The manor of Goumont lay midway between the French and British lines, which were several hundred metres in either direction.

During the evening of the 17th, Goumont had been occupied by four companies of light infantry of the British Guards. Two of these, commanded by Lieutenant Colonel Lord Saltoun (Maitland's Brigade), had taken up position in the orchard and in the eastern end of the wood. The two others, under the orders of Lieutenant Colonel Macdonell (Byng's Brigade), had brought the buildings and the garden up to a defensive state. The greater part of Maitland's and Byng's brigades remained behind the Chemin des Vertes Bornes.

On the morning of the 18th, Wellington reinforced the garrison with three hundred Hanoverian riflemen and a Nassauer battalion from Saxe-Weimar's brigade, which occupied the edges of the wood.

As Wellington saw it, the role of the Goumont position was to present an obstacle to any attack mounted on his right, towards Braine-l'Alleud. For him, this village was of the great-est importance, for it commanded his line of retreat towards Hal, which he had caused to be occupied by 17,000 men on the morning of 17 June. In addition, he kept Chassé's division of Netherlanders at Braine-l'Alleud until the evening.

At around ten o'clock the Duke examined the position at length and surveyed the French preparations. The menacing presence of Jérôme's division, less than three hundred metres from the Goumont wood, caused panic in the ranks of the Nassauers, who began to fall back. This was halted by the arrival of Wellington himself, although as he rode off again several shots were fired in his direction by the very troops he had just rallied.

The manor or chateau and farm of Goumont might be better-known to English-speaking readers by its more recent name of Hougoumont; though at the time of the battle it was probably known as either Gomont or Goumont.

The attack on Goumont did not figure in Napoléon's initial plans. However, according to what he wrote on Saint Helena, its purpose was to attract Wellington's attention to his right and to prevent him from reinforcing his centre-left, where the French effort was intended to be applied. It consisted therefore of no more than keeping the enemy occupied by maintaining a substantial line of skirmishers and of taking possession of the wood. The man charged with this operation was Prince Jérôme Bonaparte. Preceded by a large body of skirmishers, his division began to advance on the wood at Goumont. At the same time – it was now half-past eleven – the British artillery opened fire. Bauduin's brigade advanced on the wood and after a hard fight ejected the Nassauers, the Hanoverians and the British Guards, but was unable to capture the south gate. Under fire from the farm's defenders to its front and from those in the garden on its flank, the brigade fell back into the shelter of the wood.

Wellington, following the progress of the struggle from a little way to the north, ordered Bull's battery to fire shrapnel over the heads of the château's defenders, causing heavy casualties among the attackers. With the failure of this first attack, Wellington now reinforced the garrison; he withdrew the Nassauers, in whom he had little confidence, and placed the majority of Byng's brigade on the northern approaches to the farm, with Plat's brigade (KGL) to their rear.

Half an hour later, ignoring the advice of his chief of staff, Guilleminot, and the orders of Reille, who judged it sufficient to occupy the wood with skirmishers, Jérôme Bonaparte stubbornly decided upon a second attack.

View of interior ruins of Hougoumont near Waterloo.
Watercolour attributed to James Rouse, *c*.1817. Musée Wellington, Waterloo.

The château-farm of Goumont

This place name is most usually known to Waterloo historians as Hougoumont. This version of the name originates from an entry on Ferraris' map (1777), the surveyors having deduced "Hougoumont" phonetically from "au Goumont". This euphonic change left Victor Hugo free to invent an entirely whimsical explanation: 'Hougoumont', he wrote, 'derives from Hugomons and recalls a manor built by Hugo, Lord of Somerel.' The earliest record of the place-name Goumont is in 1358. Traces of a château and a farm in the sixteenth century may be found, whose lands in the following century covered more than 160 bonniers, a considerable estate for that time. In 1815 the property belonged to the chevalier *Gouret de Louville, an officer who had retired from the Austrian service.*

The farm of Hougoumont.
Unsigned watercolour. General view of the ruins of the château, looking west from the Nivelles
road. Musée Wellington, Waterloo.

*He resided at the château only occasionally. The farmer, Antoine Demonceau, had
abandoned the site when it was occupied by the British troops, but one of his servants,
Van Cutsem (called Vankilsom by Victor Hugo) claimed not to have followed his master.
The property consisted in those days of the château, which was completely destroyed
except for the chapel, and the farm buildings, of which only the gardener's dwelling
remained intact.*

*Victor Hugo's imagination transformed the well on the estate into a tomb. No less
than three hundred corpses had been thrown down it, he claimed in* Les Misérables.
Excavations carried out in 1980-1982 revealed no sign of any human bones.

Goumont Wood. Aquatint engravings with watercolour. Plate XIV of the book by Robert Hill, *Sketches in Flanders and Holland.* London, 1816, published by J Haines & J Turner.

Closing the Gate at Hougoumont. Oil on canvas by Robert Gibb, National Museums of Scotland, Edinburgh.

Once more, the infantrymen of General Bauduin, who had been killed in the wood during the first attempt, launched an assault on the southern gate, but met with no more success than before, while the 1st light infantry regiment, moving round the eastern side, advanced on the north gate. This had not been barricaded, to allow ammunition, and reinforcements if need be, to be brought to the garrison.

Lieutenant Legros, a giant of a man, smashed down the gateway with an axe and the attackers burst into the courtyard. In hand-to-hand fighting, Macdonell himself, with a handful of men, repelled them and succeeded in closing the gate again. The *1er Léger* were driven out, leaving their severely wounded colonel behind.

Meanwhile, Jérôme's second brigade, which had been concentrating its efforts on the eastern side, took possession of the orchard. But it was assailed by fire from the British

Defence of the Hougoumont château.

Watercolour by Denis Dighton. National Army Museum, London.

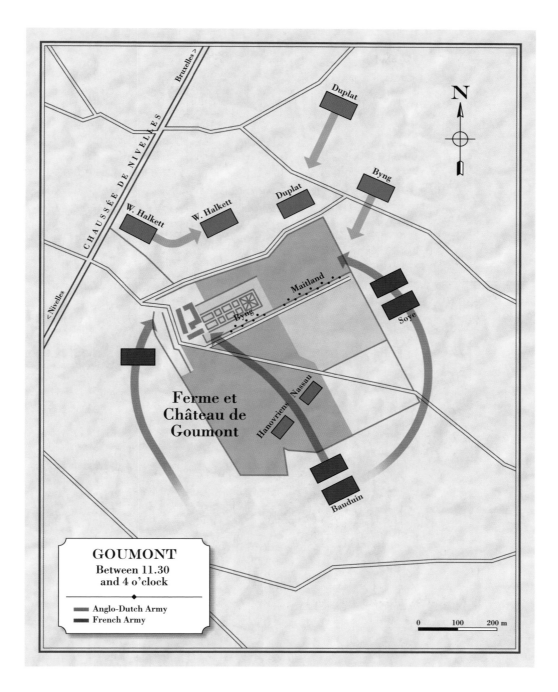

artillery, as well as flanking fire from the defenders of the garden from the shelter of its walls. It was then subjected to a counter-attack by four companies of the Coldstream Guards, from Byng's brigade and was unable to hold its ground. The time was then half-past one. The losses had been heavy, particularly amongst the French.

Taking advantage of the lull in the fighting, Wellington reorganised the garrison. The companies from Maitland's brigade returned to their parent unit, leaving the defence of the château, both internal and external, in the hands of Byng's two regiments of the Guards and a battalion of the German Legion. In support, Hew Halkett's Hanoverian brigade was sent to take up its position alongside Plat's brigade to the north, while one regiment of Mitchell's brigade moved

◄ *The French Attack at Hougoumont. 18th June 1815, Waterloo.* Coloured etching after Ernest Crofts, 1897. Musée Wellington, Waterloo.

The south gateway of the château of Goumont. Unsigned wash-tint, c.1830. Musée Wellington, Waterloo.

into position along the lane which led from the château to the Nivelles road.

Towards two o'clock, almost simultaneously with the attack by I Corps, Jérôme's division launched a third assault on Goumont, supported this time by several battalions of Foy's division. Once more the orchard was occupied by the French, but though they hurled themselves against the walls of the garden and the various buildings, they got no further. An attempt to outflank the position was foiled by Plat's brigade.

Jérôme then realised that the only way to dislodge the British infantry would be to bombard the buildings in which they were established. As three o'clock approached, Napoléon, in response to his request, placed at his disposal a howitzer battery, whose shots set fire to the château and

to all the barns and stables. Only the chapel and the farmer's house were spared. Despite the blaze, which rendered the defenders' position even more arduous, the sporadic and ill-directed attacks of the French infantry made no headway, though they continued throughout the afternoon.

The garrison of the château itself never exceeded two thousand men, but in their support Wellington had to set aside the brigades of Hew Halkett, Plat and Mitchell – approximately four thousand men. On the French side, Jérôme's division and one of Foy's brigades, some eight thousand men, devoted all their efforts towards the unsuccessful attempts to overcome this strongpoint, which secured Wellington's right wing.

The attack by Drouet d'Erlon

Wellington had stationed two infantry divisions along the length of the Chemin de la Croix and the Vieux Chemin de Wavre, from the gravel pit opposite La Haie-Sainte as far as Papelotte.

Hidden below the shelter of the ridge, between fifty and a hundred metres to the rear of the lane, were Kempt's and Pack's brigades with, further on towards Papelotte, those of Best and von Vincke. Forward of the ridge, between Kempt and Pack, Picton, commanding the Allied left wing, had placed Bijlandt's Dutch-Belgian brigade.

To the rear of this line, in the valley near to the roadway, were massed Ponsonby's cavalry, while to the north, on the west side of Mont-Saint-Jean Farm, was Lambert's infantry brigade.

At about half-past one, the attack of the French I Corps was preceded by a preliminary artillery barrage. A powerful *Grande Batterie*, composed of about 80 pieces, a goodly number of which were 12-pounders, positioned forward of the lane between La Belle Alliance and La Marache, opened fire on the Allied left at a range of approximately 800 metres[89].

The skilful placing of the infantry on the reverse slope and the fact that, as an additional precaution, they were lying down limited the effect of this violent bombardment. In accordance with Wellington's orders, the Allied artillery did not reply to the French battery's fire[90].

At about two o'clock, the French infantry began to move forward in columns, preceded by a crowd of skirmishers. The formation of these columns has been the subject of much controversy.

Drouet d'Erlon, having served in the Peninsular War and experienced the firepower of the British infantry, had formed up his four divisions – in order, from west to east, Quiot, Donzelot, Marcognet and Durutte – by deploying each battalion three ranks deep, giving a front of 180 men. The other battalions followed six paces to the rear. This arrangement allowed the use of the complete firepower of the leading battalion, as well as a rapid deployment of a column into line. In that way he aimed to compensate for their inferior firepower compared to the British infantry, which was deployed in two ranks.

This formation has been criticised for rendering the column vulnerable to artillery fire, given its depth, each column covering a front of one hundred and forty metres.

At that time, the advance in column was the most favourable arrangement against the formidable attack by the *arme blanche*. It was believed that, in broken ground, columns acted more rapidly and with greater vigour and coherence than when deployed into line. The risk lay in the vulnerability to cavalry attacks, but this threat did not appear to be a serious one, since the assault was to be supported by a brigade of *cuirassiers* (Dubois). Furthermore, the reputation gained by the British cavalry during the war in Spain was not such as to strike terror into an opponent's heart.

The four French divisions, eight infantry brigades strong, a total of 17,000 muskets, attacked in four columns disposed in echelon. The Quiot division devoted all its efforts to the capture of La Haie-Sainte and was not involved in the main action. The supporting brigade of *cuirassiers* under Dubois was to sweep through the western approaches to the farm and threaten the brigades of Ompteda and Kielmansegge which occupied the crossroads.

The garrison installed by Wellington in La Haie-Sainte Farm initially consisted of the second light battalion of the German Legion (Ompteda's brigade) – 376 men commanded by Major Baring. Since the evening of the 17th, the farm had been placed in a state of defence, with loopholes knocked through the walls and staging arranged behind them for the defenders to stand on. In addition, the roadway through the entry porch to the farmyard had been barricaded.

At about half-past two in the afternoon, Quiot's division, led by Marshal Ney himself, began the assault on La Haie-Sainte. The division was divided into two brigades: the first, commanded by Quiot, attacked the orchard; the second, advancing along the road under the orders of General Bourgeois, drove before it the skirmishers of the 95th Rifles, who were entrenched in the gravel pit opposite the farm.

Wellington sent the Luneburg battalion of Kielmansegge's Hanoverian brigade to reinforce the little garrison, but to no effect. Propelled by the impetus of their charge, the French carried the orchard south of the farm and the garden to the north, leaving the defenders to barricade themselves in the buildings. One party of the latter, which had attempted to rejoin the bulk of Ompteda's and Kielmansegge's brigades on the north side of the Chemin de la Croix, were sabred by Dubois' brigade, as it came up in support to the west of the farm.

However, the repulse of I Corps' attack brought about the general withdrawal of the French infantry, which was obliged to give up the ground it had gained. The garrison, reinforced by two companies of the 1st light battalion of the German Legion and two hundred Nassauers, reoccupied its original positions.

The attacking force proper consisted of the Donzelot and Marcognet divisions. Preceded by skirmishers, they set off two hundred metres apart, with the second four hundred metres in rear of the first. They advanced under cover of intensified fire from the *Grande Batterie* stationed forward of the lane leading from La Belle Alliance to La Marache.

The British artillery held their fire until the French emerged from the valley, when the range was approximately four hundred and fifty metres. Bijlandt's brigade, weakened by the losses suffered at Quatre-Bras and harassed by the artillery fire and by the skirmishers in front of the attacking columns, did not wait to meet the enemy, but retired in haste, a withdrawal which obliged Kempt's troops to extend their front.

When he was less than forty metres short of the Vieux Chemin de Wavre, Donzelot halted his troops and deployed them into line. At the same moment, Picton ordered his men to fire a volley and then charge. The British infantry burst through the hedge and surged forward. The French first wavered and then began to fall back.

During the assault, Picton was killed by a ball in the temple. A hero of the war in Spain, he had barely arrived from

Battle of Waterloo. Acid and aquatint engraving by M Dubourg, after J H Clark, published in London on 18 April 1817. Musée Wellington, Waterloo.

Death of Sir Thomas Picton. Coloured aquatint engraving by M Dubourg, after J A Atkinson, published in London on 1 January 1817. Musée Wellington, Waterloo.

The Charge of the Household Brigade.
Unsigned watercolour. Musée Wellington, Waterloo.

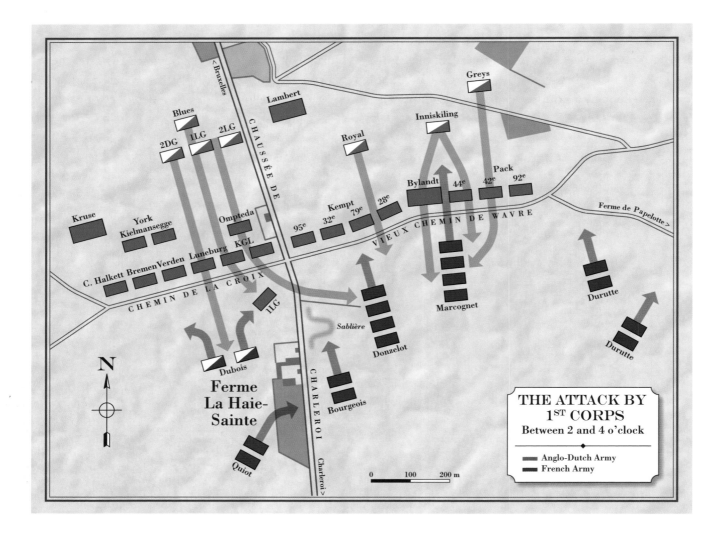

THE ATTACK BY
1ST CORPS
Between 2 and 4 o'clock

■ Anglo-Dutch Army
■ French Army

England in time and had gone to war in civilian dress and top hat. He had been wounded at Quatre-Bras, but had concealed the fact in order to remain at the head of his men.

Marcognet's column had more success than Donzelot's; it breasted the ridge, crossed the *chemin* and began to deploy, brushing aside the Scottish regiments in its path.

This was a critical moment, for the thrust of the French infantry had succeeded and it seemed as if nothing could stand in their way. It was then that Uxbridge gave the order to charge to the two brigades of heavy cavalry, waiting on either side of the road.

On the western side, Somerset sent four regiments (1st and 2nd Life Guards, the 1st Dragoon Guards and the Royal Horse Guards – the Blues) against Dubois' *cuirassiers*, who had just charged Kielmansegge's battalions and those of the King's German Legion, positioned behind the Chemin de la Croix.

The fighting turned in favour of the British: one body of

French cavalrymen escaped along the Chemin de la Croix and around La Haie-Sainte before regaining their own lines, the others turned their horses and made for La Belle Alliance. The 2nd Life Guards rode over the crossroads and charged to the east of the roadway. Ponsonby's brigade, three regiments strong (the Royal Dragoons, the Scots Greys and the Inniskilling Dragoons), threw itself recklessly on Donzelot's already shaken column, thus halting the advance of Marcognet and causing him to withdraw hastily back across the Vieux Chemin de Wavre.

Disrupted in the midst of their deployment, the French divisions found themselves unable to form squares and yielded rapidly to panic. They poured back like a flock of sheep, to use the description of an eye-witness, leaving many dead and wounded behind. Two or three thousand men were taken prisoner, two Eagles were captured and two horse batteries were put out of action.

The British squadrons, carried away by the impetus of their charge and deaf to all calls on them to rally, then redirected their assault towards the *Grande Batterie*. To block them, Napoléon sent in a counter-charge by Jacquinot's lancers and General Delort's brigade of *cuirassiers*. Caught between the two, Somerset's and Ponsonby's riders scarcely escaped total annihilation. It needed the intervention of Vandeleur's brigade, positioned in support of Best, before the survivors were able to return to their own lines.

Out of two thousand horsemen, half were left on the field, Ponsonby being among the dead. These slaughtered regiments were unable to play any further role in the battle; however the attack by the French infantry had been repulsed.

The fourth division of d'Erlon's corps, commanded by Durutte, had followed the advance towards the Allied left wing largely to the rear, since the French infantry had moved forward in echelon. Durutte had deployed one brigade in front of Papelotte. The French had driven the Nassauer skirmishers back and had entered the hamlet of La Marache, but had not been able to capture either Papelotte or La Haie Farm.

The retreat of d'Erlon's columns had entailed the retirement of Durutte's other brigade, which had been advancing towards the Vieux Chemin de Wavre in order to attack the Hanoverian troops of Best and von Vincke. The French infantry had then been charged by one of Vandeleur's regiments, the 12th Light Dragoons, held in reserve behind Papelotte[91].

The decisive Charge of the Life Guards at the Battle of Waterloo. Coloured engraving by W Bronley after Luke Clennel, published by John Britton, 1 March 1821. Musée Wellington, Waterloo.

Scotland For Ever. Oil on canvas by Elizabeth Thompson, Lady Butler, 1881.

Leeds Museums and Art Galleries, Leeds.

Death of Major Gl. Sir Wim. Ponsonby. Coloured aquatint by M Dubourg after Manskirch,
published by Edward Orme, 1 January 1817. Musée Wellington, Waterloo.

The great French cavalry charges

At around half-past three, while the fighting around
Goumont continued without the French managing to
establish possession, Ney embarked on another attempt to
capture La Haie-Sainte. Quiot's and Bourgeois' infantrymen, supported by one of Donzelot's brigades, operating
entirely as skirmishers in front of the British left, but lacking any effective artillery support, suffered a second rebuff
before the farm's solid walls, although a brigade held on in
the orchard.

Ney now called on the brigade of *cuirassiers* under Farine
to sweep clear the approaches to La Haie-Sainte and prevent
the bringing in of reinforcements. General Delort, who
commanded the division which included Farine, forbade his
subordinate to take any action, reminding him that both of
them were answerable only to General Milhaud, commanding IV Cavalry Corps.

'During this argument, which stopped all movement on
the brigade's part', wrote Delort, 'Marshal Ney himself
arrived, bristling with impatience. He not only insisted on
the execution of his order, but he demanded, in the name
of the Emperor, both divisions (in other words, Milhaud's
entire corps). I still hesitated [...] I remarked that heavy
cavalry ought not to attack, uphill, infantry which was far
from demoralised and in a good position to defend itself. The
Marshal cried: "Forward, the safety of France is at stake". I
reluctantly obeyed [92].'

In fact, Ney had probably changed his mind; instead of a
limited action around the exterior of La Haie-Sainte, he was
providing himself with the means for a general attack on the
Allied centre-right, using Milhaud's entire corps.

While the French artillery to the west of the road redoubled its firing, Milhaud's four brigades of *cuirassiers*, which
until then had been positioned to the rear of d'Erlon's corps,

crossed the highway in front of La Belle Alliance and took up their start position in the lower ground between La Haie-Sainte and Goumont.

Either thinking that the movement also concerned his division, or because, at the moment his corps was starting to move, Milhaud had said to him: 'Support me, I am going to charge', General Lefèbvre, commanding the light cavalry of the Imperial Guard, ordered his squadrons to follow the *cuirassiers*[93].

There were thus forty squadrons, a total of five thousand sabres, which sprang up to throw themselves against the Allied position, by attacking not the brigades stationed to the east of the Brussels road, but the troops positioned on its western side, along the Chemin de la Croix and the Chemin des Vertes Bornes leading to Goumont.

It was with a certain surprise that Wellington saw the preparations being made for this large-scale cavalry attack against infantry which was almost intact and well protected by many batteries. At all events, he reinforced his line with several Brunswicker battalions, recalled from Merbraine, and Adam's and Mitchell's brigades.

From east to west, formed up in squares arranged in two lines in a chequerboard pattern, were: Alten's division, to the rear of La Haie-Sainte; Colin Halkett's division, at the junction of the Chemin de la Croix and the Chemin des Vertes Bornes; four Brunswicker battalions positioned forward of the Chemin des Vertes Bornes; Maitland's brigade, on the reverse slope; finally Adam's and Mitchell's brigades, linking up with the Goumont strongpoint[94]. In front of the Allied line were at least twelve artillery batteries, their teams sent

The Battle of Waterloo, 18th June 1815. Coloured aquatint engraving by R Reeves after W Heath, published in London by R Reeves, 4 June 1816. Musée Wellington, Waterloo.

Attack on the British Squares by the French Cavalry.

Watercolour by Denis Dighton, 1815. National Army Museum, London.

Sergeant Taylor, 18th Hussars & French Cuirassiers. Coloured engraving by J Booth
after Captain George J Jones, published in London, 23 December 1819.
Musée Wellington, Waterloo.

to the rear, with orders to fire canister. At the last moment,
their gunners were to take refuge in the squares.

Many years afterwards, General Cavallié Mercer, who
had been in command of a troop of horse artillery, recalled
those first charges: 'I saw through the smoke the leading
squadrons of the advancing column coming on at a brisk
trot, and already not more than one hundred yards distant,
if so much, for I don't think we could have seen so far. I
immediately ordered the line to be formed for action – case
shot! And the leading gun was unlimbered and commenced
firing almost as soon as the word was given…

The very first round, I saw, brought down several men
and horses. They continued however to advance… Still they
persevered in approaching us, though slowly, and it did seem
they would ride over us. We were a little below the level of the
ground on which they moved – having in front of us a bank
of about a foot and a half or two feet high, along the top of
which ran a narrow road – and this gave more effect to our
case-shot, all of which almost must have taken effect, for the
carnage was frightful. I suppose this state of things occupied
but a few seconds, when I observed symptoms of hesitation,

and in a twinkling, at the instant I thought it
was all over with us, they turned to either flank
and fled away rapidly to the rear. Retreat of the
mass, however, was not so easy. Many facing
about and trying to force their way through the
body of the column, that part next to us became
a complete mob, into which we kept a steady fire
of case-shot from our six pieces…

Every discharge was followed by the fall of
numbers, whilst the survivors struggled with
each other, and I actually saw them using the
pommels of their swords to fight their way out
of the mêlée… At last, the rear of the column,
wheeling about, opened a passage, and the whole
swept away at a much more rapid pace than they
had advanced, nor stopped until the swell of the
ground covered them from our fire[95].'

With the French breathless and their horses
blown, Wellington seized the chance to launch
his own reserves against them – the Dutch-
Belgian horsemen of Trip, van Merlen and de Gigny and
the British under Dörnberg and Arenschildt.

Surprised and disordered, the two French divisions
were forced back down the hillside. With scarcely time to
reform, they were thrown once more against the squares,
but with no more success. A young officer in Maitland's
brigade, ensign Gronow, described this charge: 'The word
of command, 'Prepare to receive cavalry', had been given,
every man in the front ranks knelt, and a wall bristling with
steel, held together by steady hands, presented itself to the
infuriated cuirassiers. I should observe that just before this
charge the Duke entered by one of the angles of the square,
accompanied by one aide-de-camp; all the rest of his staff
being either killed or wounded. Our Commander-in-Chief,
as far as I could judge, appeared perfectly composed; but
looked very thoughtful and pale…

'The charge of the French cavalry was gallantly executed;
but our well-directed fire brought men and horses down,
and ere long the utmost confusion arose in their ranks. The
officers were exceedingly brave, and by their gestures and
fearless bearing did all in their power to encourage their men
to form again and renew the attack. The Duke sat unmoved,

Death of Colonel Coenegracht. Oil on canvas by Theodor Schaepkens. Musée Wellington, Waterloo. ▶
This officer commanded the 1st regiment of carabiniers, Trip's brigade.

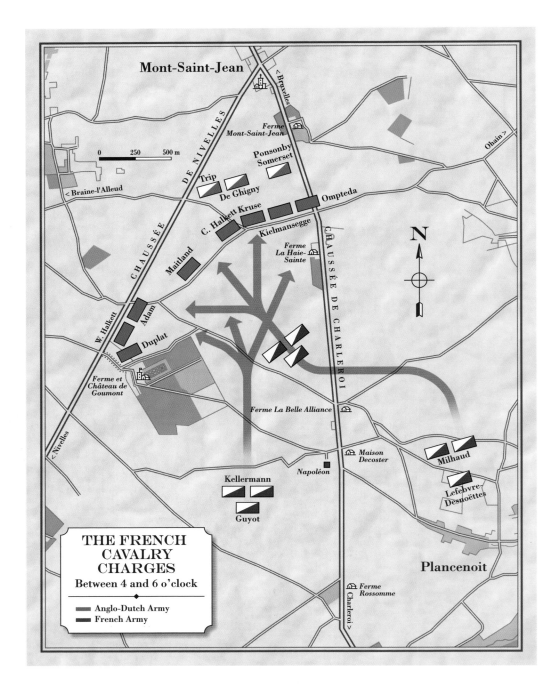

Mont-Saint-Jean

< Bruxelles

Ferme Mont-Saint-Jean

Ponsonby
Somerset

0   250   500 m

< Braine-l'Alleud

Trip

De Ghigny

Ompteda

C. Halkett Kruse

Kielmansegge

Ferme La Haie-Sainte

Maitland

N

W. Halkett

Adam

Duplat

Ferme et Château de Goumont

Ferme La Belle Alliance

< Nivelles

Maison Decoster

Milhaud

Napoléon

Kellermann

Lefebvre-Desnoëttes

Guyot

THE FRENCH CAVALRY CHARGES

Between 4 and 6 o'clock

━━ Anglo-Dutch Army
━━ French Army

Plancenoit

Ferme Rossomme

< Charleroi

mounted on his favourite charger. I recollect his asking Colonel Stanhope what o'clock it was, upon which Stanhope took out his watch, and said it was twenty minutes past four. The Duke replied, "The battle is mine; and if the Prussians arrive soon, there will be an end of the war"… The enemy's cavalry had to advance over ground which was so heavy that they could not reach us except at a trot; they therefore came upon us in a much more compact mass than they probably would have done if the ground had been more favourable. When they got within ten or fifteen yards they discharged their carbines, to the cry of "Vive l'Empereur!" but their fire produced little effect, as is generally the case with the fire of cavalry. Our men had orders not to fire unless they could do so on a near mass; the object being to economise our ammunition, and not to waste it on scattered soldiers. The result was that when the cavalry had discharged their carbines, and were still far off, we occasionally stood face to face, looking at each other inactively, not knowing what the next move might be… When we received cavalry, the order was to fire low so that on the first discharge of musketry, the ground was strewed with the fallen horses and their riders, which impeded the advance of those behind them, and broke the shock of the charge. It was pitiable to witness the agony of the poor horses, which really seemed conscious of the dangers that surrounded them: we often saw a poor wounded animal raise its head, as if looking for its rider to afford him aid…

'At four o'clock our square was a perfect hospital, being full of dead, dying, and mutilated soldiers. The charges of cavalry were in appearance very formidable, but in reality a great relief, as the artillery could no longer fire on us… I shall never forget the strange noise our bullets made against the breastplates of Kellermann's and Milhaud's cuirassiers[96].'

By then it was almost five o'clock.

Napoléon, writing on Saint Helena, claimed that the action in which Milhaud's corps and Lefèbvre-Desnouettes' division were engaged had been initiated by Ney, had been ill-timed and had not received his approval. 'This is a rash movement which could have fatal consequences', said he to Soult when he saw the masses of cavalry charging the British line[97]. He is sup-

Cuirassiers charging the Highlanders at the Battle of Waterloo on the 18th June 1815.
Oil on canvas by Felix Philippoteaux. Apsley House, The Wellington Museum, London.

The charge by Marshal Ney at Waterloo. Oil on canvas by François Flameng. Musée du Caillou, Genappe.

The sunken lane

There were on the battlefield, supposedly, a number of sunken lanes or roads, such as that which led from La Belle Alliance to Plancenoit or to La Marache. The most famous of these was Le chemin creux, *made memorable by Victor Hugo. It was the lane which ran from Braine-l'Alleud to Ohain and was called the Chemin de la Croix on the western side of the Charleroi road, then becoming the Vieux Chemin de Wavre to the east. To the west of the Brussels highway, for about a hundred and fifty metres, it took the form of a sunken lane. To the east, it was hedge-lined. Victor Hugo's account of Milhaud's cavalry charge is celebrated, but entirely imaginary: 'Between them and the English, the* cuirassiers *had just caught sight of a ditch: it was the sunken lane to Ohain. It was a terrible moment. The abyss was there, unexpected and yawning sheer beneath their horses' hooves, twelve feet deep between its two banks. The second rank pressed upon the first and the third pressed upon the second; the horses reared up, sprang backwards, fell on their rumps and slid over with all four legs in the air, throwing and crushing their riders. With no way of recoiling, the whole column was nothing but a projectile and the force built up to crush the English crushed the French instead; the inexorable ravine was conquerable only when it was filled, as a confusion of horses and riders rolled into it, one pressing down on another, the pit one mass of flesh until, when the ditch was full of living men, the rest rode over them. Nearly one third of Dubois' brigade fell into that chasm.'*

Not a single witness, neither British nor French, has been found who mentions this bloody episode, which ought to have left its imprint on the memory. None of the generals who led the charge was either killed or wounded (with the exception of Delort, who suffered a sabre cut), whereas they would have been the first to perish in the slaughter. In addition, the French charges that afternoon were directed, not parallel to the Brussels road, but on the western side of the sunken part of the Chemin de la Croix.

posed to have added: 'They are one hour too soon; however, we must stand by what has been done[98].' He gave the order for Kellermann's corps (two divisions of *cuirassiers*, dragoons and *carabiniers*) and the heavy cavalry division of the Guard (General Guyot) to support the movement[99]. Five thousand more horsemen set off to join the throng in the bowl below the plateau where the Allied infantry was standing fast.

An officer of the 7th Dragoons, squadron commander Letang, described the charge: 'The squares waited resolutely for the cavalry, determined not to fire until point-blank range. The pressure on the cavalry's spirit of the infantry's fire, more formidable than its actual effect, was never better demonstrated. The coolness of the British infantry, all the more remarkable for the absence of the fusillade which we were expecting, but which to our great surprise we failed to hear, disconcerted our riders. They were seized with the thought that they were going to be met with fire which would be all the better-sustained for being saved up and all the deadlier for being point-blank and, probably to escape such fire, the first squadron made a right turn and thus decided a similar movement by all the squadrons which were following it. The charge was unsuccessful and none of the squadrons rallied until they reached La Haie-Sainte Farm[100].'

General Kellermann himself, three years after the battle, described how his squadrons were sacrificed: 'They all arrived, in confusion, in disorder and breathless, at the screen occupied by the British artillery. The guns were instantly abandoned, but the horses were led away. To the rear a double line of infantry was formed in a square. It was necessary to halt and reform, after a fashion, under fire, but it proved impossible to persuade the cavalry, excellent though it was, to charge again. It was in the most unpleasant situation, without infantry and without supporting artillery. The enemy squares withheld their fire, but were covered by a swarm of skirmishers whose every shot found a target. In this frightful position almost our entire cavalry remained for several hours between the wood at Hougoumont and La Haie-Sainte, able neither to withdraw, for fear of taking with it the whole Army, nor to charge, for lack of space, and unable to administer the mortal blows which it was forced to receive, while also exposed to fire from our own batteries which it had left well behind[101].'

Seven times Ney launched the cavalry against the Allied line. Some squares, charged nine, ten or a dozen times, bowed but did not break; three standards were captured by the French. One regiment passed completely through the British position, carried on down the Nivelles road and regained its own lines behind Goumont.

Although jolted, shaken and wracked by heavy casualties, the Allied infantry held fast. The British batteries at the foot of the slope, many times overrun by the French cavalry, many times reformed and resumed their deadly fire. The infernal struggle went on for two hours; then, at around six o'clock, Milhaud's and Kellermann's exhausted divisions abandoned the high ground and, for about half-an-hour, a rare lull descended on that part of the field.

Ney now realised that he ought to have invoked his infantry to support these heroic but unavailing charges. To deal with them, the Allied infantry would have had to have been deployed in line, making them easy prey for the French cavalry. And Ney had infantry to spare: Bachelu's division and one of Foy's brigades which since the morning had been left forgotten, arms grounded, along the lane between La Belle Alliance and Braine-l'Alleud.

He now launched these six thousand bayonets, in columns in echelon, against the right of the British line. Confidently, with a firm step, the troops marched towards the enemy, assailed however by a redoubled fire from the British artillery, whose gunners had once more taken possession of their pieces.

One of Foy's ADCs gave an account of the brief and deadly assault: 'Within musket range, the general, still fully confident, tapped me on the shoulder and said: "Tomorrow, Brussels and a colonelcy from the Emperor!"

'Smiling at these words, I replied by pointing at Bachelu's column, which was beginning to give way and waver; onwards though, we must do our best.

'At that moment, having come within close range, the infantry's fire and that of the artillery began to shake our columns. The one on the right lost its cohesion and the men took to their heels; our own, torn by the same fire, followed their example. Everyone ran to save their own skins; we, unable to stop them, were obliged to follow…[102].'

Despite this success, the Allied situation worsened.

Capture of La Haie-Sainte

While the French cavalry was launching its attacks against the British squares to the west of the Brussels road, sporadic fighting was taking place on its eastern side.

Although the artillery never ceased to pound the British lines, only the skirmishers of Donzelot's and Marcognet's divisions were harrying the infantry deployed along the Vieux Chemin de Wavre, while Durutte's did the same before Fichermont, though without really threatening the Allied garrison.

At about half-past five in the evening, while the cavalry were vainly charging the British squares, Napoléon, who had at last realised that La Haie-Sainte remained the key to the Allied position, ordered Ney to launch a fresh attack.

The assault was marked by extreme ferocity, the French attempting frantically to scale the walls and to disarm the defenders by seizing their weapons through the loopholes. At one particular point the barn caught fire, but the little garrison extinguished the flames by means of bowls and cooking pots, drawing water from a pond in the farmyard.

Baring's battalion and the reinforcements he had received were equipped with the Baker rifle, which required car-tridges different from those used by the universal musket. Despite urgent and repeated requests for fresh supplies, Baring soon found himself short of ammunition.

The fire died down and, by climbing on to the roofs of the pigsties, Quiot's soldiers were able to get into the farmyard and begin to slaughter the garrison, which now had only its bayonets with which to fight. Refusing to surrender, Baring, who had had three horses killed under him, with no less than six balls in his saddle and two in his hat, retreated with the survivors through the small door at the rear of the main building.

It was half-past six; a few minutes earlier, the Prince of Orange, who was near enough to see the desperate situation of the strongpoint, had sent it reinforcements consisting of two new battalions of the German Legion, under the command of Ompteda himself. They had progressed scarcely

The Defence of La Haie-Sainte. Oil on canvas by A Northern, Niedersächsisches Landesmuseum, Hanover.

Watercolour lithograph by Taillois, afrer Montius. Musée Wellington, Waterloo.

The farm of La Haie-Sainte

The name of Haie-Sainte recalls the existence of a meadow enclosed by hedges, the property of a family of the name of Sainte, mentioned in a feudal return of 1386. The farm seems to have been built prior to 1536 by a family from Braine-l'Alleud, the Moitomonts. It was acquired by Jean Glibert in 1618 and then became, by marriage, the property of the Boucquéaus, a powerful farming family who also owned the farm of Le Caillou and worked that of Mont-Saint-Jean. In 1815 the farm belonged to Comte Charles-Henri Boot de Velthem, who had purchased it in 1775, and was rented by Pierre Moreau. In despair at the destruction of his crops during the battle, Moreau abandoned the farm several weeks later.

two hundred metres when a party of French *cuirassiers* fell on them, sabreing one battalion, capturing its standard and killing Ompteda, while the other, having formed square, succeeded in regaining the Allied lines.

The capture of La Haie-Sainte represented Napoléon's first significant success.

To the east, skilfully using the farm as a base, the infantry of Quiot, Donzelot and Marcognet, deployed as skirmishers, drove the 95th Rifles out of the gravel pit and exerted heavy pressure on the remains of the brigades of Kempt, Pack and de Lambert, which had been reduced to a quarter of their strength.

A horse battery was set up to the north of the farm and opened fire with its six 6-pounders on the Allied centre at a range of one hundred and fifty metres, which was also assailed from the west by the skirmishers of Foy and Bachelu.

On the extreme left of the French line, Durutte made a new effort to capture the hamlet of La Marache and the farms of Papelotte and La Haie at the same time as d'Erlon's entire corps was supporting the decisive assault on La Haie-Sainte with a swarm of skirmishers. The French managed to take La Marache, but the farms remained in the hands of Saxe-Weimar's troops, a fact which was not without its tactical importance, since the Papelotte position formed the hinge which would provide the junction between the Prussian and the Anglo-Dutch forces.

Nevertheless, Wellington's situation had never been so critical.

Ompteda's brigade had been reduced to one battalion, that of Kielmansegge had lost half its strength, while Kruse's Nassauers were not much better off and were on the point of giving ground under the torment being meted out by the French skirmishers. Of Colin Halkett's brigade, only a third remained. Halkett asked Wellington that he be allowed to take his brigade out of the firing line.

"Well, Halkett, how do you get on?"

"My Lord, we are dreadfully cut up; can you not relieve for a little while?"

"Impossible."

"Very well, my Lord, we'll stand till the last man falls"[103].

Napoléon had never been so close to victory.

What is the explanation for this sudden worsening of the Allied situation? It was in fact the result of the first use on the French side of the three arms in combination.

The infantry, which had formed square in order to resist the attacks of the French cavalry, constituted an ideal target for the artillery and the skirmishers. The latter were able to act with complete impunity, for the cavalry supporting the Allied centre were out of the fight, while if the squares were to redeploy in line, they would become easy prey for the French squadrons. Ney, sensing that the time was ripe to take advantage of the situation and administer the final blow, sent an aide de camp, Colonel Heymès, to ask the Emperor for more infantry, which drew from Napoléon the irritated response: 'Troops! Where would you like me to take them from? Do you want me to manufacture them?[104]' Nevertheless, he still had the Old Guard to call on, that supreme reserve which had been the deciding factor in many battles.

However, at that moment – it was half-past six – it looked as if Plancenoit had fallen into the hands of the Prussians. Before he could deal finally with the British, the Emperor would have to stem the enemy advance which threatened his army with encirclement.

The exhaustion of the French cavalry and the reluctance of Napoléon to employ the Imperial Guard immediately, so making the most of the fall of La Haie-Sainte, would allow Wellington to take a series of steps to save his army.

The attack by the Guard

One hour later, at about half-past seven, Napoléon, now satisfied that he had banished the threat of encirclement which Blücher's troops had posed when they seized Plancenoit, decided to finish off the Anglo-Dutch army and force it to retreat, before turning on the Prussians with all his forces.

For hours Wellington's army had been subjected to an incessant and deadly assault from the French artillery and had suffered heavy casualties. According to General Müffling, nearly half his men had been put out of action. The cavalry charges had also taken their toll, even though the squares had held firm against their hammer blows.

The capture of La Haie-Sainte had destroyed one of the strongpoints in the enemy line. This advantage should have been followed up without delay, but the Emperor failed to do so, thus giving Wellington time to call up his reserves and plug the gaps in the line.

The only fresh troops left to Napoléon were his Guards, or rather some of them. The Young Guard and two battal-

Napoleon views the Field from la Belle Alliance. Oil on canvas by Sir William Allan. Apsley House, the Wellington Museum, London.

ions of the Old Guard had been engaged at Plancenoit, the 1st battalion of the 1st *Chasseurs* was guarding the headquarters at Le Caillou and the two battalions of the 1st Grenadiers were positioned back at Rossomme. This left the Emperor with only nine battalions, concentrated between Decoster's house and La Belle Alliance.

In order to stimulate them and inject fresh courage in all the troops who would be called on to support the Guard's attack by a general assault on the Allied line, Napoléon deliberately caused false news to be circulated of the imminent arrival of Grouchy.

This notorious lie, notes Colonel Baudus, attached to the Imperial headquarters, '... not only had its effect [...] on the able-bodied but, admirably, it reinvigorated even the wounded, for all those who could still crawl arose and threw themselves on the enemy with cries of *"Vive l'Empereur"*[105].'

Wellington had reinforced his centre and his right. Aware of the impending arrival of Zieten's corps, he summoned von Vincke's infantry from the vicinity of Papelotte and posted it behind the remains of Ompteda and Kielmansegge, on either side of the roadway. Vivian's and Vandeleur's brigades were stationed in the second line, in support of the troops deployed along the Chemins de la Croix and des Vertes Bornes. Chassé's Dutch-Belgian division was brought over from Braine-l'Alleud, where it had bivouacked. Detmers' brigade was inserted behind Colin Halkett and the Brunswicker battalions, while Aubremé's brigade was placed in reserve, where the lane to Braine-l'Alleud crosses the Nivelles road.

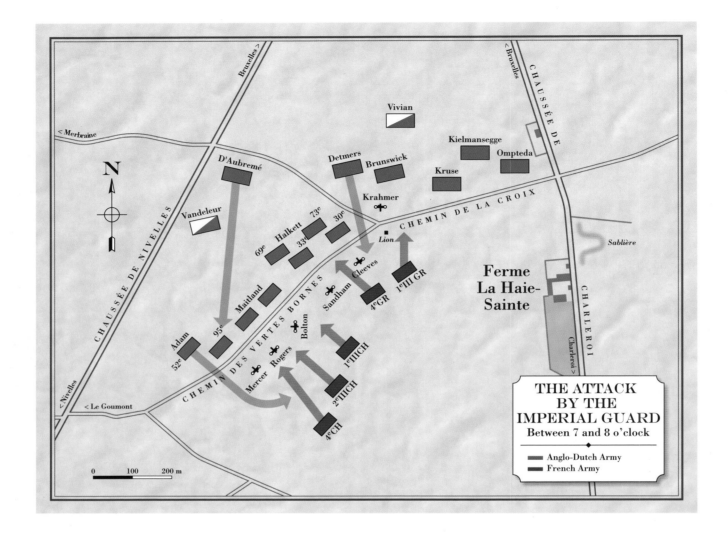

Once the Emperor had taken the decision to commit his last reserves, he left his observation point opposite the Decoster house and went forward on foot to a point halfway between La Belle Alliance and La Haie-Sainte. He decided to attack in two waves. The first, consisting of five battalions, was entrusted to Marshal Ney. The 1/3rd Grenadiers and the 4th Grenadiers (whose two battalions amounted to the strength of a single one) formed the first column and the battalions of the 3rd and 4th *Chasseurs* (two battalions of reduced strength) constituted the second. These two columns were accompanied by a battery of horse artillery. They were formed up in the grounds of La Haie-Sainte by Napoléon in person and marched off along the same line as that taken by the cavalry charges.

The second wave, of four battalions, remained in reserve at the foot of the Belle Alliance plateau. The assault was to be supported by a general attack by the troops of d'Erlon and Reille.

The Donzelot, Alix and Marcognet divisions once more mounted an assault on the Allied centre, but the movement was much slower on Reille's side. The attack by the Guard had turned away before Foy's and Bachelu's supporting divisions arrived.

The Old Guard – the *grognards* as they were dubbed – moved off, supported by intensified artillery fire. The battlefield was enveloped in mist and at times folds in the ground and clouds of smoke hid the columns from view, except when the cannon fired their flares. According to one witness, it was difficult to see further than ninety metres.

The drums beat the charge and the soldiers measured the pace of their march with shouts of *'Vive l'Empereur'*. The Allied artillery, which had been reinforced by batteries in reserve, obeyed Wellington's orders and refrained from returning the fire from the French cannon. Its ammunition stocks were, in any case, greatly depleted.

When the French columns appeared on the plateau, emerging through the smoke, a savage rain of canister shot converged on them, from in front and from the flank, causing heavy casualties. A British artillery officer recalled, '…the Column waving, at each successive discharge, like standing corn blown by the wind [106].'

As they neared the British line, the *grognards* deployed in echelon. The righthand column was led by Marshal Ney himself. He had just, for the fifth time, had his horse killed beneath him, so, sword in hand, he marched at the head of the veterans. The thrust by the 1/3rd Grenadiers was aimed at the junction between Halkett's brigade and the Brunswick battalions.

In a single thrust, despite the deadly canister fire from Krahmer's and Lloyd's batteries, the Grenadiers overpowered two battalions of Brunswickers and drove back Halkett's 30th and 73rd regiments. The latter surged back in disorder, but their retirement, which had threatened to become a rout, was brought to a halt by Vivian's cavalry.

At the same time, General Chassé, a Dutch officer who had served in all the Empire's campaigns, earning thereby a baron's title and a reputation as an intrepid warrior, sent against the grenadiers the 3,000 fresh troops of Detmers' brigade. With their bayonets fixed and shouting '*Oranje boven*' or '*Vive le roi*', as applicable, the Dutch-Belgian infantry, despite strong resistance, drove the *grognards* back down the slope.

While that was going on, the second echelon of the French column, the battalion of the 4th Grenadiers, had made for the right wing of Halkett's brigade. Supported by the fire of two guns of the horse artillery, the grenadiers' volleys caused the 33rd and 69th regiments before them to give way and retreat, Halkett being wounded as he was trying to rally his men. The reverse suffered by the other echelons of the Guard meant that this success could not be built upon and the 4th Grenadiers soon found themselves having to withdraw in good order to avoid encirclement.

The second column had directed its efforts against Maitland's and Adam's brigades. The leading echelon, composed of the two battalions of the *3rd Chasseurs*, made directly for Maitland's Guards, lying amid the corn, fifty metres beyond the crest of the ridge, sheltered from the French artillery fire.

The Battle of Waterloo. Coloured etching by J T Wilmore, after a painting by George J Jones, published in London by J Hogarth, on 21 March 1849. Musée Wellington, Waterloo.

Wellington was alongside Maitland. When the French crossed the ridge, having driven the gunners of Sandham, Bolton and Rogers from their cannon, the Duke called: 'Now Maitland, now is your chance'. The British saw the French drawing near and began to deploy, but remained hidden from their view. 'Up Guards and at them', cried Wellington[107]. Fifteen hundred men, in four ranks, rose up like a red sea before the *Chasseurs*.

At thirty metres, the volley was devastating. In less than a minute, three hundred men were disabled, while those in the rear tried to deploy in conditions of the greatest confusion.

Seizing the moment, Lieutenant Colonel Lord Saltoun of the 1st Foot Guards sent his men forward with their bayonets fixed.

Wellington signalling the general advance. Watercolour by J A Atkinson. The British Museum, London.

The Battle of Waterloo. Coloured etching, unsigned, after a painting by George J Jones. Musée Wellington, Waterloo.

In a furious hand-to-hand fight, the *grognards* were forced back, step by step, towards the orchard at Goumont. But the *3rd Chasseurs* soon found support in the form of the single battalion of the *4th Chasseurs* which constituted its left echelon. This injection of fresh troops was enough to release them from the grip of Maitland's Guards who, before combat could be engaged, were ordered by their officers to retire to their start line, in some degree of disorder. The French battalions were hastily reformed and climbed once more up the hillside in the wake of the 4th *Chasseurs*, who were crossing the Chemin des Vertes Bornes.

At that moment Lieutenant Colonel Sir John Colborne, a veteran of the Portuguese and Spanish wars and known to his men as 'the fire-eater', on his own initiative sent forward the thousand men of his 52nd infantry regiment, positioned on Maitland's right, wheeling them so that they were at right-angles to the Allied line and on the flank of the French column. The 52nd discharged a heavy volley of musket fire and then charged with the bayonet.

Seeing this movement, Wellington sent the 2nd battalion of the 95th Rifles to support Colborne[108]. Overwhelmed by numbers, under fire from in front and the side and torn by the concentrated fire of the artillery, the *Chasseurs* fell back, in good order.

The Duke rode over to Colborne's side and, while congratulating him, enjoined him to press the French without pause and give them no chance to rally. Then, spurring Copenhagen forward, he returned with Uxbridge to his observation post near the crossroads on the Brussels highway.

Napoléon had observed the reverse suffered by the first assault wave of his Guard from a small rise above the orchard of La Haie-Sainte. Nearby, to the west of the road, were the I/2nd Grenadiers (General Christiani), the II/1st *Chasseurs* (General Cambronne) and the II/2nd *Chasseurs* (General Monprez); further off, near Goumont, were the II/3rd Grenadiers (Lieutenant Colonel Belcourt). These four battalions, intended to finalise a successful assault, would have to be used in an attempt to avert disaster.

Napoléon ordered Cambronne and Monprez to extend their line out towards Goumont. He himself, accompanied only by General Drouot, remained close to the I/2nd Grenadiers, formed up in a square on the roadway. To the rear were massed the four squadrons in attendance: four hundred dragoons of the Guard, the only fresh cavalry that remained.

The repulse of the attack by the Guard had meant that Reille's divisions which, in three columns in echelon and covered in front by skirmishers, had tried, from some dis-

Defeat of the French Imperial Guards at Waterloo. Watercolour by John A Atkinson. Musée Wellington, Waterloo.

tance to the rear, to support the attack by the *grognards*, had also had to withdraw.

On their side, the Allies were determined to seize on the advantage offered, by not allowing the French to reform and renew their attack. Wellington ordered Adam, with Hew Halkett's Hanoverian brigade in support, to press forward and for Vivian to follow them up. The target of Vivian's three regiments was the remains of the French cavalry, which was rallying, as well as it could, between La Belle Alliance and Goumont and which represented a potential threat to Adam's columns.

After a brief and violent engagement, the British hussars forced the exhausted French squadrons to leave the field, but were prevented from advancing further by the fire from the Guard's squares.

Meanwhile, Adam's brigade, with Colborne's 52nd at its head, was crossing the battlefield diagonally, in the direction of La Haie-Sainte, its regiments deployed fanwise, four ranks deep. A battalion of the 95th took possession of the farm's orchard then, forming up in line parallel to that of the French, began to climb the slope to the higher ground.

By then it was well past eight o'clock. Suddenly, a shaft of sunlight and a light breeze swept away the mist and

smoke from the field of battle, which Wellington was able to survey through his telescope. The French right, yielding to the pressure applied by Zieten's corps, fell back rapidly, the majority of its units seeming to be on the point of losing their footing. Between La Belle Alliance and Goumont, Reille's troops were attempting to reform behind the shelter of the battalions of the Guard who either had returned from the high ground or were in reserve.

The Duke, reaching a decision, turned to Uxbridge, saying: 'Oh, dammit!... In for a penny, in for a pound is my maxim; and if the troops advance they shall go as far as they can[109].'

Wellington placed his hat on the point of his sword and raised it three times – this being the signal to attack by all his troops. He was answered by a triple hurrah from the Allied line then, spurring his horse, he galloped over to La Haie-Sainte. Uxbridge accompanied him, but was hit in the knee by a piece of shrapnel and carried to the rear.

Wellington reiterated to Adam the order to continue his advance and as he rode by called out: 'Well done Colborne! Well done! Go on. Never mind, go on, go on. Don't give them time to rally. They won't stand.[110].' Adam's regiments, with the 52nd at their head, continued their advance towards the Belle Alliance plateau.

In the ranks of the French, the greatest confusion was reigning: each unit was carrying on the fight independently, combined movements were no longer possible and whole regiments were succumbing to panic.

Vandeleur's brigade had joined up with Vivian's horsemen and their squadrons were once more spreading their deadly whirlwind between La Belle Alliance and Goumont.

Several troops of *cuirassiers* tried hard to repel them, but without success, one witness reporting that their horses' exhaustion placed them in such a state of inferiority that they were being unseated like young recruits[111]. Reille's infantry cut no better figure: assailed alternately by cavalry and infantry, they no longer knew what formation to adopt and some among them gave way to panic and sought safety in bewildered flight. The 2nd *Ligne*, who had fought all day before Goumont, were a particular example. One of its officers recalled: 'We were being fired on from the rear and our soldiers, already frightened, caught sight of our Polish lancers and, taking them for the British cavalry, cried out: 'We are lost!' The cry was taken up in all parts and soon we

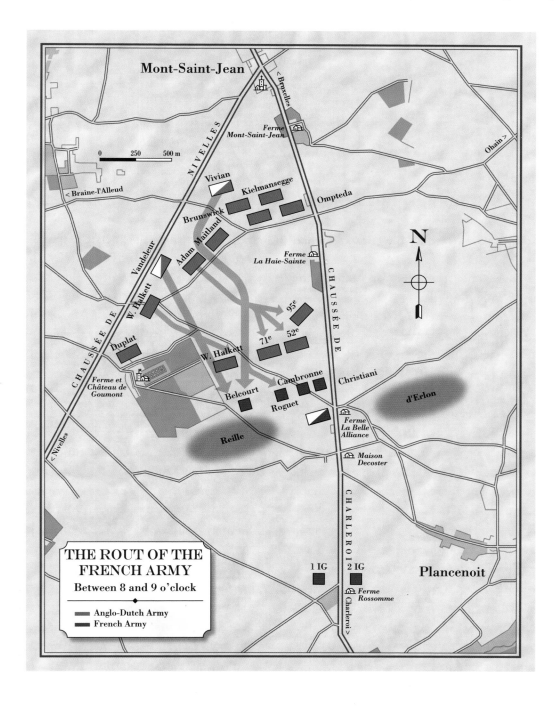

THE ROUT OF THE
FRENCH ARMY
Between 8 and 9 o'clock

▬ Anglo-Dutch Army
▬ French Army

were in complete disorder. Each man thought only of his own safety. Bewildered men are impossible to control. The cavalry followed the example of the infantry; I saw dragoons, fleeing at the gallop, bowling over unfortunate foot-soldiers and then trample over their bodies with their horses. I myself was knocked over once. Annoyed by such disorder, worn out by vain efforts, I kept shouting: 'Stop, pull yourselves together, we are not being pursued'. Seeing that my efforts were to no avail, I armed myself with a rifle and confronted two or three dragoons. Threatening them with the bayonet or the rifle, I shouted at them loudly that there was no one pursuing us and that the first one to take another step would have a bullet in him. I finally managed to persuade them to stop. In that way I collected a dozen cavalrymen and about sixty infantry[112].' Other regiments retreated in good order, moving southwards across the fields.

Amongst this mob, almost the only ones to maintain their composure were the battalions of the Guard, although at the price of heavy casualties.

The II/3rd Grenadiers, subjected to fire from Gardiner's battery, which had advanced with Hew Halkett's brigade east of Goumont, shot at by the Hanoverian infantry and charged by Vandeleur's dragoons, were destroyed as they were falling back towards the road.

In front of La Belle Alliance, the squares formed by the I/2nd Grenadiers (Christiani), the II/1st *Chasseurs* (Cambronne) and the II/2nd *Chasseurs* (Monprez), merged with the remnants of the battalions which had been ejected from the plateau, were forced to endure a pounding from Adam's brigade, backed up by the fire of Rogers' cannon and by Vivian's horse.

When Napoléon had observed the failure of the attack by the Guard and had then harangued the remnants of the battalions who were reforming as well as they could at the foot of the plateau, he returned on foot to La Belle Alliance. For a while, he stayed near a square of the 2nd Grenadiers, observing the rearward movement of his troops then, getting on his horse, he withdrew in the direction of Rossomme.

The squares were supported at first by a 12-pounder battery, which quickly ran out of ammunition and succumbed to the sabre. They were then left to themselves and slowly retreated, losing more men with every enemy salvo, stoically closing ranks and facing up to the furious charges of Vivian's regiments. Too few to form square in three ranks, they were reduced to two and then formed into a triangle.

Cambronne, wounded in the head, fell to the ground senseless and was taken prisoner by Hew Halkett. The remnants of his battalion, decimated by the fire of the artillery, joined forces with the II/2nd *Chasseurs* and the I/2nd Grenadiers, which retired step by step, with the mob of fugitives swirling around them. By the time they reached Rossomme, these two battalions had been reduced to a few score men each and they broke up. 'The voices of the officers were ignored', recounted General Christiani, 'once my men dispersed it became impossible to rally them[113].' As twilight descended on the field, conquerers and conquered were mingled together in the utmost confusion.

A Prussian battery, which had arrived somehow on the slope of the Vieux Chemin de Wavre, fired in enfilade on the British columns and Mercer's cannon had to return fire to silence it. Prussian balls intended for the stubborn defenders of Plancenoit fell amidst Adam's regiments, the British 18th Hussars exchanged sabre thrusts with a Prussian cavalry regiment emerging from Plancenoit and Vivian's and Vandeleur's men came close to slaying one another on the high ground at La Belle Alliance.

The situation of the French right wing was just as dramatic. The attack by the Guard had been supported by a general offensive movement by the French army and d'Erlon's corps had therefore advanced once more against the Allied left.

To the east of the road, Marcognet's and Donzelot's columns were unable to advance beyond the Chemin de la Croix. An officer of the 95th Rifles provided the following description of their unavailing attacks: 'It consisted of an uninterrupted fire of musketry (the distance between the hostile lines I imagine to have been rather more than one hundred yards) between Kempt's and some of Lambert's Regiments posted along the thorn hedge, and the French Infantry lining the knoll and the crest of the hill near it. Several times the French Officers made desperate attempts to induce their men to charge Kempt's line, and I saw more than once parties of the French in our front spring up from their kneeling position and advance some yards towards the thorn hedge, headed by their Officers with vehement gestures, but our fire was so very hot and deadly that they almost instantly ran back behind the crest of the hill, always leaving a great many killed or disabled behind them[114].'

To the west of the road, one of Quiot's columns had moved against the left wing of Colin Halkett's brigade, with no more

The last square. Oil on canvas, unsigned, Musée Wellington, Waterloo.

The words of Cambronne

Tradition has it that General Cambronne, when called on to surrender during the final attack on the British line, replied: 'The Guard will die, but will not yield!' Shortly afterwards, he was wounded in the head and taken prisoner. The words can most probably be attributed to the pen of a journalist, Rougemont, who, as early as 24 June 1815, published them in the Journal Général de la France. *At that date, no officer or soldier of the Guard had yet returned to Paris, which had seen only a few generals of the Imperial headquarters arriving with news of the disaster. The quotation is all the more improbable since, at the moment when it was supposed to have been uttered, the Allied troops were still very hard put to hold on and could scarcely be thinking of inviting their assailants to surrender. Furthermore, Cambronne, who commanded the 2nd battalion of the 1er chasseurs, took no part in this attack. After he died, in 1842, the son of General Michel, second in command of the chasseurs of the Guard, claimed that it was his father who had spoken the legendary words. This claim may be dismissed by referring to the testimony of the aide-de-camp to Michel, who was killed during the attack: 'When we reached the plateau, within close range of the English, who were waiting for us, not moving, we were met by a tremendous volley. General Michel fell from his horse crying: "Mon Dieu, my arm is broken!". I leapt down and unbuttoned his coat to find the wound. The general was dead; a ball had struck him in the left breast, passing right through his body.' Cambronne, who had always denied having spoken the words, did however acknowledge that he had said something else. Several years later he told a former comrade in arms: 'I didn't say that (the above words), I simply said: "Buggers like us never surrender". Diffident allusions to another response by Cambronne, coarser and more soldierly, started to appear in 1830. Victor Hugo was the first, attributing the robust reply to him in* Les Misérables. *One day, General Bachelu asked Cambronne about it, the latter replying: 'What, you too? This is too much, it is beginning to be* emmerdant!' *Bachelu added: 'In such circumstances the word was so natural that Cambronne must have uttered it five or six times that day – as I did myself.'*

success, as an officer of the 73rd Infantry Regiment described: 'Thus situated we remained for a short time inactive, when the last attacking Column made its appearance through the fog and smoke, which throughout the day lay thick on the ground. Their advance was as usual with the French, very noisy and evidently reluctant, the Officers being in advance some yards cheering their men on. They however kept up a confused and running fire, which we did not reply to until they reached nearly on a level with us, when a well-directed volley put them into confusion from which they did not appear to recover, but after a short interval of musketry on both sides, they turned about to a man and fled[115].'

The success enjoyed by the attacks of the brigades of Adam, Vivian and Vandeleur, in conjunction with the general movement of the British line, brought about the abrupt and final collapse of d'Erlon's corps. His divisions, in fear of being surrounded, degenerated into a mob, with cries of: 'Every man for himself, we have been betrayed'. 'All discipline vanished', said an officer of I Corps, 'the regiments dissolved into an indescribable disorder, in shapeless swarms of men which were broken up and dispersed by the enemy's cannon[116].'

La Haie-Sainte, so dearly captured, was abandoned without a fight, filled with its dead and wounded.

Ney, bare-headed, with sword in hand but no aide-de-camp at his side, was on foot and walking with difficulty, hampered by his heavy boots in the muddy ground, still sodden with the previous day's rain. Carried away by the destruction of his regiments, he exclaimed to Drouet: 'd'Erlon, if we escape this, you and I, we shall be hanged[117].' In vain he tried to arrest the debacle by putting himself at the head of Brue's brigade, but this broke up in its turn and the marshal was borne off towards Rossomme by the flood of fugitives. There, on either side of the road, the 1st Grenadiers of the Old Guard had formed two unshakeable squares.

By way of the lane to Maison du Roi, General Pelet arrived with what remained of the men – barely half – who had been engaged at Plancenoit. Night came down very swiftly: '...it was impossible to make anything out more than ten paces away,' remarked Pelet[118].

Napoléon, astride his horse, was in the middle of the square formed by the 1st battalion of the 1st Grenadiers.

There were fugitives everywhere. General Petit,

The last square at Waterloo. Oil on canvas by Joseph Bellangé (detail). Musée de Picardie, Amiens.

commanding the battalion, had the *grenadière* beaten and large numbers of the Guard came to swell the two squares, which were eight to ten ranks deep. But, despite vigorous supporting fire from an 8-pounder battery, it proved impossible to withstand the enemy pressure.

The Emperor ordered the retreat and left the square. The Grenadiers retired in the best of order, making frequent halts or marking time as if on parade, to allow the last cannon or the covering skirmishers to catch up. Further on, the two squares joined together and formed into columns, while Napoléon arrived at Le Caillou.

Throughout that day, Le Caillou had seen little activity. Responsibility for guarding the headquarters and the transport had been in the hands of the 1st battalion of the *1er chasseurs à pied* of the Imperial Guard, commanded by a Dutch officer in French service, Lieutenant Colonel (Major) Duuring.

Round about five or six o'clock, Saint-Denis, known as the Mameluk Ali, arrived at the headquarters in haste, calling for a small canteen, so that the Emperor and his suite could eat a light meal. He was the bearer of bad news: the incursion on to the battlefield of Bülow's Corps.

Faced with these events, Marchand, Napoléon's *valet de chambre*, after conferring with the principal equerry, General Fouler, ordered that the Emperor's bed be dismantled and loaded on to a mule. It was at about that time also that there appeared to the east of Le Caillou, on the edge of Chantelet Wood, the first Prussian units.

Duuring lost no time in evacuating the treasury and the transport, as more and more fugitives filled the road. To keep them in check, Duuring stationed two companies on the road, bayonets fixed, with orders to allow only the wounded to pass. Not without difficulty, he managed to collect some two hundred men. With this small force and a hundred *chasseurs* deployed as skirmishers, he advanced towards the enemy troops emerging from Chantelet Wood and threw them back without too much trouble.

But the flood of fugitives continued to grow: infantry, artillery and cavalry were all jumbled together. Duuring, incapable of putting a stop to the rout, contented himself with welcoming into his ranks the men of the Old Guard.

'In such unhappy disorder, and with sharp-shooters appearing to our rear', recounted Duuring, 'the Emperor arrived, accompanied by a few *chasseurs à cheval* and several generals, including Comtes Drouot and Lobau. His Majesty came up to me, asked me what I had done, what force I had mustered and its position, and then ordered me in person to form up in close order and follow him, saying: "I count on you"[119].'

Napoléon then made off in the direction of Genappe and vanished into the night.

THE FIGHT AGAINST BLÜCHER

The Prussians' march from Wavre to Mont-Saint-Jean

It was at Wavre, where the Prussian headquarters had been set up at midday on the 17th, that Blücher learnt of Wellington's intention to fall back to Mont-Saint-Jean and there to give battle the following day, provided that he was supported by his Prussian ally.

It was five o'clock when the transport waggons arrived from Gembloux, bringing fresh ammunition for the troops, and from that moment a Prussian intervention became possible. At about eleven o'clock that evening, Blücher took steps to inform the Duke of his intentions: 'I will come with not just two corps, but with my whole army, and if the French do not attack us on the 18th, we will attack them on the 19th[120].'

This message did not reach Waterloo until the morning; the marshal's desire to come to his ally's aid had still to overcome the reluctance of his chief of staff, Gneisenau. The latter's distrust of Wellington had been fostered by the promise, made on the previous day and not kept, to reinforce the Prussian army at Ligny. 'If the English are beaten', he objected, 'our army will be running a very great risk'.

Blücher, both demanding and eloquent, was insistant and in the end won the day. 'Gneisenau has given in', he told the British liaison officer, Colonel Hardinge, triumphantly, 'we shall link up with the Duke[121].'

Shortly afterwards, Müffling brought Blücher the news that the Duke was now established on the Mont-Saint-Jean plateau, between Braine-l'Alleud and Fishermont, with the intention of giving battle, with the Prussians' support.

Towards midnight, orders were issued to the corps of Bülow, Zieten and Pirch I to get under way at first light, while Thielmann's corps covered the army's movements by guarding Wavre.

Bülow (IV Corps) was given more precise instructions: 'At daybreak, you are to march with IV Corps from Dion-le-Mont, through Wavre and towards Chapelle-Saint-Lambert, where you are to conceal your forces as far as possible, in the

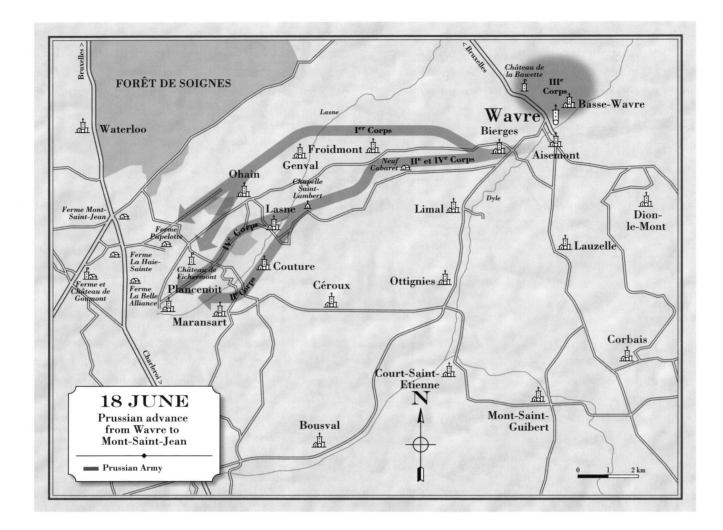

event of the enemy being not seriously engaged by the Duke of Wellington. Otherwise you are to vigorously attack the enemy's right flank. II Corps will be in support and I and III Corps will be ready to march in the same direction[122].' At half-past nine in the morning, Blücher confirmed to Müffling his intention of joining Wellington.

At about four in the morning, Bülow's corps moved out of its bivouacs at Dion-le-Mont and made for Wavre, which its vanguard reached at around seven o'clock, although the greater part of the corps was held up by a fire which broke out in the Place du Sablon (now the Place Bosch).

The Prussian troops carried on towards Chapelle-Saint-Lambert, along the Vieux Chemin de Wavre, through La Haie sous Bierges, Le Pèlerin, Neuf-Cabaret and the Saint Robert Chapel. The vanguard of IV Corps arrived at Chapelle at eleven o'clock, as mass was ending. At about that time Blücher left Wavre, reaching Chapelle at about one, at the same time as Hiller's brigade[123]. As midday approached,

the Pirch I Corps set off in Bülow's wake.

I Corps, which had bivouacked at Bierges, did not get on the road until two o'clock, having had to wait for two hours to allow II Corps to go by in front. Zieten took a more northerly route, via Rixensart sur Froidment Wood, Bourgeois and Genval. Leaving on its left the village of Ohain, it reached the Notre Dame de Bon Secours Chapel at half-past six, having covered ten kilometres in four and a half hours, along narrow and difficult tracks, where the artillery had difficulty in forcing its way through.

At about one o'clock, while the Emperor, with his staff, was at Rossomme, Soult remarked to Napoléon that, to the east, on the high ground at Saint-Lambert, he could make out what appeared to be troops.

'All the telescopes of the staff were focussed on that point. The weather was fairly misty; as happens on such occasions, some held the view that there were no troops, only trees, others that there were columns which had moved into position and some that there were troops on the march[124].'

In order to make sure, Napoléon called for General Domon and told him to take his division of light cavalry and that of Subervie and reconnoitre the army's right wing.

If there had been any doubt, it was soon removed. A quarter of an hour later, an NCO of the Silesian 2nd Hussars was brought in, who had just been captured near Lasne by the men of Colonel Marbot's 7th Hussars, which had been ranging the countryside around Lasne, Couture and Mousty. A letter from Bülow to Wellington had been found on the Prussian, announcing the arrival of IV Corps at Chapelle-Saint-Lambert. The prisoner, who spoke French, willingly gave them all the information in his possession. The mass of the Prussian army had bivouacked at Wavre and had seen nothing of Grouchy.

Napoléon immediately sent the intercepted letter on to the Marshal, with instructions to move in his direction, to take Bülow by surprise. 'This morning we have a ninety per cent chance', he said to Soult by way of conclusion, 'we are still six to four. And if Grouchy mends the terrible error he committed yesterday in loitering at Gembloux and dispatches his detachment without delay, our victory will be all the more decisive, for Bülow's corps will be completely lost[125].'

The Emperor ordered Lobau to move east with his IV Corps, to support Domon's light cavalry and to '…choose a good intermediate position where, with 10,000 men, he could hold back 30,000, should that become necessary[126].' Then he sent Ney the order to launch the attack by d'Erlon's corps. The time was nearly two o'clock.

View of the village of Plancenoit. Coloured lithograph by J Sturm, after E Pingret, published by Jobard. Musée Wellington, Waterloo.

Watercolour lithograph by Taillois, after Montius. Musée Wellington, Waterloo.

Papelotte Farm

The Walloon word 'papelote' corresponds to the French word 'papillote', which means the sheet of paper in which a lock of hair is wrapped before it is curled. It has taken on a derogatory meaning for something derisory, of little value. It was probably in this sense that it was applied to the farm's land, reputed to be of poor quality. The existence of the farm can be traced back to the end of the seventeenth century. In 1815 it was occupied by Melchior Mathieu who, according to tradition, did not abandon it despite the fighting. The present buildings date from 1860.

Bülow appears on the stage

The Prussian vanguard remained at Chapelle-Saint-Lambert, arms grounded, for more than three hours[127]. Blücher, and Gneisenau in particular, intended that, as a minimum, they should have Bülow's entire corps available (four infantry brigades, each with a strength of 6,000 muskets and 3,000 horse) before engaging in combat. Gneisenau did not wish to risk battle before he was certain that the British would not retreat, leaving the Prussians facing Napoléon alone[128].

Since the dawn, Bülow had been reconnoitring the ground through which he intended to pass, and by eight o'clock his scouts were at Chapelle-Saint-Lambert, at Maransart at nine and in Fichermont Wood at ten, revealing that the way was clear and that Napoléon had taken no steps to reconnoitre his right.

Already by eleven o'clock, a Prussian patrol had entered the hamlet of La Marache and had linked up with one of Vivian's squadrons. Even before fighting began, therefore, Wellington was aware that the Prussian advance guards were three-quarters of a league from the left of his army.

At about two o'clock, Bülow's vanguard began to cross the valley, an arduous undertaking due to the poor state of the lanes, after the damage caused by the previous day's storm. Old Blücher himself urged his men on: 'Forward', he cried, 'it can't be done, I hear, but it must be done. I've given Wellington my word – you surely don't want me to break it! One more little effort boys and victory is ours[129].'

The Prussian troops' route lay along the rue du Culot, in those days an ill-made earth track which crossed a fairly steep vale and then climbed the far side towards the hamlet of Culot and Kelle farm. From there, they went down

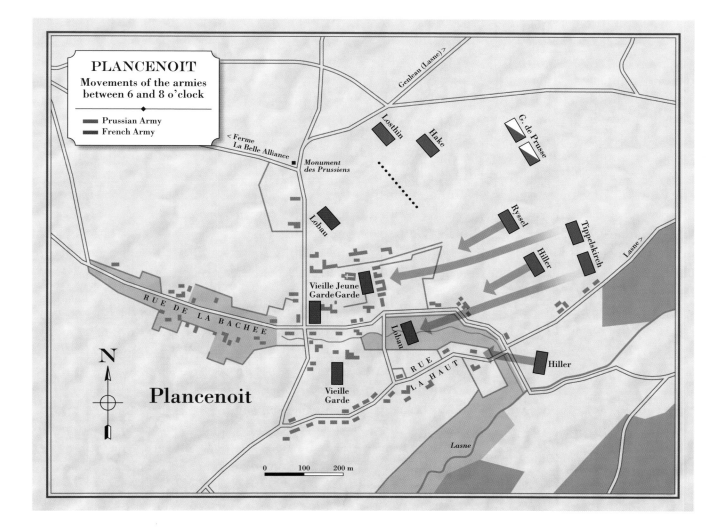

today's rue de la Gendarmerie and crossed the Lasne near to the church. There was a footbridge only and the transport had to cross by the ford, the movement being screened by the cavalry. Fichermont Wood, on the opposite bank, was occupied without difficulty.[130].

The leisurely speed of movement of the French VI Corps is hard to explain. From its starting point, to the east of the road, to the edge of Fichermont Wood was less than two kilometres. The order to confront the Prussians was passed to Lobau shortly before two o'clock. Two and a half hours later, his troops had still not occupied the wood from which the enemy would emerge. To the Prussians' great surprise, they met not a single scout and it was only on the other side of the wood that a small patrol was encountered[131].

At about half-past four, Bülow's two leading brigades began to leave the wood. They marched along the ridges from Genleau to Plancenoit, guided by the roofs of La Belle Alliance which they could see on the horizon.

At the same time, three battalions of Losthin's brigade were making for the château of Fichermont, which was occupied by an Orange-Nassau regiment, whose uniforms were very similar to those of the French troops. Thinking that they would have to deal with them, the Prussians opened fire and the garrison, taken in the rear, was forced to retire until the confusion had been cleared up. After that, a link was established with Saxe-Weimar's troops at Papelotte.

The infantry of Lobau's corps was well to the rear and the first clashes took place between the cavalry, which on both sides was shadowing the movements of its opponents. Fighting broke out at about a quarter past four; the Prussian IV Corps had numerical superiority, for Lobau had only 6,600 muskets and scarcely 2,000 sabres at his disposal. However, established behind Ranson Wood, the French offered strong resistance.

Rather than persisting in a frontal attack, Blücher, taking advantage of the arrival of Bülow's last units, slipped two brigades across to his right, along the lane running from Aywiers to Plancenoit. Faced with this threat of encirclement, Lobau was forced to retreat, taking up positions in the immediate vicinity of Plancenoit, with one of his brigades occupying the village itself.

Towards six that evening, the Prussian left wing, comprising von Hiller's 16th brigade with part of von Rijssel's 14th brigade in support, launched an attack on Bellair's brigade positioned in the village. Six batteries opened fire on Plancenoit where the French were entrenched. Some of the balls landed as far away as the Charleroi road, killing several generals of the Imperial staff.

The Prussians formed up in three columns. They found the village to be fiercely defended. In the first attack the cemetery was taken, but all around the French clung on and could not be moved. If Plancenoit chanced to fall, the French army could find itself encircled. Seeing the danger, Napoléon sent General Duhesme at the head of four thousand men of the Young Guard to restore the situation.

Half his battalions went to support Lobau to the north of the village and the other half drove the Prussians out of the cemetery. Twice more von Hiller's and von Rijssel's brigades were thrown at Plancenoit and the defenders were on the point of being overwhelmed.

Napoléon sent reinforcements in the shape of two battalions of the Old Guard, one of grenadiers and one of *chasseurs*. To General Pelet Napoléon said: 'Take your 1st battalion to Plancenoit, where the Young Guard has been completely overcome. Back them up, keep your troops together and keep them in hand. If you get up with the enemy, use the bayonet[132].'

Pelet has left us a colourful description of his experiences: 'I rushed off with the 1st battalion to Planchenoit. It might have been about six o'clock, maybe seven; anyway, I don't know how long I stayed there, but it seems to me to have been some time. As I entered the village I first met poor General Duhesme, who was being carried off on his horse, dead or dying. Then the light infantry, in sorry straits, their Colonel Chartran telling me that he could get nothing more out of them – plenty of men in fact, but all moving to the rear. I promised them that I would bring the enemy to a halt and urged them to reform to my rear. In fact, I got as far as the village crossroads and there, seeing the Prussians advancing, I ordered the leading company to rush the enemy with the bayonet, as they came down the road opposite to the one we were in. Scarcely had the enemy shown us their backs than the men started to blaze away at them. He sent in fresh troops and I called up another squad; it insisted on firing at them; I pushed them forward myself, and the enemy fled. But this squad broke up and, on every charge I made, the same thing happened. The men in the last companies shouted: 'Forward!', started to fire their muskets and the effect was scattered. I took several men myself to occupy the church and found myself face to face with these

Unsigned lithograph. Musée Royal de l'Armée, Brussels.

The Fichermont Château

The first known reference to the place name was in 1250. From the seventeenth century on, the Xaviers, lords of Fichermont, also held the title of Baron de Lasne. At the time of the battle, the old château had retained its feudal appearance, with a massive square tower. Since 1805, the property had been in the hands of a Brussels lawyer, Jean-Charles le Hardy. The old Fichermont château was demolished and rebuilt in 1859. By 1960 these structures, too, had finally disappeared.

gentlemen, who fired at me point-blank and then made off. Then, seeing how much resistance they were meeting, they lobbed a great many shells into the village and tried to get round it along the gullies of the Lasne and through the nearby woods, so I sent an officer there. In the course of all these attacks, we took many of their men prisoner but our men slaughtered them in a state of frenzy. I ran to stop them from doing so and, even as I ran, I saw one die in front of my eyes (they had butchered and hung our own fellows in cold blood). I was more revolted than infuriated. I took several under my protection, particularly an officer who grovelled and spoke of his French friends and those of his family. I led them behind my horse and then handed them over to my sappers, who would answer to me for their safety. However, the length of the fighting had turned all my men into sharp-shooters and I could no longer raise even a half-company. The enemy could not penetrate the village, but he stretched in front of me on both sides; in every gap I saw muskets aimed at me from forty paces and I could not imagine how he had been unable to fall on us twenty times over. At last, when I was at full stretch, sorely pressed and short of men, there arrived a company of grenadiers, sent by an unknown hand, and for which I was more than grateful. I stopped them while I got together a few *chasseurs*, then I sent them in with the bayonet, without firing a single shot. They went off like a wall and bowled them all over. I hung on amidst a hail of shells, fires which were started in various houses and musketry which was both terrible and continuous; there was a multitude of sharp-shooters all around us. No matter, I held on like a demon; I could no longer keep my men together, but they had all found themselves some cover and poured a deadly fire on the enemy, which held him off. They would have stopped him completely, but for his overwhelming numbers[133].'

By seven that evening, the outcome of the fighting – and Gneisenau's own agreement – was still uncertain. Bülow's right wing was being worn down by the unsuccessful attacks on Plancenoit, while his left wing was kept at arm's length, to the north of the village, by the firm countenance displayed by Lobau. Between the two, the mass of IV Corps' cavalry stood exposed to the fire from the French batteries.

Half-an-hour later, the battle swung back to the Prussians, with the arrival of their II Corps. At about six o'clock, marching in Bülow's wake, Pirch I received the order to cover the Prussian army's left by sending infantry and cavalry through Caturiaux, Couture-Saint-Germain and Maransart. At seven thirty, the two leading brigades reached the fighting zone and were immediately dispatched to the left wing, which was in most urgent need of help.

After a brisk cannonade, the 5th brigade (Tippelskirch) formed up in two columns and, with nine battalions from the 14th and 16th brigades in support, launched another attack on the village while, further north, the 13th and 15th brigades advanced on Lobau.

There was a considerable inequality of numbers: Bülow was fielding 23,000 infantry, 2,200 cavalry and 86 guns and he was supported by Pirch I with 8,000 fresh infantry, 2,600 cavalry and 24 guns. To oppose them, the French could find only 12,500 infantry, 2,000 cavalry and 52 guns.

At the same time, Zieten's corps, coming into the line at Papelotte, were driving Durutte out of La Marache and making d'Erlon fall back in disorder.

Lobau's troops, yielding to the general panic around them, gave way abruptly: 'The enemy suddenly stopped firing, as if he had been struck by a thunder-clap', wrote Pirch in his report, 'only our cannon continued to scatter his ranks as they fled in disorder[134].'

In Plancenoit, however, the struggle went on relentlessly. Entrenched in the church and the cemetary, a battalion of the Young Guard was annihilated, after inflicting considerable casualties on the infantry of Pirch I.

The Prussians seized the rue La Haut, so rendering resistance impossible, and forced the defenders into a precipitate retreat to avoid encirclement. 'Outside the village', Pelet recounted, 'I found myself in a terrible chaos of people who were running away and shouting: "Stop! Stop! Halt! Halt!". And those who were shouting loudest were those who were running the fastest. These sounds were mixed with the noise of cannon fire and of canister, which lent wings to the greatest sluggards among them. The enemy also sent skirmishers after us, particularly near Maransart Wood, through which I lost the beggars[135].'

The Prussian cavalry spread out in the direction of Rossomme and Maison du Roi, sabreing the fugitives as they went. It was then nine o'clock in the evening.

Zieten - the decisive act

While the fierce fighting for possession of Plancenoit was going on, the Prussian I Corps had been continuing its march to the north, aimed at linking up with the left wing of the Anglo-Dutch army. At about seven o'clock, the columns of Zieten's corps began to appear on the plateau between Papelotte and Ohain, in the vicinity of the Jacques chapel.

Wellington was preparing to face the attack by the Guard and had weakened his left by recalling to the centre Best's infantry and the brigades of Vivian and Vandeleur. He sent an aide-de-camp, Colonel Freemantle, accompanied by Müffling, with the object of obtaining from Zieten the urgent dispatch of reinforcements, even though it be no more than three thousand men.

'The Duke is anxiously waiting for your arrival, otherwise he will be obliged to retire', Müffling explained to the chief of staff of I Corps, Lieutenant Colonel von Reiche. Wellington's left was indeed showing signs of imminent collapse.

Ludwig von Reiche was highly embarrassed. 'Just at that moment', he related, 'as I was seeking out General Zieten to acquaint him with the situation, Captain von Scharnhorst happened on me and cried out that I Corps must be immediately sent to Fichermont, in other words in Blücher's direction, for whom things were not going too well. I tried to explain to him that all had been agreed with Müffling, that Wellington counted on our joining in with him, but von Scharnhorst would not listen, insisting that those were Blücher's orders and that if I did not obey them it would be on my responsibility. I had never been in such a difficult

The arrival of Zieten's cavalry. Watercolour engraving by M Dubourg, after John H Clark, published in London by E Orme on 18 April 1816. Musée Wellington, Waterloo.

The bridge at Genappe. Watercolour lithograph by Taillois, after Montius. Musée Wellington, Waterloo.

situation in my entire career. On the one hand, our troops were in danger at Plancenoit, on the other, Wellington was counting on our help. It was a dilemma which filled me with despair. General Zieten could not be found, yet the head of I Corps' column needed to be told what it should do. It had even advanced beyond the point where it ought to have turned off in Blücher's direction, when General Steinmetz, in command of I Corps' vanguard, seeing me in discussion with the head of the column, swooped down on me, questioned me aggressively, in his usual manner, and without attempting to hear my explanations ordered his vanguard to retrace their steps to the turning and move in the direction of Plancenoit. Fortunately, at that very moment General Zieten turned up and, after hearing my report, restored the direction of march towards the left[136].'

This indecision had cost at least half-an-hour and it was past seven thirty when Steinmetz' brigade deployed. It was none too soon, for the pressure exerted by Durutte's troops had been such that the French had seized La Marache, only Papelotte and Fichermont remained in the hands of the Nassauers and the link between Bülow's extreme right and Wellington's left had been broken.

Four batteries arrived to relieve the Hanoverian artillery on the Papelotte ridge and opened a fierce fire. Steinmetz' battalions, having deployed, retook La Marache from Durutte's men after desperate fighting. The Prussians pressed on and took their assault up the slopes of the plateau, supported by a brigade of cavalry. Durutte, seeing Donzelot and Marcognet withdrawing on his right, ordered a retreat also, for fear of being surrounded.

Brue's brigade gained the higher ground at La Belle Alliance in good order, but the other one, under Pegot, with the Prussian cavalry all about them, took to their heels and mixed with the other divisions of I Corps which, instead of facing the front, sought safety in flight.

At that moment, the pernicious nature of the false news of Grouchy's arrival, which Napoléon had allowed to circulate an hour earlier, was revealed. Instead of finding themselves reinforced by their own comrades, the French saw surging towards them the Prussian masses. Exhausted and shaken by six hours of fighting, they felt themselves betrayed and d'Erlon's corps began to crumble, to cries of '*Sauve qui peut*'.

Marshal Ney, displaying wherever he went his remarkable energy, attempted to arrest the stampede. Placing himself at the head of Brue's brigade, which was still maintaining a steady posture, he cried: 'I will show you how a Marshal of France can die!', but his gesture was instantly buried in a surge of fugitives and confusion was his sole reward[137].

THE EVENING OF 18 JUNE

Accompanied by several officers, Napoléon arrived on horseback at Genappe, where indescribable disorder reigned. Carriages and artillery pieces blocked the Grand-rue, jostling to cross the three-metre-wide bridge over the Dyle. Locating his own carriage, the Emperor, overcome with fatigue, threw himself into it.

The Prussian cavalry, commanded by Gneisenau in person, was sent in pursuit of the rout of the French army. Now and again a few regiments could be found marching in an orderly manner amongst the mob of fugitives.

The meeting of Wellington and Blücher. Coloured etching, after the painting by J Maclise. Musée Wellington, Waterloo.

On the evening of the Battle of Waterloo.

Oil on canvas by Ernest Crofts. National Museums and Galleries on Merseyside (Walker Art Gallery), Liverpool.

At the entry to Genappe, two or three hundred men reassembled and attempted to bring the enemy to a halt, but the Prussians deployed a horse battery which fired sufficient balls to spread panic. In a single rush, the Prussians swept away isolated points of resistance and entered Genappe.

Napoléon had barely enough time to remount his horse and escape, leaving his carriage to be seized by the enemy. His coachman, after suffering several sabre cuts, was taken prisoner. Inside the coach, Major von Keller found the Emperor's hat, together with his sword, telescope and cloak. A pouch contained 800,000 francs' worth of diamonds and 2,000 napoléons[138].

Between two and three o'clock in the morning, the Emperor rode hastily through a Charleroi congested with fugitives, arriving at nine o'clock before the gates of the Place de Philippeville, where he was at last able to find some rest. He had been in the saddle for twenty-four hours.

Throughout the day, Wellington had not spared his own person from danger, exposing himself continually in the front line. He watched the advance by Adam's brigade, accompanied by several officers, including General de Constant Rebecque.

'We were near Rossomme Farm', the latter remembered, 'and the Duke asked me, concerning the battle:

'"Well, what do you think of it?"

'I replied: "I think, Sir, it is the finest thing you have done as yet."

'He added: "By God, I saved the battle four times myself!"

'I then said to him: "I suppose the battle will take the name of Mont-Saint-Jean."

'"No", he replied, "Waterloo"[139].'

Having halted his leading troops near Maison du Roi and ordered them to bivouac, Wellington returned to his headquarters, accompanied by a small group of officers.

It was between half-past nine and ten in the evening when the meeting between himself and Marshal Blücher took place: 'On nearing the farm of La Belle Alliance', an eyewitness related, 'a group of horsemen were seen crossing the fields on our right; on seeing them, the Duke left the road to meet them. They proved to be Marshal Blücher and his suite. The two great chiefs cordially shook hands, and were together about ten minutes; it was so dark that I could not distinguish Blücher's features, and had to ask a Prussian officer whom the Duke was conversing with, although I was quite close to him at the time, but of course not near enough to hear what was said. On leaving Blücher, the Duke rode at walk towards Waterloo[140].'

Twenty-five years later, in the course of a dinner, Wellington recalled this meeting: 'Blücher and I met near La Belle Alliance, we were both on horseback, but he embraced and kissed me, exclaiming *Mein lieber Kamerad*, and then *Quelle affaire!* which was pretty much all he knew of French[141].'

By the time that Wellington got back to the inn at Bodenghien, the time was eleven o'clock. His aide-de-camp, Alexander Gordon, had been severely wounded in the thigh at about half-past six, while he was accompanying the Duke encouraging the Brunswick battalions, which were crumbling before the intense fire of the French skirmishers and artillery. His leg had been amputated and he had been carried to the headquarters at Waterloo. As soon as he heard he was there, the Duke went to his bedside[142]. 'Thank God you are safe,' murmured Gordon[143]. Wellington told him that victory had been won, just as the other sank into a coma.

Accompanied by Don Miguel de Alava, a Spanish general attached to his headquarters, Wellington ate a light meal. Alava was the only one among his officers and staff who had not been either killed or wounded in the course of the day. The Duke said to him: 'The hand of Almighty God has been upon me this day.' Then he raised his glass to the memory of the war in Spain.

At three o'clock in the morning, Dr Hume, the surgeon who had operated on and watched over Gordon, woke the Duke who, overcome with fatigue, had thrown himself on a bed in the next room, without even washing, in contrast to his usual well-groomed appearance.

Sitting on his bed, Wellington shook his hand. Hume then told him that Gordon had just died in his arms and went on to read out the long list of dead and wounded officers. Tears ran down Wellington's face and fell upon the surgeon's hand. In a voice breaking with emotion, the Duke said: 'Well, thank God, I don't know what it is to lose a battle, but certainly nothing can be more painful than to gain one with the loss of so many of one's friends[144].'

Unable to return to sleep, the Duke changed his uniform, consumed a cup of tea and a little toast and then sat down to write his report on the campaign and the previous day's events for submission to his government. This report is known as The Waterloo Dispatch, taking the name which Wellington had decided to confer on the battle of the 18th June, possibly,

Wellington writing the Waterloo Despatch. Oil on canvas by Lady Burghersch. Private collection.

The Waterloo Despatch and the Rothschild fortune

One of Wellington's ADCs, Major Henry Percy, was charged with carrying the news of the victory at Waterloo to London. He left Brussels by post-chaise at about midday on 19 June, carrying with him the Eagles of the 45th and 105th regiments of the line, captured during the attack by d'Erlon's corps, but it was the following day, at about one o'clock in the afternoon, before he arrived in Ostend. A brig of 200 tons, the Peruvian, *had just disembarked some troops. He persuaded its captain to return to sea, although they did not get under way again until half-past six. At eight o'clock on the morning of the 21st, the wind dropped and the sailing ship lay becalmed in mid-Channel. Percy, impatient to reach England, had a dinghy launched, sat himself in it and ordered it to be rowed towards the coast, which was visible on the horizon. Fortunately, an hour later the wind got up again, the* Peruvian *took the officer back on board and at three o'clock in the afternoon landed him at Ramsgate, Percy arriving in London by post-chaise at about ten o'clock. Lord Bathurst, Secretary for War, was dining at the house of Lord Harrowby, in Grosvenor Square. There, the exhausted officer presented his dispatch and, near to fainting, answered the questions with which he was plagued. Six days had passed since the Duchess of Richmond's ball, during which time he had had no sleep. Legend has it that Nathan Maier Rothschild, having learnt of the victory at Waterloo before anyone else, built his fortune by speculating on the rise in the Stock Exchange. Rothschild himself was not in Belgium in June 1815, but his firm was nevertheless concerned by the outcome of the campaign, since it had made the necessary advances to the British Government to enable it to place Wellington's army on a war footing. One may also discount a message by carrier pigeon, for the Rothschilds had set up a link only as far as Calais, while the news would have to come via Ostend, being nearer. The identity of the messenger and his starting point are unknown, but he arrived in London during the night of 19 June. The next morning Nathan Rothschild passed on his information to the Prime Minister, who refused to believe it. Rothschild may have profited from the news by purchasing bonds on the London Exchange, speculating on their inevitable rise when the victory was made public, but the tightness of the market would not have permitted an operation of great scope. The resultant profit would have been very much less than the million pounds sterling which legend has calculated to be the banker's gains.*

Blücher at Genappe. Etching by L Arndt, after Rich. Eishstaedt. Musée Wellington, Waterloo.

as the poet Southey later said, because 'Waterloo' rings so well in English ears. Müffling, however, had informed him shortly before midnight that Blücher intended to call the battle 'The Victory of La Belle Alliance'.

On the 19th June, at about half-past five, the Duke mounted his horse and rode to Brussels, where news of the Allied victory had arrived during the night. There Wellington completed his dispatch and also wrote an almost identical report for the King of the Netherlands.

Blücher arrived at Genappe towards midnight and also found lodging, in his case at the *Roi d'Espagne* inn where

General Duhesme, seriously wounded at Plancenoit while commanding the Young Guard, had also been taken. There is a story that this officer was slaughtered by the Prussians. Very much to the contrary, Blücher, learning of his presence in the inn, paid him a visit and had him cared for by the surgeon belonging to his own headquarters, Dr Bieske. Sadly, it was to no avail, for Duhesme succumbed two days later and was buried in the cemetery at Ways, the nearby village.

Before taking some rest, Blücher wrote to his wife: 'I have held to my promise. On the 16th, superior force obliged me to retreat, but on the 18th, together with my friend Wellington, I annihilated Napoléon's army[145].'

9. THE DEAD AND THE WOUNDED – THE CASUALTIES OF WATERLOO

On the morning of 18 June, a field hospital for the Allied armies was set up in Mont-Saint-Jean Farm and it was there that the surgeons attached to Wellington's head-quarters, namely Doctors Gunning, Hume, Hyde, Taylor and Woolrich, carried out their work. The majority of the wounded senior officers were carried there and were given first aid. The Prince of Orange, Colonel Delancy, chief of staff of the Anglo-Dutch army, and Colonel Gordon, one of Wellington's ADCs, had their wounds dressed there, before being evacuated to Waterloo.

Hundreds of the wounded were dealt with in this field hospital. During the fighting, class discrimination was no less in force when it came to the care of the wounded. According to Lieutenant Howard of the British 33rd Regiment of the Line: 'We faced charges which were so fierce that we had difficulty in moving wounded officers to the rear, and it was even more so in the case of the men[146].'

The medical orderlies in Alten's, Cooke's and Clinton's divisions had also set up reception centres and first aid posts in a number of houses in Mont-Saint-Jean and Joli-Bois, out of range of the enemy's fire.

'Wherever the opportunity was offered, the wounded were either carried or crept back from the crest of the position; and the worst cases, if they survived long enough for the proceedings, were removed into the houses; for almost all the buildings along the rear of the line had been converted into temporary hospitals. Straw covered the earthen floors, and coarse but wholesome sleeting was spread over it. There, the wounded and mangled lay down, crowd upon crowds, with scarce interval between; while the medical man and their assistants gave to each in his turn such attention as it was in their power to bestow', noted one observer[147].

On the French side an ambulance had been installed at La Belle Alliance, where Larrey, the renowned chief surgeon of the Imperial Guard, worked. According to tradition, Wellington, spotting him occupied in caring for the wounded in the front line, ordered a short cease-fire and, doffing his hat, saluted him with the words: 'I salute the honour and loyalty displayed[148].'

Once the Imperial army had taken flight, British surgeons took the place of the French at La Belle Alliance and oper-ated there throughout the night.

The physical courage of the soldiers of those days was astonishing. There were no anaesthetics available and 'pri-mary amputation' – in other words, that carried out during the first four or five hours after the wound was incurred – was considered to be the safest way of saving the life of a victim of a complex fracture.

Wounds caused by musket balls or case-shot were par-ticularly dangerous, for often splintered bone, crushed flesh and shreds of clothing forced into the wounds made an ideal location for a microbic invasion such as gangrene or tetanus. The possibility of paralysis had also to be borne in mind if the nerves had been damaged by the impact.

Asepsis was unknown and neither the lancet nor the saw received any sterilisation, while the unfortunate custom of bleeding reduced still more the resistance of wounded men, already weakened by the loss of blood through trauma.

Amputation, the dominant remedy, was submitted to with the greatest courage. As an example, Lord Fitzroy Somerset, Wellington's secretary and nephew by marriage, whose arm was shattered near La Haie-Sainte, was taken to Mont-Saint-Jean, where the member was amputated immediately by Dr Gunning. The patient endured the operation without

The field of Waterloo after the battle. Water colour engraving by M Dubourg,

after John H Clark. National Army Museum, London.

Coloured lithograph by Mogford. Musée Wellington, Waterloo.

Mont-Saint-Jean Farm

The place name derives from a farm belonging to the Order of the Knights of Saint John, which can be traced back to the end of the eleventh century. From 1654, the farm was occupied as a tenancy by the Boucquéau family and then later was purchased as a national asset by one of its members, Grégoire Boucquéau, who was its owner in 1815.

complaint then, once it was over, called to the surgeon: ' Hey, don't throw my arm away until I have removed the ring that my wife gave me[149].'

Another example is provided by the astonishing attitude displayed by the wounded Frenchman who collected his leg and flung it in the air crying: '*Vive l'Empereur!*'; or that of a British officer who, refusing all help, dragged himself under the operating table and hopped one-legged on to a hand-cart to be carried to the rear.

The medical services on both sides were rapidly overwhelmed. It was in the collection and evacuation of the wounded that the problems lay. None of the Allied regiments possessed a sufficient number of vehicles to be able to transport the wounded, after they had been given first aid, to the hospitals in the rear and it was therefore necessary to commandeer waggons and hand-carts. The unfortunate men endured veritable agony on the roads of those days, shaken about by their uneven cobbles and treacherous ruts.

That evening after the battle, the plain was strewn with thousands of the dead, the dying and the wounded. Captain Mercer of the Royal Horse Artillery has left us a graphic description of that tragic night of 18 June: 'The night was serene and pretty clear; a few light clouds occasionally passing across the moon's disc… Here and there some poor wretch, sitting up amidst the countless dead, busied himself in endeavours to staunch the flowing stream with which his life was fast ebbing away… From time to time a figure would half raise itself from the ground, and, with a despairing groan, fall back again. Others, slowly and painfully rising, stronger, or having less deadly hurt, would stagger away with uncertain steps across the field in search of succour. Many of these…alas! after staggering a few paces, would sink again on the ground, probably to rise no more… Horses, too, there were to claim our pity – mild, patient, enduring. Some lay on the ground with their entrails hanging out, and yet they lived. These would occasionally attempt to rise, but, like

Battle of Waterloo. Watercolour engraving by M Dubourg, after John H Clark, published in London
by E Orme on 18 April 1816. Musée Wellington, Waterloo.

Watercolour by Tallois, after Montius. Musée Wellington, Waterloo.

The Maison Paris

Henry William Paget, Lord Uxbridge and later Marquis of Anglesey, stayed here on 17 June. After he was wounded, towards the end of the battle, Paget was taken to the Maison Paris, approximately one hundred metres north-west of the church, on the road to Brussels. The surgeons examined his injured leg and recommended amputation. Uxbridge replied: 'Very well gentlemen, I accept your opinion. I place myself in your hands; if amputation it must be, then the sooner the better.' His operation took place on the dining room table and, although anaesthetics did not exist, he suffered it without the least complaint, although at one point he did remark that it seemed to him that the instruments were not as sharp as they might be. When all was over, he limited himself to observing: 'I have had my day, for 47 years now I have been a "beau". It would not have been right to have gone on any longer competing with the young.' Paris, the owner of the house, buried the amputated leg in the garden, planting a willow above it, to which he attached a plaque citing the memory of the leg of the '… valiant Lord Uxbridge […] who, through his heroism, took part in the triumph of the cause of the human race'. The poet Southey, who visited Waterloo in the autumn of 1815, composed a less pretentious epitath: ' This is the grave of Lord Uxbridge's leg. Pray for the rest of his body, I beg.' Uxbridge died in 1854, but his right leg remained at Waterloo, where a storm had uprooted the willow and exposed the bones. The descendants of Paris displayed them in a sort of shrine, where visitors could pay to gaze on a few bones tied to a boot by a rather dirty cord. In 1878, Uxbridge's heirs, learning of this unseemly state of affairs, prevailed upon the British Embassy in Brussels to put an end to this most unbecoming exhibition. It took nearly two years for an agreement to be reached and for the hero's leg to be interred in the Waterloo cemetery, where all trace of it has been lost.

their human bedfellows, quickly falling back again, would lift their poor heads, and, turning a wistful gaze at their side, lie quietly down again, to repeat the same until strength no longer remained, and then, their eyes gently closing, one short convulsive struggle closed their sufferings[150].'

The gathering and evacuation of the wounded represented an immense task; it placed a burden on the local communities, who were conscripted by the civil authorities. On 19 June, the *Intendant* of Nivelles wrote to the Mayor of Braine-l'Alleud: 'In the name of humanity, I call upon you, immediately, to send people to remove the wounded who are still lying helpless on the field of battle and to at least get them under cover and give them a little comfort, without leaving them any longer exposed to the ravages of the weather. If you have any conveyances, have them brought immediately to Nivelles[151].'

The majority of the regimental surgeons had followed the Allied armies in their march towards Paris and their pursuit of the French troops. To make up for these departures and to deal with the needs of the hospitals to the rear, the British and Dutch medical authorities conscripted civil surgeons and brought leading practitioners from England.

The names of some of these are worth mentioning: Gunning, who distinguished himself in the field hospital at Mont-Saint-Jean; Grant, head of the medical service in Wellington's army, who organised the rear hospitals; the Dutchmen Brugman and Kluyskens; a young surgeon from Nivelles, Seutin, who on 28 June was designated head of a travelling ambulance to visit the makeshift hospitals around Brussels and who, after the Revolution of 1830, became an eminent practitioner and, later on, the head of the medical services of the Belgian army.

The Allied wounded were often given priority treatment. The staff officer Basil Jackson testifies to this discrimination: 'The truth is that, as far as our means allowed, the wounded of the British and King German Legion were first thought of, and those of the Hanoverians. The Brunswickers, Dutch and Belgians, all had ambulances, or hospital waggons, for the

Battle of Waterloo. Watercolour engraving depicting the arrival of the wounded in the Place Royale, Brussels, by M Dubourg, after John H Clark, published in London by E Orme on 16 April 1816. Musée Wellington, Waterloo.

use of their own wounded, but the French were left for the waggons of the country to gather in, and the poor fellows, being in great numbers, lay long on the ground; this was very sad, as it was only on the fourth day after the battle that the last were got in. No food was supplied to them save what the peasant women, who went about with pitchers of water and bread, were able to afford, the humble offering of true Christian charity. The villages and hamlets adjacent received the French who filled the churches, barns, and outhouses, each little community clubbing contributions of meat, bread, and vegetables, to make soup for their sustenance[152].'

The consequences of this discrimination in the recovery of the wounded were to be seen in the hospitals. The British surgeon Bell, who arrived in Brussels to lend his assistance on 1 July, wrote: 'I found that the best cases, that is, the most horrid wounds left totally without assistance, were found in the hospital of the French wounded. This hospital was only forming; they were even then bringing these poor creatures in from the woods. It is impossible to convey to you the picture of human misery continually before my eyes… At six o'clock [in the morning] I took the knife in my hand, and continued incessantly at work until seven in the evening; and so the next day, and again on the third. And all the decencies of performing surgical operations were so neglected, while I amputated one man's thigh, there lay at one time thirteen, all beseeching to be taken next; one full of entreaty, one calling upon me to remember my promise to take him, another execrating. It was a strange thing to feel my clothes stiff with blood, and my arms powerless with the exertion of using the knife. And more extraordinary still, to find my mind calm amidst such variety of suffering… The force with which the cuirassiers came on is wonderful. Here is an officer wounded; a sword pierced the back and upper part of the thigh, went through the wood-work and leather of the saddle, and entered the horse's body, pinning the man to the horse[153].' It was not until he arrived at the hospital that he could be separated from this 'harness'.

After being given first aid, the wounded were sent in different directions. The Prussians were evacuated via the hospitals in Namur, Louvain, Liège and Maastricht; the British wounded were spread out between those in Antwerp, Ghent, Bruges and Ostend, while others were sent to Nivelles. But it was above all Brussels which, at least in the first few days, served as a transit centre. Apart from the military hospital, once a Jesuit convent, the hospitals of Saint Pierre and Saint Jean and the barracks took in wounded. The Abbey of the Cambre, the church of the Béguinage, the temple of the Augustinians, the church of the Madeleine, the Mint and the Variety Theatre were transformed into temporary hospitals and huts were erected for the same purpose on the site of the old town walls.

Many families gave shelter to the wounded, who often had been billetted with them prior to the campaign. In a great surge of solidarity, linen, lint, rugs and bedding were collected. The whole of Belgium, to use an expression from the newspapers of the day, was 'the sister of charity to wartorn Europe'.

A woman of letters, Madame d'Arblay, described the scenes: 'The immense quantity of English, Belgians, and Allies, who were first, of course, conveyed to the hospitals and prepared houses of Brussels required so much time for carriage and placing, that although the carts, wagons, and every attainable or seizable vehicle were unremittingly in motion – now coming, now returning to the field of battle for more – it was nearly a week, or at least five or six days, ere the unhappy wounded prisoners, who were necessarily last served, could be accommodated. And though I was assured that medical and surgical aid was administered to them whenever it was possible, the blood that dried upon their skins and their garments, joined to the dreadful sores occasioned by this neglect, produced an effect so pestiferous, that, at every new entry, eau de Cologne, or vinegar, was resorted to by every inhabitant, even amongst the shopkeepers, even amongst the commonest persons, for averting the menaced contagion[154].'

Another word concerning the looters who haunted the plain of Waterloo after the battle. The best-known image is that of Thénardier, deserter from the French army and robber of corpses, described by Victor Hugo in *Les Misérables*.

Looting was part of the military tradition; soldiers looted not only in the course of their marches, but also during the fighting. One of Uxbridge's aides-de-camp, Captain Seymour, was thrown from his horse near Picton, who had just been killed, and saw a grenadier of the 28th Fusilliers rummaging in his general's breeches pockets, trying to steal

◄ *After Waterloo. The wounded.* Oil on canvas, unsigned. Musée Wellington, Waterloo.

The Horse Guards at the Battle of Waterloo. Watercolour engraving after W Heath, published in London
by E Orme on 4 June 1817. Musée Wellington, Waterloo.

his spectacles and his purse. In the British bivouacs, in the evening after the battle, a mass of objects was being offered for sale – gold, silver, watches, rings. An officer of Picton's division confessed: 'I could have bought it for a pound, but I don't think that any officer did so, probably believing that, in a few days or so, in another battle, our pockets would be emptied as those of the French had been[155].'

During the night, there were soldiers, mostly Prussian, but some Anglo-Dutch also, who remained in the rear, where they stripped the dead and sometimes finished off those wounded who attempted to protect their property.

General Frederick Ponsonby, wounded at the start of the battle, was lying on the ground when, while the fighting was still going on, a French skirmisher approached him: 'He stopped to plunder me, threatening my life: I directed

him to a small side-pocket in which he found three dollars, all I had; but he continued to threaten, tearing open my waistcoat, and leaving me in a very uneasy posture...' He lay wounded and waiting to be rescued for the whole day and a part of the night: 'It was not a dark night and the Prussians were wandering about to plunder; many of them stopped to look at me as they passed; at last, one of them stopped to examine me: I told him that I was a British officer, and had been already plundered. He did not however desist, and pulled me about roughly[156].'

Jolyet, a battalion commander in the French 1st Light Infantry, was wounded at Goumont and took refuge in a little house at Genappe: 'It was scarcely daylight when there was a hammering on our door. We would have been unwise not to have opened it, whereupon a Prussian officer and NCO came in and made me surrender my watch and some of my money (the rest was hidden in one of my shoes). They also took my epaulettes and everything which was of any value. In robbing me, they seemed to be implying that I was extremely fortunate that they were prepared to leave me my life. Hardly had they departed when others arrived, also demanding money and turning us over all ways, searching everywhere. I ought to add that some of them, on seeing my blood-stained clothing and my roughly dressed wound, went away without touching me. However, one Prussian drummer was determined to pull off my boots and dragged me twice round the room trying to tear them off me. His comrades were indignant and threw him outside. I remained in this condition until midday; in other words, rolled over, jostled and threatened with death by soldiers of all the regiments which passed by. They took my braces, my cravate, my belt and my shirt, but were kind enough to leave me my greatcoat and my breeches[157].'

The figures for the casualties suffered by both sides are difficult to establish. Although we have accurate assessments for the majority of the Allied troops, the Dutch-Belgian losses can be estimated only by deduction from the figures covering all the casualties for both Quatre-Bras and Waterloo. Similarly, it is impossible to furnish figures for the French army, since a large number of soldiers deserted when Napoléon's second abdication was announced on 22 June and figure as missing in the regimental returns[158].

With these reservations, the following table may be drawn up[159]:

	Killed	Wounded	Missing	Total
British troops	1747	4923	592	6932
German Legion	362	1009	218	1589
Brunswick contingent	154	456	50	660
Hanoverian contingent	294	1028	210	1532
Nassau contingent	254	389	-	643
Prussian Army of the Lower Rhine	1226	4287	1373	6885
Army of the Netherlands[160]	352	1550	1228	3130

The total casualties for the Allied armies thus amounted to 4,389 killed, 13,642 wounded and 3,671 missing, giving a grand total of 21,702. The estimated French casualties were approximately 5,000 killed and 18,000 to 19,000 wounded, to which may be added 8,000 to 10,000 prisoners.

On the evening of Waterloo, there were thus still lying on the field of battle nearly 9,500 dead and 31,000 or 32,000 wounded, not to mention several thousand dead or mortally wounded horses.

Shock and loss of blood accounted for the most seriously wounded; where it had not been possible to distribute water, the more lightly injured succumbed to dehydration[161]. It is likely that the proportion of the wounded who died where they fell was very large. As an example, the British 32nd Regiment of Foot lost 28 men killed, while of the 146 wounded, 26 had died by 26 July, 18 of them on 19 June[162].

On the day after and on subsequent days, the local population occupied themselves in cleaning up the battlefield. The burial of the dead was undertaken by the inhabitants of Plancenoit, Waterloo, Maransart and Braine-l'Alleud. The task of interment of the corpses, as rapidly as possible as a precaution against disease, had always fallen to the communities which bordered the scenes of combat. The bodies were thrown anyhow into common trenches dug wherever it was convenient, with no attempt at identification.

'Military deaths thus remained different to civilian ones, since the decree of the 23 *Prairial* year XII, 12 June 1804, for the control of cemeteries required the provision of both a separate interment and also a coffin. Since that time, although paupers were still buried in common graves, they were placed side by side and were no longer piled upon one another[163].'

Coffins were thus used only exceptionally and probably reserved for the burials of certain officers. Only one example can be given with certainty, that of the interment of General Duhesme at Ways, whose death – also very exceptionally – was recorded in the Ways parish register[164].

All the locals who could be found were thus brought together and formed into teams which, under the direction of NCOs of the Dutch army, dug trenches at various places all around the area. The usual procedure before burial was to strip the corpses of their clothes and to recover anything which could be reused, such as boots and uniforms, unless the wounds involved had rendered them unusable[165].

Weapons and other military equipment, as well as cannon balls, were recovered and payments made to those who brought them to the civil authorities. However, despite the inspection of dwellings carried out during the following

Farm of La Haie-Sainte. Watercolour engraving and coloured etching by James Rouse, after C C Hamilton. Plate K of the work by W Mudford, *An historical account of the Campaign in the Netherlands in 1815...*, published in London by H Colburn, 1817. Musée Wellington, Waterloo.

weeks on the orders of the Dutch authorities, articles of a military nature were still being sold to tourists as souvenirs fifteen years later.

The dead were sometimes covered in quicklime. After a few days, the resultant stench meant that the bodies were dragged away by means of hooks at the ends of ropes pulled by horses.

At Goumont, enormous funeral pyres were built; a witness described the scene on 28 June: 'The pyres had been burning for eight days and by then the fire was being fed solely by human fat. There were thighs, arms and legs piled up in a heap and some fifty workmen, with handkerchiefs over their noses, were raking the fire and the bones with long forks. The devastation of the farms, the smell of the

corpses and the thick smoke from the pyres, which spread itself over fallen trees, formed a scene of horror which will never be eradicated from my memory[166].'

Several days after the battle, a young man from Brussels visited the plain of Waterloo and described the scene of desolation offered by the farm at La Belle Alliance: 'At the entrance we saw several cartridge pouches, from which I took a few cartridges. Inside the farm, some soldiers were cooking their stew; I think they were wounded. At the back door was a wounded man who was near his end. He was fighting against death. On the dung-hill and on the floor of the yard were several corpses. When we emerged from the farm we saw, in a pond, the body of a Dutch dragoon, the biggest man I have ever seen in my life; he was still fully dressed and had been struck through the breastplate. In the garden of La Belle Alliance, two or three troopers were cleaning their equipment. The garden was full of cartridge pouches, bayonets, muskets and shakos. This farm was pretty dilapidated; its area covered no more than one *bonnier* and was not fully levelled. There were no longer any cows or horses and there was not a single tile unbroken[167].'

Although the trenches were supposed to be dug to a depth of five feet, the bodies were hastily buried, very often at barely a couple of spade depths, so that a few weeks later an eyewitness was able to describe these hastily-dug trenches,

covered with a thin layer of earth '…protruding from which an arm or a face could be seen, with pestilential discharges emerging from them[168].'

One year later, in April 1816, the Mayor of Ohain wrote: 'Every day there still arrive on the battlefield a large number of people, some of them drawn by greed; these latter go so far as to dig up the corpses, in the hope of discovering some who, having been buried before the battlefield had been completely looted, had retained their clothing and whatever might be in their pockets.' To deal with this, he requested the *gendarmerie* to patrol the countryside[169].

Hougoumont. Watercolour engraving and coloured etching by James Rouse, after C C Hamilton. Plate Q of the work by W Mudford, *An historical account of the Campaign in the Netherlands in 1815…*, published in London by H Colburn, 1817. Musée Wellington, Waterloo.

Grouchy. Watercolour engraving, enhanced in gold, by Louis-François Charon, after Charles Aubry.
Bibliothèque royale Albert 1er, Brussels.

10. GROUCHY'S OPERATIONS, 17 – 20 JUNE

During the night of 17 June, Grouchy's troops were concentrated at Gembloux. A protective screen was provided by Exelmans' dragoons at Sauvenière, with a detachment at Perwez.

From information the Marshal had received after ten o'clock that evening, he was convinced that the Prussians were retreating in the direction of Brussels, but he believed them still to be within his reach, although they were already in the neighbourhood of Wavre.

At six the next morning he wrote to Napoléon: 'All my reports and information confirm that the enemy is retiring on Brussels, either to concentrate there or to stand and fight after linking up with Wellington. The first and second corps of Blücher's army appear to be making for Corbais and Chaumont respectively. They seem to have left Tourinnes at about half-past eight yesterday evening and to have marched throughout the night. Happily, it was such a bad one that they cannot have got very far. I leave immediately for Sart-à-Walhain, from where I shall make for Corbais and Wavre[170].'

Once more, the French troops were late in setting off: Exelmans, with the vanguard, did not leave Sauvenière until six o'clock in the morning and did not arrive at Walhain until eight. III Corps left its bivouacs at about half-past seven, with IV Corps following behind, thus forming one long single column instead of marching in parallel along side roads. Despite the early hour, it was very warm and a fine rain was occasionally falling.

At Walhain, Exelmans received an order to push on to Nil-Saint-Vincent and La Baraque, while Pujol, who had bivouacked well to the rear at Mazy, was to proceed to Tourinnes, where it was nearly one o'clock by the time he arrived. At ten o'clock, Exelmans, who had caught sight of the Prussians near Neuf-Sart and La Plaquerie, notified Grouchy, who sent III Corps to support him. The head of the column reached Walhain at around eleven o'clock, at the same time as Grouchy himself.

The Marshal called at the house of the lawyer Hollert in Walhain in order to send to the Emperor the information – some of it incorrect – which he had gathered: 'Blücher's I, II and III Corps are marching in the direction of Brussels… A Corps from Liège has joined up with those which were engaged at Fleurus. Some of the Prussians which are in front of me are proceeding towards the plain of the Chyse, situated near the road to Louvain and two and a half leagues from that town.

'It seemed that the intention was to concentrate there, either to join battle with the troops pursuing them, or to link up with Wellington, a plan revealed by their officers… This evening I shall concentrate at Wavre and shall lie between Wellington, whom I presume to be retreating before Your Majesty, and the Prussian army. I am in need of further instructions concerning what Your Majesty might order me to do…[171].'

After sending this dispatch, Grouchy accepted an invitation to lunch with the lawyer. They had reached the dessert, a dish of strawberries, when the muffled sound of far-off cannon-fire was heard[172]. General Gérard arrived, preceding his troops. He advanced the opinion that they should march towards the sound of battle. Grouchy deemed it to be no more than a rearguard action.

The rain had ceased; some officers went into the garden and applied their ears to the ground to determine the direction of the gun-fire. It was nearly one o'clock and the rumbling went on increasing. Gérard repeated: 'We must march towards the gun-fire and join up with the Emperor.'

'I told him', wrote Grouchy, 'that when he had dispatched

me the previous day, he had announced that, if the Duke of Wellington decided to fight, it was his intention to attack the British army.

'Therefore, general, I am not surprised by the engagement which is taking place at this moment. Besides, if the Emperor had wanted me to take part, he would not have detached me from him, at the very moment when he was moving towards Quatre-Bras.

'I also remarked to General Gérard that, according to the local people, the cannon-fire which we heard was taking place six or seven leagues from Sart-à-Walhain and that therefore I should not arrive in time, since there was no passable road leading to it, that the lanes were narrow and muddy and that one would have great difficulty in getting the artillery along them. My opinion was shared by General Baltus, commanding the artillery in Comte Gérard's corps, who had campaigned in that region before.

'General Valazé, commanding the engineers in IV Corps, maintained that, with the sappers, he could open passages and deal with the lanes so that the march could be swift and easy. However this view of the matter was based more on hope than on reality.

'Finally, I ended my discussion with General Gérard by observing that my instructions enjoined me not on any account to lose touch with the Prussians once I had found them and that it would be disobedience to conform to his views. I was anxious to rejoin my vanguard and I made to take leave of Comte Gérard, but he retained me once more, asking that, if I found myself unable to share his opinion, I should allow him at least to move off in the direction of Soignes Forest.

'That, I replied, would be to commit the unpardonable military error of dividing my forces and having them operate at the same time on both banks of the Dyle, which at that time was unfordable. I was pursuing an army three times the size of my own and I would expose one or other of its parts, unable to act in support of each other, to being crushed by such a disproportionate force[173].'

Grouchy returned to Exelmans, whose regiments had taken up positions at La Plaquerie Farm and at Neuf-Sart. In front of them, they could at last see the Prussian rearguard. The detachment under Ledebur, left as a forward look-out post at Mont-Saint-Guibert, withdrew hastily into the ranks of Brause's brigade to avoid encirclement. Grouchy sent the head of III Corps' column to support the cavalry, which flushed out the Prussians entrenched in Lauzelle Wood. The

Marshal ordered Vandamme to pursue them as far as the hills above Wavre and there to await his orders. The time was then about two o'clock.

THE BATTLE OF WAVRE

While his columns were closing on Wavre, Grouchy galloped off to Limelette, in the direction of the cannon-fire, the sound of which had increased in intensity. He quickly became convinced that it was a real battle and not some rearguard action which was unfolding at Mont-Saint-Jean.

On his return to Wavre at half-past three, he received the dispatch sent by Soult at ten o'clock that morning: 'The Emperor requires me to tell you that at this time His Majesty is intending to attack the British army, which has adopted a position at Waterloo, near Soignes Forest. His Majesty thus desires you to direct your movements towards Wavre, so as to bring yourself closer to us, place yourself in operational contact and maintain communications, while pushing back the enemy corps which have taken that direction and should have halted at Wavre, which you should reach as soon as possible. Inform me immediately of your arrangements and of your order of march, as well as any news which you possess about the enemy, not failing to maintain communications with us...[174].'

To Grouchy, if he had felt misgivings about not marching towards the cannon-fire from Walhain, this letter was reassurance. 'I am glad that I obeyed the Emperor's instructions by marching on Wavre, rather than listening to the advice of General Gérard', he said to his aide-de-camp[175].

His tasks now were to capture Wavre and to close with the Imperial army. He left III and IV Corps to continue their advance on the little Belgian town and recalled Pajol, who informed him that there was no longer the least trace of any Prussians in the region of Tourinnes, Obaix and Malèves. This cavalry force, reinforced by Teste's division, was ordered to return with all speed to Limal and there to cross the Dyle.

Meanwhile, the cannon had begun to thunder on the Wavre hills. Towards four o'clock, Vandamme, without waiting for Grouchy's orders, had sent Habert's division into the attack. Up until then, the slow, hesitant approach of Grouchy's troops had scarcely been such as to cause disquiet in the Prussian headquarters and the last corps, Thielmann's, was preparing to leave Wavre for Mont-Saint-Jean when Vandamme's regiments attacked.

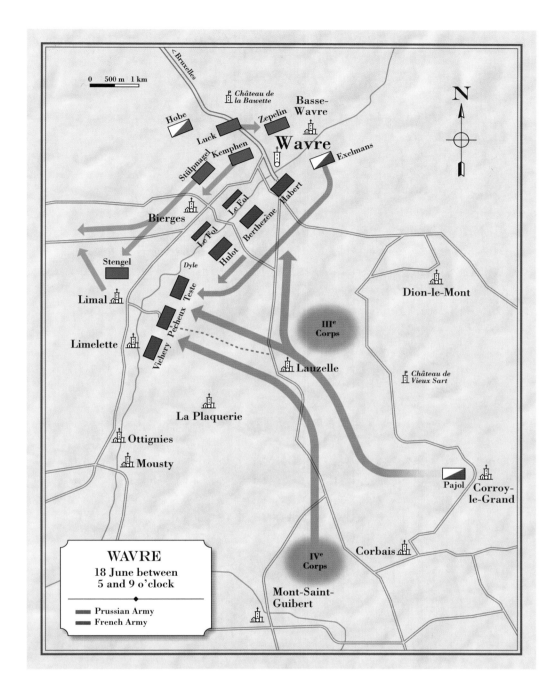

WAVRE

18 June between
5 and 9 o'clock

◆

Prussian Army
French Army

In those days the little town (4000 inhabitants) was mostly established on the left bank of the Dyle, with the suburb formed around the Place du Sablon, on the right bank, joined to it by two stone bridges. The larger bridge, called the 'Pont du Christ', was in the centre of the town; the smaller one, taking its name from the 'Moulin de Wavre', was to the south.

The Dyle could also be crossed by a wooden bridge, downstream of the town at Basse Wavre, and this was also the case upstream, at Bierges, Limal and Limelette. The river was not very deep but, swollen by the heavy rain of the previous day, had overflowed its banks and transformed the adjacent meadows into marshland.

Without delay, Thielmann made his defensive arrangements; a detachment destroyed the bridge at Basse Wavre and guarded the bridgehead. Three battalions, under the command of Colonel von Zepelin, entrenched themselves in Wavre and its suburb, barricading the Pont du Christ as well as they could.

Stülpnagel occupied Bierges and the hills above it, Kemphen took possession of the slopes to the north-west of the town, Luck positioned himself in the rear, astride the Brussels road, while Stengel, with 1,200 men, installed himself at Limal. The cavalry waited in reserve at the château of Bawette, where Thielmann had set up his headquarters. With 18,000 men and 34 cannon, the Prussian general prepared himself for assault by forces which outnumbered his own by nearly two to one.

After a short artillery barrage, Habert's division opened the attack and, having taken possession of the suburb, launched itself at the barricade on the Pont du Christ. However, assailed by the fire from Prussian troops sheltering in the houses, it was unable to break out into Wavre itself.

General Fantin des Odoards gave an account of this unsuccessful and bloody attack: 'Instead of crossing the Dyle above or below Wavre, where it is fordable in many places, General Vandamme, who had been charged with the crossing in order to drive the enemy back, chose to take a bridge, in the very

middle of the town, which had been thoroughly barricaded and protected by thousands of sharp-shooters posted in the houses on the opposite bank. Such a strong position needed to be outflanked, but this general obstinately insisted on attacking it frontally with massed troops which, engaged in a long road perpendicular to the bridge, were open to all the Prussian fire without being able to deploy their own. In that place we lost many men, while gaining nothing. The 70th Regiment, the very one which had been discomfited two days before, had been given the task of storming the bridge under a hail of shot and was thrown back.

'It was rallied by its Colonel Maury, then, as it continued to hesitate, that brave officer, seizing the Eagle, cried: "What, you scum, having dishonoured me two days past, will you repeat the offence today? Forward, follow me". Grasping the Eagle,

The Pont du Christ at Wavre. Coloured lithograph by Sturm. Musée royal de l'Armée, Brussels.

he threw himself on the bridge and, as the drums beat the charge, the regiment followed. But that fine leader had scarcely reached the barricades when he fell dead, whereupon the 70th fled faster than before, indeed so rapidly that, had it not been rescued by men of my own 22nd Regiment, their Eagle, which lay on the ground in the middle of the bridge beside my poor lifeless comrade, would have become the prize of the enemy skirmishers who were already intent on seizing it[176].'

Meanwhile, Grouchy had taken possession of the hills above Wavre. A brisk conversation ensued between himself and Vandamme, whom he rebuked for mounting his attack without proper consideration and without attempting to outflank the enemy position. To repair the error, the Marshal ordered one of Lefol's battalions to cross the Dyle at Bierges Mill and Exelmans to move to Basse Wavre.

At five o'clock a new dispatch arrived from Soult, which had been sent off at half-past one: 'Your movements comply with His Majesty's intentions, which have previously been communicated to you. However, the Emperor has ordered me to say to you that you must continually manoeuvre in our direction and seek to get closer to the army, so that you will be able to join us before any corps can come between us. I will not suggest any direction to you; it is for you to see the place where we are, so as to make the appropriate dispositions and to maintain communication with us, as well as to be ready at all times to fall on any enemy troops who attempt to interfere with our right wing and to crush them.

'At this time, battle has been joined on the line of Waterloo, in front of Soignes Forest. The enemy's centre is at Mont-Saint-Jean; move therefore so as to join up with our right.

'PS. A letter which has just been intercepted indicates that General Bülow will attack our right flank; we believe we have seen this corps on the high ground at Saint-Lambert. Do not therefore lose a moment in moving in our direction and in joining us, nor in crushing Bülow, whom you will catch in the act[177].'

Grouchy sent an order to Pajol to move to Limal without delay and himself went to La Baraque in the rear, in order to divert Vichery's and Pécheux' divisions, which were marching towards Wavre, in the same direction. However, contrary to his expectations, he could find no sign of those units there, so after half an hour he left an officer on the spot, to pass on to them the order to go straight to Limal.

Grouchy returned to Bierges, where Lefol's attack had not succeeded. He sent one of Hulot's battalions to help him,

but with no greater effect. Gérard then went forward with further reinforcements. The men floundered about in the muddy meadows and in the ditches brimming with water, all the while under a murderous fire from Stülpnagel's brigade, established in the mill and the village. While he was leading one of these assaults, Gérard was hit in the chest and was carried to the rear, gravely wounded.

Grouchy gave the command of his corps to General Baltus, who refused it point-blank. The Marshal, leaping astride his horse, then put himself at the head of the battalions preparing to resume the attack, crying: 'If under difficult circumstances one cannot make oneself obeyed by one's subordinates, one must know how to be killed in order to achieve it[178].'

Grouchy was no more successful than Gérard in taking Bierges and the Marshal thereupon altered the disposition of his troops. Leaving one of Hulot's brigades in position, he moved with the other against Limal. It was then nearly seven o'clock in the evening.

The Prussians were defending the approach to the Limal bridge from positions in the houses and the mill, but they had omitted to barricade it. Pajol, who had just arrived with Vallin's cavalry, summed up the situation immediately: mounting a strong charge, the French crossed the bridge and occupied the village. A Prussian counter-attack, by the greater part of Stengel's detachment and Stülpnagel's brigade, which had been replaced at Bierges by Kemphen, was repulsed, reinforcements having now arrived in the shape of the divisions of Teste, Pècheux and Vichery.

After heavy fighting, the French also took possession of Limelette and advanced as far as the top of the plateau, which they occupied at about eleven o'clock. With the two sides bivouacked within musket range of each other, Grouchy passed the night in the front line.

The Marshal was now able to communicate with Napoléon. Since nightfall the cannon had fallen silent and optimism was high in the French ranks: 'Many people thought that the Emperor had beaten the British army and was marching on Brussels[179].'

GROUCHY'S RETREAT

Thielmann, learning at two o'clock in the morning of the victory at Waterloo, took steps to recover the initiative as soon as the sun rose. Stengel's detachment had bivouacked in Bierges Wood, Stülpnagel lay between the wood and Bierges, Kemphen between Bierges and Wavre and Luck at Wavre and Basse Wavre, while Hobe's cavalry was in reserve, behind Bierges Wood.

Grouchy, for his part, meant to build on his success of the previous day by completing the encirclement of Wavre. To this end, he ordered Vandamme to rejoin him '… leaving his fires burning, to make the enemy think that his corps was still in position [180].' Once more disobeying orders, the latter sent to Grouchy only Hulot's and Exelmans' divisions, holding back those of Berthezène and Lefol.

At three o'clock in the morning, the Prussian cavalry attempted to take the bivouacking French by surprise, but were beaten off. While the cavalry of Soult (the Marshal's brother) and Vallin reconnoitred to the left towards Chapelle-Saint-Lambert, the divisions of Pécheux, Teste and Hulot pushed forward between Bierges Wood and the village, with Vichery and Exelmans in reserve. The wood was taken and the Prussians fell back on all sides.

At that point, Thielmann received confirmation of Blücher's victory and notification of the arrival of Pirch I, marching on Grouchy's flank. He desperately tried to hold his ground until joined by these reinforcements, but to no avail. The turning movement carried out by Grouchy had placed the opposing troops in a tactically impossible situation. By half-past ten that morning, the French offensive had succeeded in outflanking the enemy; Teste had taken Bierges and Vandamme had entered Wavre. Thielmann was obliged to order a retreat towards Louvain.

The French vanguard was snapping at the Prussians' heels near Rosières when an aide-de-camp, haggard and exhausted, presented himself to Grouchy. He had been sent by Soult to report the grim result of the Battle of Waterloo and the ruin of the French army. He bore no written message and his appearance did not inspire confidence. At first, he was supposed to be drunk, but the incoherence of his speech was due only to exhaustion.

Grouchy called an urgent conference of his corps commanders to discuss the action to be taken. Vandamme proposed that the march on Brussels be continued, to release the prisoners there, harass the enemy's communications and thence to return to French soil via Enghien, Ath and Lille. It was an enterprise both rash and hazardous. Rightly, the Marshal chose to take the shortest line of retreat, via Namur, Dinant and Givet. It was necessary to move fast if they were not to be cut off.

The withdrawal began between eleven o'clock and midday. Exelmans was sent ahead to secure the bridges at Namur, while IV Corps and Vallin's cavalry recrossed the Dyle at Limal and marched via Gembloux to Mazy. Vandamme remained in position at Wavre until fairly late in the afternoon, then made for Namur via Dion-le-Mont, Tourinnes and Grand-Leez, taking up its quarters near Temploux. The retreat was completed without the firing of a single shot.

To Thielmann, who had been pushed back to Rhode-Sainte-Agathe and sorely tried by the fighting at Wavre, the French withdrawal went unnoticed, while Pirch I, reaching Mellery towards midday, judged his men to be too weary and bivouacked there. It was dawn on the 20th when Thielmann finally realised that the French had gone and sent Hobe's cavalry in pursuit, which caught up with Vandamme's rearguard at half-past nine near Falise. At the same time, Sohr's brigade made contact near Temploux with Vichery's division, which was bringing up the rear of Gérard's corps, on the road between Gembloux and Namur.

The Marshal, recognising the danger, immediately caused the withdrawal to continue to Dinant, leaving Teste with the task of covering the army's retreat by holding the Prussians at Namur. With 2,000 men and 8 cannon, the latter general held the assaults of Krafft's and Brause's brigades throughout the afternoon, inflicting heavy casualties, as he related: 'On the morning of the 20th, a Prussian corps of 12,000 to 15,000 men arrived before Namur, intending to seize it by force. This attack was pressed home with vigour, principally against the iron gate, where I had two companies of grenadiers of the 75th, and was repulsed, the enemy leaving many dead in the moats. Shooting went on at long range until midday, when the Prussians tried again, with the same result. At three o'clock, the enemy appeared in greater numbers and with greater tenacity; men who appeared to have consumed *eau-de-vie*, their officers also, threw themselves against our barricades to die on our bayonets. At half-past four, our assailants withdrew, leaving the ground before us strewn with their dead [181].' At about half-past eight that evening, having set fire to a pile of faggots at the Porte de France, on the other side of the town, to prevent any pursuit, the French made good their escape and reached Profondeville and Dinant without further trouble.

On the following day, Grouchy's army recrossed the frontier and mustered on the Place de Givet. The Marshal had saved his troops and brought back in good order his wounded, his baggage train and his artillery.

11. EPILOGUE

Napoléon, after a brief halt at Laon, arrived in Paris at five o'clock on the morning of 21 June. The news of the disaster at Waterloo had spread through the political world and to the Chamber of Deputies, where the intrigues of Joseph Fouché, denouncing the Emperor as the sole cause of the war, found their echo.

Apprehensive about the possibility of a *coup d'état*, the Chamber of Deputies voted to sit in permanent session. On 22 June, despite the reproaches of his brother Lucien, who urged him to seize power and govern by appealing to the lower classes, Napoléon abdicated in favour of his son. This was ignored by the Legislative Assembly, which appointed a governmental commission to negotiate peace terms with the Allies, who were marching on Paris.

The former Emperor travelled to Rochefort, with the intention of embarking for America, in the hope that this voluntary exile would be approved of by England. On 3 July, Paris, besieged by Blücher and Wellington, capitulated and three days later Louis XVIII made his entry into the capital.

Threatened with arrest by the new authorities, Napoléon decided to surrender himself to the British fleet, for he had failed to receive any safe-conduct to travel to America. On 5 July he went on board the *Bellerophon*.

Deported to Saint Helena, he died there on 5 May 1821, aged fifty-one.

With Waterloo, Wellington's fame was at its peak. The British Parliament voted to purchase for him in 1817 the estate of Stratfield Saye, together with a subsidy of £200,000 for its upkeep. He would eventually receive field marshal batons from no less than twelve countries.

As Commander-in-Chief of the Allied forces of occupation, he presided over the restitution of the works of art seized by France during the twenty years of war and over the indemnification for the damage caused by French occupation over the greater part of Europe.

With the peace, the Duke's career pursued its brilliant path. Commander-in-Chief of the British Army and Prime Minister from 1828 to 1830, he attracted attention through his opposition to the Reform Bill, a stance which on three occasions resulted in the stoning of Apsley House, his London residence. For its protection, Wellington had iron shutters installed, giving rise to his nickname of the 'Iron Duke'.

In 1846 he retired from political life, having played a major role in the activities of the Tory Party. He died at Walmer Castle on 14 February 1852, at the age of eighty-three. He was given a state funeral and interred in Saint Paul's Cathedral.

Blücher had had the satisfaction of seeing Paris capitulate to him a second time. Bent on revenge, he imposed on the city a levy of one hundred million francs and prepared to take steps to blow up the Pont d'Iéna, symbol of the humiliating defeat at Jena. Pressure from Wellington and Louis XVIII obliged him to abandon these plans.

Disappointed, the old general retired for the last time from military life. He passed his final years as he always had, living the life of a country gentleman, hunting, gaming and overseeing the management of his estates. In the winter he lived at his town house in Berlin, passing the summers on his lands in Silesia, where in 1819 he died, aged seventy-seven.

Church at Waterloo. Unsigned watercolour.

12. DEBATES AND CONTROVERSIES

For a hundred and fifty years, both praise and blame have been heaped on the heads of the army commanders involved, by historians and men of letters of all nationalities. The greatest of the military critics of their day, Clausewitz and Jomini, have brooded over the four days of the campaign[182].

Appraisal of dispositions adopted in the uncertainty of the moment is always a delicate task, when one is in possession of information which was not available to the men in the field. However, to avoid disappointing (and indeed shortchanging) the reader, these controversies must be examined.

THE EVENTS OF 15 JUNE

The military critics are in agreement in considering that Napoléon's strategic plan, the concentration of his army on Beaumont and Philippeville and the advance on Charleroi in three columns is beyond reproach. One is however entitled to wonder whether the route chosen was the best one, since it resulted in the Emperor's 120,000 soldiers becoming jammed, as in funnels, at the bridges at Marcinelle, Charleroi and Châtelet, at the cost of many hours' delay before they could cross the Sambre.

The delay suffered by Vandamme's corps, who had not received the movement order, has been cited as an example of Soult's negligence in performing his duties as chief of staff, compared with the zeal and efficiency of Marshal Berthier in the same role. However, accusations of similar failings may also be levelled against the Duc de Neufchâtel, notably at Wagram and at Bautzen. The absence of Berthier on the Imperial general staff in 1815 cannot be advanced as the cause of certain failures in the transmission of orders, particularly since his deputy, Bailly de Monthion, was assisting Soult[183].

By the evening of 15 June, the Emperor could pronounce himself satisfied in having concentrated his army on either side of the Sambre, in the centre of the enemy host, after marching a distance of thirty-five to forty kilometres, in overpowering heat.

The decision of the Emperor to give the command of part of the right wing to Ney was not perhaps the most advisable. The Marshal, who had rejoined the army lacking both staff and retinue, was placed in command of two army corps, which were unaware that they were under his orders and which found themselves spread out over more than twenty kilometres to the rear.

Napoléon blamed Ney for not gaining control of Quatre-Bras on 15 June, but there is nothing to show that he had given the order – verbal under the circumstances – to the marshal. Indeed, it is even likely that the Duc d'Elchingen did *not* receive such instructions since, at three in the afternoon, when the Emperor entrusted his left wing to Ney, he lacked knowledge of the enemy's positions and was trying to find this out before he made any decision against which of his adversaries he should direct the greater part of his forces.

The Marshal had no information concerning what was happening on his right, whence came the thunder of cannon; he was still facing a threat from the Prussians who, though thrown out of Gosselies, were still standing at Gilly. Furthermore, as night fell, he had no infantry to call upon. Under such circumstances, it was reasonable that he should make no attempt to push further forward and take possession of the crossroads.

The Prussian concentration was carried out with remarkable speed. The sole error to have been committed seems to have been in the dispatch of imprecise instructions to

Bülow, which delayed the commencement of his operations by twenty-four hours.

In contrast, it is permissible to ponder the sluggishness of Wellington's reaction. Although he was informed of the French attack at around three o'clock, it was after five before his first orders, which went no further than for the assembly of the army, were sent. He would seem to have hesitated for several more hours, while considering that the French movement on Charleroi was no more than a diversion.

This uncertainty, coupled with a wish to reassure the population, explains why he should have remained in Brussels to attend the Duchess of Richmond's ball while, had he made up his mind earlier, his place would have been at either Nivelles or Braine-le-Comte.

The initiative taken by Generals Constant Rebecque and Perponcher in occupying the strategic crossroads of Quatre-Bras in force was of capital importance for the campaign which followed, since it secured the Brussels road and rendered possible close collaboration between the Allied armies by ensuring that a wedge of several leagues was not driven between them at the very start.

16 JUNE

In the morning, Napoléon did not believe that he would be required to fight that day. His eight o'clock letter to Ney clearly reveals that he thought he was facing no more than Zieten's rearguards. His intention was to march on Brussels, for he attached great importance to that city, as the symbol of the French presence in Belgium. The order to Ney was therefore to wait until the Emperor had reached his decision, which he expected to do at about three in the afternoon, or possibly that evening.

What a loss of valuable time! Why did Napoléon not contemplate attacking the Prussians at midday? By dawn he had available to him Vandamme's corps before Fleurus, that of Gérard at Châtelet, the Guard between Gilly and Charleroi, Pajol's and Exelmans' horse in the front line and Kellermann's at Châtelineau, making 45,000 muskets and 10,000 horse. Whereas, up to midday, Blücher's forces amounted to no more than a single corps under Zieten, 28,000 men at the most, taking the casualties of the previous day into account.

The Emperor's procrastinations before Fleurus cost him all the advantage he had gained from his unexpected march of 15

June. A morning attack would have had the effect of obliging Zieten to fall back on Gembloux or to join battle, while awaiting reinforcement by the other corps. This second choice would have resulted in the destruction of the Prussian army, whose units, arriving piece-meal on the battlefield, would have been in a constant state of numerical inferiority.

Ney has been criticised for his inactivity on the morning of the 16th. True, he was awaiting orders from the Emperor, which he did not receive until about eleven o'clock. But why did he not use these long hours of uncertainty in order to concentrate on Frasnes the two infantry corps which he had been given?

Only Bachelu's division was available and capable of marching on Quatre-Bras. The other divisions of II Corps were decidedly in the rear: Foy and Jérôme at Gosselies, Girard at Wangenies. d'Erlon's troops were even farther away, Durutte and Donzelot between Jumet and Gosselies, Marcognet at Marchienne, Quiot at Thuin!

The cost of this casualness amounted to three hours delay to the attack on Quatre-Bras, saving Wellington by enabling his reinforcements to arrive. Ney, with the advantage of a considerable numerical superiority, would have been able to seize Quatre-Bras and, in the afternoon, perform the sideways manoeuvre against the Prussians envisaged by Napoléon.

The Battles of Ligny and Quatre-Bras differed from one another. Facing Blücher, the Emperor's tactics consisted of holding the enemy down with Vandamme's corps and then encircling him from the left by bringing in all or a part of Ney's troops and, on the right, pushing him back on Ligny with Gérard's troops. At Quatre-Bras, the Duc d'Elchingen contented himself with a frontal attack for the seizure of the crossroads.

Despite the failure of the task allotted to Ney, Ligny was a French victory. At eight o'clock that evening, many of Napoléon's troops were still fresh, while all of Blücher's had been engaged. The Prussian line gave way to superior numbers in the classic manner and Blücher's right, threatened with encirclement due to the fall of Ligny village, was obliged to retreat.

The Battle of Quatre-Bras fell out in completely the opposite manner. At the end of the day Wellington had more troops at his disposal than Ney who, still lacking I Corps, had exhausted his resources. However, the firm stand put up by his men enabled the Marshal to halt the Allied attack and to maintain his initial position.

Although the Duc d'Elchingen had fought a battle in which he was twice nearly victorious, his decision to countermand the movement of d'Erlon's corps, in defiance of the Emperor's orders, deprived the latter of a decisive victory against the Prussians.

17 JUNE

This day was the last on which victory lay within the Emperor's grasp, but, as on the previous day, his chances were jeopardised by his laxity.

One must question why Napoléon did not order a pursuit of the Prussians on the evening of the 16th. Lobau's corps had not fired a single musket ball and the numerous French cavalry had been scarcely engaged all day. Such a tactical pursuit would have prevented the Army of the Lower Rhine from regrouping and recovering its operational capability as rapidly as in fact it did.

The time wasted by Napoléon on the morning of the 17th had serious consequences throughout the rest of the campaign. From eight o'clock onwards, Grouchy was begging for orders, yet received them only between eleven and midday. It was nearing three o'clock when the first Prussian columns reached Wavre, at which time Vandamme's leading units were just leaving the battlefield at Ligny.

There is no justification for this negligence. Napoléon cannot be excused on account of his troops' tiredness, when Blücher's, all of them just as weary, were on the march at three in the morning! Moreover, the Emperor could call on troops which had not fought on the previous day and which could have moved off at daybreak. During the night of the 16th and the morning of the 17th, the Prussians gained a lead of a day's march over Grouchy, a gap which the latter was never able to make good.

The Prussian retreat on Wavre was accomplished swiftly and skilfully. Gneisenau increased the pace of progress of his regiments by having them march in parallel columns, while Grouchy sent Vandamme's and Gérard's corps one after the other, along the same road.

The decision to place Gérard and Vandamme under Grouchy's command failed to take into account the rivalries and jealousies which put these two at loggerheads with the Marshal, whom they obeyed only with reluctance.

The withdrawal of the Army of the Lower Rhine went unnoticed by the French scouts, while Gneisenau left a party of cavalry, under Major Gröben, on watch near Tilly. These Prussian observers were never detected and were able to monitor the French movements with impunity, thus providing Gneisenau with hour-by-hour information about the enemy's comings and goings.

On the morning of 17 June Wellington had no knowledge of how his Prussian ally had fared in the battle of the previous day and it was he who dispatched Gordon to find out. It was seven thirty when he found out that Blücher's army was retreating to Wavre; he himself decided to fall back on Mont-Saint-Jean and did not fail to inform his ally of this intention. Reassured by the immobility of Ney's troops, he did not hurry and the withdrawal was not begun until ten o'clock.

Napoléon scarcely bothered to advise Ney of the day's outcome at Ligny, the Marshal not being told of it until about nine o'clock on the morning of the 17th. Despite the Emperor's order to occupy Quatre-Bras and to inform him if he met any resistance, the Marshal remained immobile until two o'clock that afternoon and Wellington was thus able to effect his retreat free from any interference.

The inaction of the Duc d'Elchingen is culpable, but that of Napoléon is every bit as much. If, that morning, the French columns had encircled the Allied left by advancing along the Namur road, combined with a frontal attack by d'Erlon's and Reille's corps, the British army would probably have been destroyed.

One major criticism has been made concerning the provisions made by Wellington on the morning of the 17th, namely his instructions to Prince Frederick of the Netherlands to occupy Hal with 18,000 men. These troops would have constituted a considerable reserve at Mont-Saint-Jean the following day. Several years later, the Duke explained his reasons: 'I never had any intention of withdrawing on Brussels. Had I fallen back from my position, my retreat would have been to the right, towards the sea, the ships and my stores[184].' A defeat on the 18th would have seen the British army retiring towards Antwerp.

18 JUNE

Through Napoléon's dilatoriness the French had lost the initiative. In his writings on Saint Helena, the Emperor has tried to make his subordinates the scapegoats for the defeat at Waterloo. In his version, the two great sinners were Ney and Grouchy, the one for having squandered his cavalry, the other for having allowed the Prussians to escape. The responsibilities for the defeat are more complex and more widely attributable.

Military critics are agreed in considering the massed cavalry attacks inappropriate, under the conditions in which they were made, without adequate support from the horse artillery and without being coordinated with the infantry. Responsibility for this fault has been laid at Ney's door, but is this fair?

In the morning, the Emperor had the intention of using his cavalry in a less than orthodox manner. He said to Foy, during the headquarters conference at Le Caillou: 'The battle which is about to take place will save France and will become famous in the annals of the world. I shall bring my ample artillery into play, then I shall send in my cavalry to force the enemy to show himself and when I am sure of the English deployment, I shall fall on them directly with the Old Guard[185].'

This plan, which was certainly simplistic, implied a mass attack by the cavalry. Napoléon's criticism of Ney for sending in Milhaud's corps was therefore unwarranted, since this attack accorded with his own intentions that morning. Furthermore, the Emperor, positioned at that moment opposite Decoster's house, could not fail to see the five thousand horsemen five hundred metres away, moving forward to reach their starting places in the grounds of La Haie-Sainte. If the engagement of the cavalry had really been premature or inappropriate, he had only to dispatch an aide-de-camp to bring the movement to a halt.

A second criticism may be levelled against Napoléon: that of having supported Milhaud's first charges with Kellermann's and Guyot's corps, instead of using the infantry divisions of Bachelu and Foy, which since the morning had been stood with ordered arms forward of the lane to Braine-l'Alleud. The engagement of his cavalry was scarcely justified. The distance between La Haie-Sainte and Goumont was not more than a thousand metres, so that, with the vicinity of these strong-points being unapproachable on account of fire from the infantry occupying them, the French charges could be deployed over no more than seven to eight hundred metres. There could thus be scarcely more than 12 squadrons in line, representing a front of approximately 650 horsemen. Merely by using Milhaud's corps and the light cavalry division of the Guard, Ney's manpower was

already sufficient, even superabundant, if the different arms had acted in conjunction; in other words, a joint supporting action by the horse artillery and the infantry.

Nor does Grouchy deserve the criticisms which have been levelled against him. His task was difficult, if not impossible. The enemy columns had a start of fifteen or sixteen hours over his own men, while his job was further complicated by the erroneous information supplied by Napoléon concerning Blücher's supposed line of retreat. Although he found the Prussians at Wavre, their movement in the Mont-Saint-Jean direction escaped him completely. Should Grouchy have marched towards Waterloo, as Gérard pressed him to do? A decision to do so was not justified. The Marshal had no reason to be concerned because he could hear cannon fire, since the Emperor had told him of his intention of joining battle with Wellington. Why should he disobey the orders which stipulated that he should catch up with the Prussians, in order to lend assistance to Napoléon?

The essential error was the Emperor's; convinced that Blücher's troops were out of the fight for several days, he completely neglected any reconnaissance of his right wing. Had he discovered the threat from Bülow earlier, he would have been able to recall Grouchy in good time. The order dispatched at half-past one was too late for the marshal to be able to reach the battlefield in time. Military critics all cite the ambiguity of the orders received by Grouchy on 18 June, since they required him both to continue his movement towards Wavre and to march in the direction of Chapelle-Saint-Lambert. In other words, the Emperor had set him two goals which were mutually incompatible. When Grouchy received the order, it was impossible for him to insert himself between Napoléon and the Prussians, for the latter were already at Plancenoit.

Napoléon's dishonesty in the accusations he levelled at the Marshal is clear. In his *Mémoires* and in Gourgaud's account, he claimed to have ordered Grouchy, at ten o'clock on the evening of 17 June, if Blücher were to retire on Brussels or Liège, to join up with the army's right wing with his entire force, and, if he held fast at Wavre, to detach a party to make the link-up. The Emperor maintained that he had sent off a copy of this order, before three in the morning, as soon as he had received the first report from Grouchy.

These alleged orders have never been found: no mention of them appears in the records of Chief of Staff Soult. Grouchy denied that such instructions existed. The order issued at ten o'clock on the morning of the 18th makes no reference to them. Lastly, Soult's recommendation that a part of the troops under Grouchy's command should be recalled, as reinforcements for the morrow's battle, was rejected.

In the end, these accusations levelled by Napoléon at his lieutenants need not constitute an obstacle to any analysis of the manner in which the Battle of Waterloo was conducted by the Emperor.

The formation of d'Erlon's corps has been wrongly criticised, for it was frequently used during the last campaigns of the Empire, but d'Erlon's divisions were not supported by cavalry to accompany the columns to the east of the Brussels road. Only Dubois' brigade marched to the west of La Haie-Sainte, but it was swept away by Somerset's squadrons.

Why did the first engagements around Goumont not begin until around half-past eleven and why was d'Erlon's full-scale attack deferred until two? Certainly, the French troops' quarters during the night of the 17th did not allow them to be assembled in mass before nine o'clock on the morning of the 18th. But if battle had been joined at that time, it would have been possible to beat the British before the Prussians arrived, for Napoléon would have been able to use against Wellington the infantry reserves which were later employed against Blücher.

Bülow, who reached Chapelle-Saint-Lambert at eleven o'clock, did not reveal himself until about half-past four. Assuming that he quickened his pace on first hearing the cannon-fire at nine, it would have been difficult for him to have played any part before three o'clock. At that time, however, there is every chance that Napoléon could have had Wellington on the run. In those circumstances, would Gneisenau have taken the risk of confronting a victorious French army?

Some writers, basing themselves on the declarations of General Drouot, explain this delay by arguing that the state of the ground, made sodden by the previous day's storm and the overnight rain, would not have allowed the movement of the artillery before the end of the morning. This attempted vindication lacks foundation, for in his *Mémoires*, Napoléon acknowledged '… that at eight o'clock that morning, the gunnery officers, who had gone over the ground, announced that the artillery could be manoeuvred, albeit with a certain difficulty which in an hour would be reduced[186].' Furthermore, the Allied battalions and their artillery had been taking up their positions since the dawn, without difficulty.

As early as 1816, Drouot blamed himself for having, by his advice, provoked the disaster and implicitly confirmed that it was Napoléon's tardiness which allowed the Allies to win at Waterloo: 'Had he taken no notice of my remarks, Wellington would have been attacked at seven and beaten by ten, with victory complete by midday, while Blücher, who could not have arrived before five, would have fallen into the hands of a victorious army[187].'

When the Prussians were discovered at Chapelle-Saint-Lambert, at about one in the afternoon, Napoléon must have known that he was now directly threatened by the junction of the two armies. From that point on, he had either to withdraw or beat the Anglo-Dutch before Blücher's troops were in a position to add their support. It was probably a combination of his fear of the political consequences of a strategic withdrawal and the lack of regard which he felt for Wellington which led him to accept the risk of fighting on two fronts.

But the essential requirement was to crush Wellington as soon as possible; the attack by d'Erlon, suitably supported by the cavalry, would have been able to achieve this objective. However, with regard to tactics, Waterloo was one of the worst battles ever fought by the Emperor, with no concept of manoeuvring and a poorly coordinated frontal attack.

As has been seen, collaboration between the arms was sadly missing. The French artillery, with a numerical superiority over Wellington's of nearly 50%, was badly used[188]. The strong-points at Goumont and La Haie-Sainte were bombarded only belatedly or not at all. Why was the attack of the Foot Guard not directed at the top of La Haie-Sainte, where the Allied line could have been pierced at least cost?

The attack at seven in the evening by several battalions of the Old Guard had the character moreover of a gamble, a fight-to-the-finish approach, the result of which was the destruction of the army.

Napoléon, who had just experienced the greatest difficulty in halting Blücher's advance at Plancenoit, could have been in no doubt about an early return to the offensive by the Prussians, as soon as further reinforcements arrived. The only troops remaining intact on the French side were some ten battalions of the Guard, which could have been used as a dike to shelter the retreat of the army, overwhelmed as it was by the concerted actions of its adversaries. Instead of opting for the retreat of d'Erlon's and Reille's divisions, progressively and in good order, the Emperor threw into the fight 3,500 veterans, who had not the least chance of succeeding where the day-long efforts of the whole army had not.

The behaviour of Lobau, too, cannot escape criticism. By failing speedily to take up his position to the east of Paris Wood, he left himself unable to prevent the Prussians from breaking out of Lasne and fulfil the essential task which he had been given by the Emperor.

The glaring deficiencies of command on 18 June and the Emperor's sluggishness during the Waterloo campaign have sometimes been attributed to ill-health, but no witness has ever been found who made reference to an indisposition of Napoléon of any kind during these critical days. His man-servant Marchand, his factotum Saint-Denis, known as Ali, his doctors – none of these breathed a word of any deterioration in his state of health.

Against Napoléon's errors, there may be set the perfect organisation of the Allied army and the well-judged dispositions of Wellington who, risking his own skin, on each occasion took the necessary steps to fill the breaches in the line.

The fire-power of the British infantry broke up the French attacks, but there is no doubt that the Duke's army, hard-hit by the fire of the French artillery, would not have been able to resist a third attack, carried out by Lobau and the Guard and supported by the cavalry of Kellermann and Guyot.

The Prussian march from Wavre, of three army corps proceeding along three parallel routes, remains a model of concentration on the battlefield and the decisive factor in the Allied victory at Waterloo. The credit for this is to be ascribed to Gneisenau, for his ability, and to Blücher, for his energy.

If the French had won at Waterloo, would the course of the war have been different? With Wellington forced either to retreat northwards or to re-embark, Blücher would probably have retired towards Liège, but with the risk of being crushed between Napoléon and Grouchy.

The disproportionate size of the forces aligned against France would inevitably, sooner or later, have tipped the balance in favour of the Allies. The weak armies stationed along France's frontiers would not have been able to hold back the Russian and Austrian troops which would have begun to move at the beginning of July and Napoléon, as in 1814, would have had to come to his lieutenants' rescue, one after the other, while the first serious defeat would have brought about a political crisis, with fatal results for the regime. This situation, of which Napoléon was aware, reveals the constraints which his position as Head of State imposed on his direction of the army during the campaign in Belgium. To maintain the regime, he needed successes, of greater or lesser importance, but successes none the same. An Emperor could not permit himself the strategic withdrawal which an army commander would have proposed.

13. SHORT BIOGRAPHIES OF THE PRINCIPAL PARTICIPANTS

ADAM, Frederick (1781-1853). Son of a titled family, he became an ensign in 1795 and then pursued his studies at the Woolwich Military Academy. He took part in the campaign in Holland in 1799. He was promoted major in 1803 and, at the age of 24, purchased the command of the 21st Regiment of Foot. Appointed an ADC to the Prince Regent in 1811, he commanded a brigade in Spain in 1813. He became a major-general in 1814. After Waterloo, he was appointed governor of the Ionian Islands.

ALTEN, Charles Augustus, Count (1764-1840). ADC to the Hanoverian Field Marshals von Reden (1790) and von Freitag (1793), he entered British service in 1803 and campaigned in Spain and Portugal (1810-1813). As a lieutenant-general, he commanded the Hanoverian troops in the Netherlands (1815), was wounded at Waterloo and created a Count after the battle. He was a member of the Allied forces of occupation in France until 1818. On his return to Hanover, he became Inspector-General of the Army and then Minister for War.

BRUNSWICK, Frederick William, Duke of (1771-1815). Son of the author of the *Manifeste de Brunswick*, he ascended the throne in 1806, but by the Treaty of Tilsit his Duchy was abolished and his lands sequestered. In 1809, in Bohemia, he formed a free corps, with which he marched right across north Germany and sailed to Great Britain. His troops fought in Spain and Portugal and he himself was killed at Quatre-Bras.

BÜLOW, Friedrich Wilhelm, Count von Dennewitz (1755-1816). Prussian general of great ability, he distinguished himself during the campaign in Germany in 1813, defeating Ney at Dennewitz, and during the campaign in France in 1814.

CHASSÉ, David Hendrik (1765-1849). A cadet in the army of the United Provinces, he sought refuge in France after the defeat of the patriotic movement and joined the French army as a captain in 1788. After Pichegru's invasion, he served first the new Batavian Republic and then the Kingdom of Holland. He fought in Austria, in Spain and during the campaign in France, being created a Baron of the Empire. After the first abdication in 1814, he returned to the Netherlands, where he pursued his military career. Military Commandant of Antwerp from 1819 to 1832, he defended the town against the Belgian insurrection of 1830 and withstood the siege conducted by the French army under Marshal Gérard in 1832. He was a member of the States General from 1833 to 1848.

COLLAERT, Jean-Antoine, Baron de (1761-1816). Entering the service of Austria in 1778, he later served the United Provinces and continued his career as an officer of the Batavian Republic and then of King Louis of Holland. A major-general in 1806, he passed into French service after the amalgamation of the Kingdom of Holland with the Napoléonic Empire and served in the campaigns in Dalmatia, Germany and France. In 1814, he entered the Netherlands army with the rank of general and during the Waterloo campaign commanded the Netherlands cavalry division.

CONSTANT DE REBECQUE, Jean-Victor, Baron de (1773-1850). Of Swiss origin, he was the cousin of Benjamin Constant, the liberal writer and French politician. Enlisted at a very young age in the Swiss regiments of Louis XVI, he defended the Tuileries on 10 August 1792 and continued his fight against the French Revolution and Napoléon by serving in turn the Swiss Cantons, the United Provinces,

Prussia and Great Britain. Appointed as tutor to the Prince of Orange after Jena, where he fought in the Prussian army, he accompanied his pupil to England and then took part in the Spanish campaign, on Wellington's staff. He organised the army of the Kingdom of the Netherlands (1813-1814) and, as Chief of Staff of the Netherlands army, was sent to Brussels in September 1830 and during the Ten Days campaign (1831). In 1837 he resigned from his duties as Inspector-General of the Army and retired to live with his daughter in Silesia.

DROUET, Baptiste-Jean, Comte d'Erlon (1765-1844). He became a soldier in 1783 and distinguished himself in the Revolutionary Wars. A general of division in 1803, he fought in all the campaigns of the Empire. Implicated, with Lefèbvre-Desnouettes, in a conspiracy in the Spring of 1815, he was imprisoned until the return from Elba. Condemned to death after Waterloo, he escaped and ran a brewery at Munich until 1830. Under Louis-Philippe, he became Governor of Algeria and a Marshal of France.

EXELMANS, Remi-Joseph, Baron (1775-1852). A volunteer in 1791, he rose through the ranks, being promoted to colonel after Austerlitz, general of brigade after Eylau and head of staff to Murat in Spain in 1808. He was taken prisoner at Valencia in 1808, but escaped from England after three years of captivity (1811). He distinguished himself at the Moskva and took part in the campaigns in Germany, Holland and France as a general of division. He was appointed Inspector-General of the Cavalry by Louis XVIII, but sided with Napoléon during the Hundred Days. After Waterloo, he won the last battle of the wars of the Empire at Rocquencourt. Exiled in 1816, he returned to France in 1819. As a supporter of the Second Empire, he was appointed Grand Chancellor of the *Légion d'Honneur* in 1849, a Marshal of France in 1851 and was elected to the Senate in 1852. He died as a result of falling from his horse.

FREDERICK, William Charles, Prince of the Netherlands (1797-1881). He was the second son of William I, the future King of the Netherlands. After military studies in Prussia, he took part in the campaign of 1813 and was with Bülow's corps when it liberated Holland. Grand Master of the artillery from December 1813, he exerted only nominal command during the Waterloo campaign. Colonel-General and

Admiral (1829), he commanded the expedition to Brussels in September 1830 and took part in the Ten Days campaign (the Belgian War of Independence) in 1831. On the abdication of William I, he gave up all his official functions and devoted himself to philanthropic works.

FREDERICK, Wilhelm, Prince of Prussia (1797-1888). Son of Frederick Wilhelm III, King of Prussia, he took part in the campaigns of 1814-1815. At Waterloo, he commanded the cavalry reserve in Bülow's corps. Regent of Prussia due to the illness of his brother Frederick Wilhelm IV, he succeeded him in 1861 and was proclaimed Emperor of Germany at Versailles, taking the name of Wilhelm I, on 18 January 1871.

GÉRARD, Etienne (1773-1852). A volunteer in 1791, he made his mark at Austerlitz. General of brigade in 1806, he served at Wagram in 1809 and in Portugal (1810-1811). Appointed general of division during the campaign in Russia (1812), he distinguished himself at Bautzen and during the campaign in France. Proscribed after Waterloo, he did not return to France until 1817. A Deputy for the liberal opposition in 1822, he became Minister for War in 1830 and was created a Marshal of France. He marched into Belgium in 1830 at the head of a French army, and again in 1832 for the siege of Antwerp. Created a peer of France in 1833 and President of the Council the following year, he was Grand Chancellor of the *Légion d'Honneur* from 1842 to 1848. Napoléon III made him a senator in 1852. His quarrel with Grouchy over the movements of the French right on 18 June 1815 is still notorious.

GNEISENAU, Augustus Wilhelm, Count von Neithardt (1760-1831). He took part on the British side in the war in America. In 1806, he was only a captain in the Prussian army. He assisted in the reorganisation of the army, under the orders of Scharnhorst, whom he succeeded as Blücher's chief of staff in 1813. He was raised to the peerage after Leipzig. Governor of Berlin, field marshal in 1825, he died of cholera while in command of the army ordered to repress the Polish insurrection in 1831.

GROUCHY, Emmanuel, Marquis de (1766-1847). Born into a titled family, he was a lieutenant of Gardse du corps (1783), but sided with the Revolution. General of division in 1794, he took part in all the campaigns of the Empire and was created a Comte by Napoléon. On half-pay during the first Restoration, he sided with the Emperor in 1815. His brief campaign in the Midi against the Duc d'Angoulème earned him the title of Marshal of France. Proscribed after the Hundred Days, he took refuge in Philadelphia. He was pardoned by Louis-Philippe, who appointed him to the Chamber of Peers.

HALKETT, Colin (1774-1856). He raised the King's German Legion and served in the Peninsular War. He was wounded at Waterloo, later became Lieutenant Governor of Jersey and Commander-in-Chief in Bombay. At the time of his death he was governor of Chelsea Hospital in London.

HILL, Rowland, Viscount (1772-1842). An ensign in the British army in 1790, he studied at the military college in Strasbourg. He participated in the siege of Toulon and in the campaign in Egypt. He took part in the expedition to the Weser and served throughout the Spanish campaign at Wellington's side. At Waterloo, he commanded the Allied right wing. He became Governor of Plymouth in 1827 and Commander-in-Chief of the British army in 1828.

KELLERMANN, François-Étienne, Comte de Valmy (1770-1835). Son of the victor of Valmy. General of brigade in 1796, he led the charge which won the day at Marengo and was appointed divisional commander the next day. A brilliant horseman, he distinguished himself at Austerlitz, in Portugal and during the campaigns in Germany and France. Having acquired liberal ideas, he was left in the shadows under the Second Restoration and gave his support to Louis-Philippe.

MAITLAND, Peregrine (?-1854). He began his military career in 1792 and in 1814 commanded a brigade of Guards at the Battle of the Nive. He was Commander-in-Chief at Madras in 1836 and then at the Cape of Good Hope in 1843.

MILHAUD, Jean-Baptiste, Comte (1766-1833). A second lieutenant in a colonial regiment at the time of the Revolution, he became a Deputy in the Convention of 1792 and voted in favour of the King's execution. Leaving politics, he resumed his service as a squadron commander

in the Army of Italy. He involved himself in the *Brumaire coup d'état*. Rising through the ranks, he took part in the campaigns of Austerlitz, Jena, Friedland, Spain, Germany and France. He gave his support to Louis XVIII and was appointed Inspector-General of the cavalry, but was sent into retirement at the beginning of 1815. Exiled for regicide in 1816, he did not return to France until 1830. He was one of the most intrepid heavy cavalry generals of his era.

MOUTON, Georges, Comte de Lobau (1770-1838). A volunteer in 1792, he served in the Army of the North, then in Italy and became one of Bonaparte's ADCs. He took part in the campaigns of Austerlitz, Jena and Friedland. A general of division in 1807, his conduct at Essling earned him the title of Comte de Lobau (1809). He was taken prisoner after Leipzig. His support of the Emperor resulted in his banishment after the return of Louis XVIII. Appointed General commanding the Parisian National Guard by Louis-Philippe, he dispersed the Bonapartist demonstrations of 1831 and was appointed a Marshal of France the same year. His bravery was legendary.

MÜFFLING, Frederik-Karl, Freiherr von (1775-1851). This officer on the Prussian general staff distinguished himself during the campaigns in Germany and France. Liaison officer with Wellington's Anglo-Dutch army, his memoires, *Aus meinem Leben*, are of great interest. In 1832 he commanded the Prussian army of observation on the Belgian frontier.

NEY, Michel, Duc d'Elchingen, Prince of Moskowa (1769-1815). Son of a cooper of Sarrelouis, he enlisted as a soldier in 1788 and rose through the ranks in the Revolutionary Wars to the top. Marshal of France in 1804, he took part in the campaigns of 1805, 1806 and 1807. He fought in Spain before distinguishing himself in the Russian campaign.
In 1814, he forced the Emperor to abdicate and went over to the Bourbons. In 1815 he was condemned to death for treason and shot for having returned to Napoléon's side on the return from Elba. As a general very popular in the ranks, he was known as 'the bravest of the brave'.

PAGET, Henry William, Lord Uxbridge, Marquis of Anglesey (1768-1854). Entering the army in 1793, he participated in the campaigns in Flanders and Holland. In 1802, as a major-general commanding a cavalry brigade, he took part in the first Spanish campaign, under Sir John Moore. His military career was interrupted until 1815 by his affair with and eventual marriage to Wellington's sister-in-law. Lord-Lieutenant of Ireland in 1828, his support for Catholic emancipation resulted in his recall, but was restored to the same office under the Liberal government led by Grey (1829-1832).

PAJOL, Claude-Pierre, Comte (1772-1844). Enlisting in 1791, he was one of Kléber's ADCs. A colonel in 1803, he was famous for his audacious cavalry rides during the campaigns of Austerlitz, Jena and Wagram. A general of brigade in 1807, general of division in 1812 and gravely wounded in Russia, he took part in the Leipzig campaign, where he was left for dead. Created a comte by Louis XVIII, he went over to Napoléon during the Hundred Days. In retirement after 1815, he played a new role in 1830, by assuming command of a column of National Guards, whose object was to persuade Charles X to leave French territory. Under Louis-Philippe, he was a peer of France and Governor of Paris.

PERPONCHER-SEDLINTZKY, Hendrik George de (1771-1856). This Dutchman served in the British army from 1800 to 1813. After the Battle of Leipzig, he found a place in the young army of William I. In 1815, as a lieutenant-general, he took part in the fighting at Quatre-Bras and Waterloo and ended his career as a diplomat, in the post of Ambassador in Berlin from 1815 to 1842.

PICTON, Thomas, Sir (1758-1815). He served in Gibraltar (1773-1777) and in the West Indies, where he took part in the Caribbean campaign, becoming Governor of that region. In 1803, accused of corruption, he resigned. After various vicissitudes, he was absolved of these accusations. He won renown in Spain and Portugal under Wellington and was killed at Waterloo.

PIRCH I, Georg Dubislav Ludwig von (1763-1838). He was a member of von Schlieffen's army which put an end to the Liègois Revolution in 1790. Adjutant to the Prince of Hohenlohe in 1797, he took part in the Battle of Jena, where he was taken prisoner. As a regimental commander in 1809, he fought in the campaigns in Germany and France, where he was marked out for his bravery. As general of brigade,

he commanded II Corps at Ligny and Waterloo, replacing General Borstell. Promoted to lieutenant-general after the campaign, he resigned in 1816 and retired to Berlin.

REILLE, Honoré (1775-1860). Enlisting as a volunteer in 1792, he took part in the Italian campaign of 1796. A general of brigade in 1803, he took part in the campaigns of Jena and Friedland. Aide-de-camp to Napoléon in 1808, he distinguished himself at Wagram and then saw service in Spain. He sided with the Bourbons in 1814, but served at Waterloo. In temporary disgrace at the Second Restoration, he was created a peer of France in 1819, then made a Marshal of France by Louis-Philippe (1847) and a senator by Napoléon III.

SOULT, Jean de Dieu, Duc de Dalmatie (1769-1851). This son of a notary enlisted as a soldier in 1785. He was a sergeant in 1791 and a general of brigade in 1794! He took part in the Rhine and Danube campaigns. He was a general of division in 1799 and made a Marshal of France in 1804. Described by Napoléon as 'the leading tactician in Europe', he distinguished himself at Austerlitz, Eylau and Friedland. Duc de Dalmatie in 1807, he campaigned in Spain with mixed fortunes. He established a fabulous collection of paintings, by dint of commandeering them. Siding enthusiastically with the Bourbons, he was Minister for War in 1815, a fact which did not prevent him from serving during the Hundred Days. Banned under the Second Restoration, he returned to France only under Louis-Philippe, for whom he was successively the Minister for War and for Foreign Affairs.

THIELMANN, Johann Adolf, Baron von (1765-1824). This Saxon officer was involved in the Revolutionary campaigns and at Jena in the Prussian army, then served the King of Saxony from 1806 to 1812. During the campaign in Russia, he distinguished himself at the Moskva. After Lutzen he resigned, rather than surrender Thorgau to the French, and re-entered the service of Prussia. At his death he was commanding the army's VIII Corps at Coblenz.

VANDAMME, Dominique, Comte d'Unebourg (1770-1830). A soldier before the Revolution, he was made a general of brigade in 1793, but was often in disgrace due to his pillage of occupied countries. Wounded at Wagram, he did not return to the colours until 1813. Commanding I Corps during the campaign in Germany, he was beaten at Kulm and taken prisoner. Proscribed after Waterloo, he lived in exile in the United States until 1819.

WILLIAM, Prince of Orange (1792-1849), elder son of William I, King of the Netherlands. After studying at Oxford, he was attached to Wellington's staff during the Peninsular War. He was in nominal command of I Corps in Wellington's army during the 1815 campaign and was wounded at Waterloo. He married the sister of Tsar Alexander I of Russia and played a principal role in the events of 1830 and 1831 which led to the break-up of the Kingdom of the Netherlands. After the abdication of his father in 1840, he assumed the crown with the name of

William II. Following the former's death he promulgated a liberal constitution, setting up the parliamentary monarchy of the Netherlands.

ZIETEN, Hans Ernst Karl, Count von (1770-1848). Son of a cavalry general, he took part in the Seven Years War against France and fought at Jena. He commanded a brigade during the campaigns of 1813 and 1814 and played a notable part at Leipzig. After the second Treaty of Paris he commanded the Prussian contingent of the army of occupation in France and was appointed field-marshal in 1835.

PART TWO

AFTER WATERLOO

There are aspects of the battle's aftermath, from earlier days up to the present day, which are little-known or even unrecorded.

The Waterloo medal. Lithograph by Félicien Rops, after the original drawing, 1858, in the Musée Curtius, Liège.

14. MEDALS AND DECORATIONS COMMEMORATING THE CAMPAIGN

Numerous medals pertaining to the 1815 campaign were struck in the course of the nineteenth century. A list of them, which attempts to be as comprehensive as possible, has been produced by R Chalon[1]. Below are listed and described only those medals which have an official status.

MILITARY MEDALS

The British medal

On the day after the battle, General Vivian expressed the wish that every British combatant should receive a medal bearing the name of Mont-Saint-Jean[2].

On 11 July 1818, the Prince Regent decided to award a medal to every combatant – officer, NCO or private soldier – who had taken part in the 1815 campaign in Belgium. This was the first time in the British army that such a decoration had been given to all the participants in a military campaign, and it was also presented posthumously to all those families with a relative who had been killed during the fighting. The medal (36 mm in diameter) was called the *Waterloo Medal*, and was of silver with a ring and was worn with a crimson ribbon with dark blue borders. The names of the recipient and his regiment were engraved around the edge.

Obverse and reverse of the Waterloo medal
The head of the Prince Regent in left profile, wreathed with laurel: GEORGE P. REGENT.
Below the neck: T-WYON : JUN : S.
The Angel of Victory seated, wings spread, with a laurel palm in the right hand and an olive branch in the left; above in large type: WELLINGTON; below, in a rectangle: WATERLOO; underneath:
JUNE 18-1815 T . WYON.S.

The Brunswick medal

Instituted on 11 June 1818, by a decree of the Prince Regent, acting as protector of the young Duke Charles of Brunswick. It was awarded to those who had served in the troops of the Duchy between 16 and 18 June 1815 and was in memory of his father killed at Quatre-Bras. The name of the recipient was marked around the edge. The medal, in gilded bronze (35 mm) with a ring, was worn with a ribbon which was yellow edged with blue.

The Hanover medal

Instituted in December 1817, by the Prince Regent in the name of his father, King George III of Great Britain and Hanover, for the Hanoverian troops who had fought at Waterloo. The medal was of silver (35 mm) with a ring and was worn with a silk ribbon, crimson with dark blue borders.

Obverse of the medal:
Bust in left profile: Duke Frederick William with the signature of the engraver C. Häseler.
On the reverse:
1815 with a crown of oak and laurel leaves:
Braunsweich seinen kriegern.
Quatrebras und Waterloo.
The inscriptions are in Gothic script.

Obverse of the medal:
Head of the Prince Regent in right profile, wreathed with laurel: GEORG . PRINZ . REGENT. 1815.
Below the neck: W. WYON.
On the reverse: two laurel branches
framing the words:
WATERLOO JUN.XVIII. Above, a breastplate reposing on two swords and two flags crossed:
HANNOVERSCHER . TAPFERKEIT.

The Nassau medal

Created on 23 December 1815 by Duke Frederick for the soldiers in the Nassauer division. The medal was of silver (29 mm) and was worn with a narrow dark blue ribbon with orange borders.

The Prussian medal

On 24 December 1813, King Frederick-William III decided to confer on his soldiers a medal which would commemorate the wars of liberation. By a decree of 3 October 1815, it was also awarded to the combatants of the Waterloo campaign. The medal was of bronze (29 mm) with a ring and an orange ribbon with two black and white borders.

Obverse of the medal:
The head of Duke Frederick surrounded
by the inscription:
Friedrich August Herzog zu Nassau with, below the
neck, the initials J.L. of the engraver
Johan Lindenschmit.
On the reverse: a winged Angel of Victory
bearing a palm and crowning an ancient warrior
surrounded by the legend:
Den nassauischen Streitern bei Waterloo,
with an inscription: *Den 18 juni 1815*

Maltese Cross with rays of light between the arms.
In the centre, the year 1815, within a crown of oak and
laurel. Around the edge: *Aus erobertem Geschütz.*
On the reverse: the cipher of the King of Prussia F.W.
surmounted by a royal crown; below on two lines:
Preussens tapfern kriegern. Circular legend: *Gott war
mit uns. Ihm sey die ehre.*
The inscriptions are in Gothic script.

In a certain number of small German States, medals or crosses were also bestowed on the combatants in the 1814 and 1815 campaigns (Anhalt-Bernburg; Anhalt-Dessau; Anhalt-Köthen; Hesse-Homburg; Hesse-Cassel; Mecklemburg-Schwerin; Oldenburg; Saxe-Coburg-Saalfeld; Saxe-Gotha-Altenburg; Saxe-Weimar-Eisenach; Schwarzburg Rudolstadt; Schwarzburg Sondershausen; Waldeck; Wurtemberg).

On 30 January 1816, the Senate of the city of Frankfurt created an 1815 commemorative medal for the soldiers levied by that city.

THE MILITARY ORDER OF WILLIAM I

On 30 April 1815, William, the ruling prince of the Netherlands, created a military order bearing his name, as

Obverse of the medal:
White-enamelled 8-point cross, bearing on its arms
the inscription: *VOOR MOED BELEID TROUW.*
Between the arms, the cross of Burgundy enamelled
in green. In the centre, the letter "W" within a blue
medallion surrounded by gilt laurels.
On the reverse, in the centre, the tinder box of the
Golden Fleece.

a form of recompense for armed service on land and sea and for outstanding feats of arms. The order was directly inspired by the Napoléonic *Légion d'Honneur* and was similar in form. It comprised four classes: Grand Cross, Commander, Knight third class and Knight fourth class. Membership of the order was associated with an annual pension. The cross was surmounted by a crown of gold and hung from an orange ribbon with a blue stripe at each side.

At the end of the 1815 campaign in Belgium, eight hundred and ninety-seven crosses were distributed to members of the Belgian-Dutch army.

At the instigation of the Fund for the Encouragement and Support of Military Service in the Netherlands, a medal was awarded to the men of the volunteer company of fusiliers of Rotterdam and to the light cavalry volunteers of Amsterdam who had served in 1815.

COMMEMORATIVE MEDALS

After Napoléon III had created the so-called *Sainte Hélène* medal in 1857, which was awarded to all surviving combatants in the campaigns of the Empire, including those in Belgium, certain countries riposted by striking their own medals commemorating the victorious Allied campaign of 1815.

The Dutch Waterloo Cross

On 10 May 1865, King William III of the Netherlands instituted a Waterloo Cross, which was distributed to all those who had fought against the French in 1813 and in particular to those who had taken part in the Waterloo campaign. It consisted of a silver star (35 mm) with five points, similar to the *Légion d'Honneur*. It was worn hung from an orange ribbon with two white threads.

On the obverse, in the centre: 1813.
On the reverse, in the centre: 1815.

The Hanoverian medals

As a result of public subscription, the town of Hanover struck a medal in bronze (30 mm), to be awarded to survivors of the Battle of Waterloo.

On the obverse: in the field, the arms
of the town of Hanover:
STADT HANOVER DEN SEIGERN V.
WATERLOO. 18 JUNI 1815.
On the reverse: within a wreath of laurels:
ZUR 50 JAHRIGEN JUBELFEIER AM 18 JUNI 1865.

A second commemorative medal in silver (33 mm) was struck in Hanover, probably at the instigation of the King.

On the obverse: head in left profile: *GEORG V V. G.G.*
KOENIG V. HANNOVER. Below the neck: *BREHMER*
F. In the field, at the bottom, the letter *B.*
On the reverse: within a wreath of laurels,
on seven lines:
DEN SIEGERN BEI WATERLOO GEWIDMET AM 18
JUNI 1865.
Around the edge *NEC ASPERA TERRENT*

The Waterloo medal of Félicien Rops

Given its controversial nature, which sliced through the patriotic and militaristic consensus of its time, one cannot pass over this original work, which created a great stir.

The painter-engraver Félicien Rops (Namur 1833-Essonnes 1898), well-known for his illustrations of the works of Baudelaire and Barbey d'Aurevilly, was scarcely an admirer of Napoléon. He therefore created a medal (35 mm), in either silver or tin, which cast derision on the *Sainte Hélène* medal and which is illustrated in the centre of the lithograph on page 180.

On the obverse: a one-legged soldier occupies the middle of the piece. Above him are the words: MÉDAILLE DE
WATERLOO.
On his right, within the field: DU DERNIER DES CHAUVINS and on his left: VOILÀ TOUT CE QUI RESTE.
At the bottom, the name of the artist: F. ROPS.
On the reverse: in the field, in large type:
REVERS DE LA MÉDAILLE – 15 JUIN 1858.
Circular legend: À SES COMPAGNONS DE RACLÉE SA
DERNIÈRE
PAROLE … SIGNÉ CAMBRONNE.

15. WELLINGTON, PRINCE OF WATERLOO AND HIS INHERITANCE

Amid the euphoria which reigned at government level in the young monarchy of the Netherlands after the battle, King William I, by a decree of 20 July 1815, conferred on Arthur Wellesley, Duke of Wellington, the title of Prince of Waterloo.

It was granted as '… a public and lasting recognition of esteem and gratitude' for having gained '… a brilliant victory which routed the common enemy and banished all danger from Dutch soil'. This title was declared to be transferable to his male descendants, by right of primogeniture.

On 29 September 1815, in response to a royal proposal, the States General passed a law associating with '… the title of Prince of Waterloo an inheritance comprising an annual income of approximately 20,000 Dutch florins, to be possessed irrevocably and in perpetuity by the Prince of Waterloo and his legitimate descendants'. Three parcels of land situated between Nivelles and Quatre-Bras, on both sides of the Nivelles-Namur road, covering an area of approximately 1,083 hectares, were included in this inheritance[3].

In law, the inheritance was similar to the property entailments created by Napoléon, in other words, in the event of the line becoming extinct, the ownership of the property should revert to the State, with the title-holder enjoying only its periodic fruits.

In 1817, the Duke of Wellington, wishing to clear away the woodland on his property, obtained authorisation to do so, provided that he used the profit from the sale of the trees to purchase other land, or deposited their value in the hands of the State, to be shown as an entry in the record of the Public Debt.

These woodland clearances continued throughout the nineteenth century, the greater part after 1830. By an agreement between the Duke of Wellington and the Belgian State, dated 7 June 1872, the revenue, which amounted to 80,106 francs, would henceforth be entered in the record of revenues, without including the capital, to prevent the Duke being able to claim reimbursement of that capital, which then amounted to 2,339,692 francs.

Farms had been established on the cleared land and the sixty-two farmers working them were among the most enthusiastic supporters of the continuation of the Wellington inheritance.

For more than a century, the latter has generated parliamentary questions, the trend of which is to persuade the Government to negotiate the abolition of the inheritance, emulating France which, by its Act of 22 April 1905, sanctioned the repurchase of entailed property[4].

From a legal point of view, the position of the defenders of the Wellington inheritance seems fairly secure. The Act of 29 September 1815 assigns the profits from it to all the legitimate descendants of Arthur Wellesley, and the present Duke of Wellington, the eighth to hold the title, is undoubtedly the descendant of the second son of the first Duke.

The legality itself of the inheritance under Belgian law is also contested by some, who consider it a privilege attached to a title and for that reason unconstitutional[5].

Without wishing to become involved in the controversy in detail, it has to be said that the legal basis of the inheritance derived from international law and from treaties. The undertaking voted by the States General in favour of the Duke of Wellington constitutes an obligation of the Kingdom of the Netherlands, which became an obligation of the Belgian State, by the principle of the succession of states, being located on the territory of the successor state.

The rewarding of a victorious general with material benefits, often considerable, was common currency at the time of the Napoléonic Wars. Had not Wellesley himself in 1813 received from the King of Spain an estate near Grenada, still in the possession of his descendants, as a reward for driving the French out of his country? Had not Napoléon created many sumptuous inheritances in favour of his marshals?

The survival of these ancient practices may be an affront to a society which has become profoundly democratic and which is less and less disposed to cultivate the veneration of victorious generals. Will it therefore become necessary to negotiate the re-purchase of the Wellington inheritance? Attempts towards this end were made several years ago by a burgomaster of Nivelles, but they came to nothing[6]. The question has therefore become a political one and a solution will only be found in that sphere.

16. THE WATERLOO BOUNTY

Article 5 of the agreement attached to the Second Treaty of Paris, signed on 20 November 1815, provided that a sum of 50 million francs should be drawn from the war tax levied on France and allotted half to Great Britain and half to Prussia, since the burden of the war had fallen mainly upon the armies of Wellington and Blücher.

The British share, by Wellington's wish, was distributed among all those who had fought in his army, including those in the Netherlands army and in the Hanoverian, Brunswicker and Nassauer contingents. For those who had died, the bounty was paid to the heirs. Sir Archibald Campbell, for Great Britain, Baron Jean Victor de Constant Rebecque, for the Netherlands and the Nassauer contingent, and Colonel Heise, for the Hanoverians and the Brunswickers, were made responsible by Wellington for the distribution.

The beneficiaries were divided into six classes, from generals to private soldiers. The generals received 30,589 francs, senior officers 10,394 francs, captains 2,168 francs, subalterns 833 francs, sergeants 461 francs and corporals and privates 61 francs.

The bounties paid to the senior officers were thus quite large, while those given to privates represented barely a few weeks' pay. They mirrored the social inequities of the age.

The sums not allocated on account of the disappearance of the Dutch beneficiaries (approximately 350,000 francs) were paid into the Waterloo Fund.

17. THE WATERLOO FUND

On 9 November 1815, William I signed a royal decree to organise the management of the monies which had been collected in the weeks following the battle, for aiding the military victims of the campaign. To this end he established an official body called the *Fund for the Encouragement and Support of Military Service*, commonly known as the *Waterloo Fund*, which celebrated its 150th anniversary in 1965[7].

Its function was either the payment of disabled pensions or the provision of assistance to the next-of-kin of those who had lost their lives in action. The fund was to be subsidised both by governmental grants and by sums collected from the public.

The aim was to provide the victims with a standard of living which was, as far as possible, comparable with that which they enjoyed before they were wounded. The principle was not, however, extended to families in comfortable circumstances, who were unable to claim the same help. Provision of assistance was to be based on the genuine needs of the claimants, the number of children being cared for, etc. The allowances could be drawn in addition to retired pay or a pension. In being granted this assistance, the recipients were not allowed to beg, to play musical instruments at fairs or markets or to peddle.

In the main town of every district a commission was appointed, responsible for the administration of the allowances.

When it was first created, the value of the Fund was already 1,115,234 florins, acquired by means of collections. In 1819, the sums invested had risen to 2,304,000 florins, bringing in an annual income of 57,607 florins, while collections brought in a further 29,000 florins[8].

So far as its charity work was concerned, the Fund's activities were fairly limited. During that same year of 1819, it rendered assistance to only 523 disabled soldiers, 407 injury claimants and 402 children, of whom 18 were orphans. In fact the main focus of the Fund's activities was on the upkeep of the *Maison des Invalides*, the pensioners' hospital founded at Leyden in 1817.

After 1830, the Convention of Utrecht of 19 July 1843 placed responsibility for the payments and bounties previously awarded to Belgian subjects by the Fund with the Belgian State, which received the sum of 80,000 florins in compensation.

18. WAR DAMAGES

The passage of armies, with their commandeering, their looting, the destruction of crops by the marching and foraging of the troops, as well as the destruction or burning of civilian buildings which resulted from the fighting itself, was always in the nature of a plague for the local inhabitants. Until the end of the eighteenth century, its victims obtained assistance only through the charity of the public.

The first case in which reparation for damage was initiated and organised by the public authorities occurred during the Prussian invasion of 1792, which culminated in the Battle of Valmy.

The decree passed by the National Assembly on 11 August 1792 had its basis in a new inspiration, the national solidarity which ' … seeks to give to other nations the first example of the brotherhood which unites the citizens of a free country and which renders any damage caused to one of its members a damage which is common to all[9].' The principle of the indemnification being proportional to the need was retained, but losses sustained by servants of the State and 'those who bear arms in the name of the motherland' were to be made good in their entirety.

One month after the Battle of Waterloo, King William I passed a decree which introduced the first legislation concerning war damage for the lands which in 1830 were to become Belgium. The purpose of the decree of 15 July 1815 invoked a solidarity which was widespread and very new in those days: 'Considering that the cause which was defended on the fields of Fleurus and Waterloo is that of the entire Kingdom and of Europe as a whole, it is therefore just that the inhabitants of the districts which have recently been the seat of the war should not alone bear the losses occasioned by the presence and the clashes of the armies.' As a consequence, in order to satisfy the most urgent needs,

the King made a gift of 50,000 francs out of his own funds and ordered the distribution of the foodstuffs held in the military stores. In addition, at the beginning of 1816 a sum of 400,000 francs from the national treasury was allocated for the repair of damages.

The Commission charged with the distribution of military assistance to the wounded, enlarged by the addition of one member of each of the administrative councils of the *départements* affected, namely the Dyle, Jemappes and Sambre-et-Meuse, supervised the application of the sums intended for the victims[10].

The evaluation of the destruction in each *commune* was to be carried out by Commissioners appointed by the municipal authority '… from inhabitants who were unaffected by the destruction', under the surveillance of the *intendants*, *sous-intendants* and mayors. This procedure was found to be unworkable, for '… the small number of educated inhabitants to be found in the villages led to fears that the evaluations would be anything but impartial'. The Commission therefore made use of these municipal experts only in *communes* reasonably distant from their own, under the supervision of *conseillers d'intendance* or their delegated representatives[11].

The decree of 15 July 1815 stipulated that only losses resulting from fire or looting would be considered for the granting of assistance, to the exclusion of requisitions, billeting and food which had been supplied to the troops.

To facilitate the experts' work, the Commission drew up a precise grid for the evaluation of land or of property destroyed and of either standing crops or that stored in barns which had been destroyed. This was done to guard against any attempt to swindle the scheme.

The *curé* of the parish of Finistère in Brussels, who played a leading role in the Commission, related: 'Imagine the loyalty of the people of Genappe. They backed one another up marvellously; one would testify to the losses of another with great charity, but always on a reciprocal basis. They [the Commissioners] were certain that the value of the property claimed as destroyed could never have existed in the whole of Genappe and that the affair was a culpable and scandalous exaggeration in order to deceive the Government[12].'

Nevertheless, the extent of the destruction was considerable. In 1817 it was estimated that more than 20,000 persons had suffered from damage[13]. The Commission of Evaluation for the province of Namur, in its report of 30 March 1816, reported that it had indemnified 4,888 households spread around 51 villages[14] while, in the district of Nivelles, the inhabitants of seventy-three *communes* had suffered from damage.

The distribution of the assistance followed the principle of ensuring that it went first to those least provided for. Priority was given to those persons ' ... reduced to poverty by the severity of the losses they have suffered in relation to their means and who possess neither solvent guarantors for these losses nor any means of repairing them'. Those who had other means and who, despite the losses sustained, were continuing to enjoy a level of affluence, were to receive indemnification only if there were funds left to distribute. If the money available were found to be insufficient, as was the case, the funds were to be distributed on a pro rata basis (articles 5 to 8 of the decree of 15 July 1815)[15].

A part of the losses sustained in the countryside ravaged by the war was represented by the livestock carried off or slaughtered by the troops. The size of this item in the damage claims led to it being excluded from indemnification by a decree of 6 July 1816; and also meanwhile a proportion of the livestock which had disappeared had been restored by the provision of cows and oxen drawn from the military depots and stores. By this means, in the province of Namur 753 oxen and cows were distributed.

Considerable food aid was provided. Again in the province of Namur, 1,352,692 pounds of wheat and rye flour, 166 hectolitres of dried peas and beans and 95,368 pounds of salt were given to the population, in three distributions, between October 1815 and February 1816[16].

Cash indemnifications were not made until the Spring of 1816, when the Commission had received all the declarations of losses, duly checked, and when the total value of the funds available for distribution was known. It seems that the rates of indemnification were set at one fifth of the value of buildings burnt down or destroyed, one tenth for crops looted or ruined and one twentieth for furniture lost. In addition, the victims received the refund of their taxes for the year 1815, although their request that this measure be extended to following years did not meet with any success.

Despite this assistance, conditions in the villages which had been visited by the contending armies remained very difficult. Thus, at Chapelle-Saint-Lambert, which had suffered the passage of two Prussian corps, famine threatened the inhabitants in June 1816: 'They have seen their fields devastated and have been able to harvest but little corn, while the high price of that foodstuff precludes them from procuring any and the situation in which they find themselves can only grow worse between now and harvest time.' To counter this, the mayor requested the distribution of some bread or other foodstuffs for persons in straitened circumstances[17].

King William visited Wavre in July 1815 and, seeing the extent of the destruction (54 houses burnt down or demolished), he granted to the inhabitants of the town and of the adjoining *commune* of Basse Wavre the favour of procuring from the national forests the timber necessary for the rebuilding work. This measure was not put into effect due to the hostility of the official responsible for *Eaux et Forêts*, so on 10 February 1818 the King granted a compensatory indemnity of 10,000 florins and ordered the municipal authorities to distribute it amongst the most needy[18].

In July 1815, authority to procure timber for the rebuilding of houses destroyed by fire was also granted to the inhabitants of Ligny and Grand-Manil.

PART THREE

WATERLOO'S CULTURAL HERITAGE

From the first months following the battle, the ferocity of the fighting and the importance of its consequences, perceived or otherwise, had seized the imagination. Curiosity was the first impulse which brought the visitors to the sites of Mont-Saint-Jean, La Belle Alliance and Plancenoit, which they explored from all directions, trampling down the corn and exciting the anger of the farmers, to the point where a police regulation, translated into English and prohibiting traffic across the battlefield, was demanded[1]. The battle sounds of 1815 echoed loudly down the following years, as the name of Waterloo was bestowed on many villages or new towns across the world. In June 2003, a Convention of the Waterloos of the world was even held, in Eastern Germany at Waterloo-Blüthen, a village of eighty-eight inhabitants!

The renown of the victory at Waterloo was such that all who visited the Low Countries made sure that they included a pilgrimage to the battlefield. Amongst the most famous of such visitors were, in 1815, Tsar Alexander I, the King of Prussia and his three sons, the poets Robert Southey and Walter Scott; in 1816, Lord Byron; in 1821, King George IV.

For nearly two hundred years, Waterloo has remained a tourist venue of primary importance, more on account of its symbolic value in the history of Europe than for the attraction of anything which the visitors may discover there. For many, the visit to Waterloo is in the nature of a pilgrimage devoted to historical personalities and the images of a battle fought in times gone by[2]. Some take the attraction and the enthusiasm to the lengths of donning the uniforms of the soldiers who fought one another on 18 June 1815 and of parading at the sites every year to the sound of fifes and drums, the boom of cannon and the crackle of muskets. This third part presents some of the aspects of these physical – and cultural, imagined – memorials.

The Gordon and Hanoverian monuments. Oil on canvas, unsigned. Private collection.

19. IN MEMORIAM: THE MONUMENTS

The battlefield of Waterloo and, to a lesser extent, of Quatre-Bras are strewn with commemorative monuments. The stories of these monuments reveal the different approaches taken in these places of memory at different times[3].

The first monuments on the battlefield of Waterloo were those erected by well-to-do families over the tomb of a relative who fell in action.

Such monuments were an outward manifestation on the battlefield of the social privilege which provided for some officers an individual place of interment, compared to the communal grave which was the lot of all the other dead. They also suggested that the place of burial was known or identifiable – a rare thing in the dismal confusion of the days following the battle – a fact which accounts for the rarity of individual graves. Examples are the tomb of Major Rowley Holland at Mont-Saint-Jean, that of Lieutenant-Colonel Edward Stables at Joli-Bois and of Major John Luci Blackman in the orchard of Goumont.

Several months, or sometimes several years might pass before a grave was marked by a monument, as was the case for the monument to General Duhesme, which was not erected at Ways until 1826.

Other officers were interred individually in the cemeteries of Waterloo and Braine-l'Alleud, in the Protestant cemetery in Brussels and in that which existed at the time outside the Porte de Hal, their graves marked only by a name-plate[4].

Another expression of family respect was the erection of a monument at the place where a relative or husband was *believed* to have met his death, whether his mortal remains were buried there or not. This was so for those dedicated to the memory of Alexander Gordon, Wellington's ADC, built in 1817 to the south of the crossroads between the Chemin de la Croix and the Charleroi road, and Count von Schwerin in the hamlet of Aquinot à Lasne in about 1818.

Officers' families also honoured the memory of their late relatives by having marble plaques put up in Waterloo church. The votive plaque dedicated to Major John Dorset Bringhurst is an example of these. It states that he was killed in a charge by his regiment, the First King's Dragoon Guards, and was buried on the spot, to the east of the farm of La Haie-Sainte.

Other kinds of plaques were also mounted in the church, by regiments who wished to perpetuate the memory of brothers-in-arms killed at Waterloo. In this respect the *Chapelle Royale* may be considered as a temple dedicated to the British and Dutch military tradition. These illustrations of regimental comradeship lead us from the commemoration of individuals to that of the group, of which two major monuments are examples.

The Hanoverian Monument, erected in 1818, takes the form of a truncated pyramid and is located to the east of the Brussels-Charleroi road and south of the old gravel pit, nearly opposite to La Haie-Sainte farm. It was built at the behest of officers of the King's German Legion, using money collected by subscription, to perpetuate the memory of the role played in the battle by that regiment.

It was another private initiative which produced the monument erected by the Waterloo Society in the *Chapelle Royale*. This association, whose aim was to consecrate the memory of the battle by means of a monument and to celebrate its anniversary each year, was founded in 1815. Its members were those loyal to the House of Orange and to the new regime, the majority being government officials, officers or office-holders at the Court. Until 1830 they met annually to celebrate the anniversary with a banquet and, up to 1828, to make the pilgrimage to Waterloo on 18 June.

The monument to the Prussians at Plancenoit. Coloured lithograph by Jobard at Brussels. Musée Wellington, Waterloo.

The first stone of the monument in the chapel was laid on 19 June 1828, although it was not finished until much later. It consisted of a representation of a portal in white marble, within which is a bronze bas-relief depicting Victory holding a laurel branch in the right hand and a crown in the left[5].

In addition to these memorial or commemorative monuments erected by private initiative, the governments of the Allies also sought to provide reminders of their victory.

The first of these monuments was erected by Prussia in 1818, to the north of the village of Plancenoit. This gothic spire, surmounted by an iron cross, bears a simple inscription in German: 'To fallen heroes, the grateful King and people. Belle Alliance, 18 June 1815[6].'

The second and most well-known was the Waterloo Monument, erected by the government of the Netherlands between 1824 and 1826[7]. On 18 June 1849, on the anniversary of the battle, the King of Hanover had a commemorative plaque mounted on the eastern gable-wall of the farm at La Haie-Sainte, in memory of the officers and men who fell defending that position[8].

The last memorials to be erected in the nineteenth century appeared in 1890, the 75th anniversary of the 1815 conflict. The government of Brunswick decided to honour the memory of the young Duke of Brunswick, Frederick William, who fell at Quatre-Bras on 16 June.

By the decision of a committee set up in Great Britain, the remains of twenty British officers killed at Waterloo were exhumed and laid beneath a monument by the Belgian sculptor J de Lalaing, which was erected in the cemetery of Evere in Brussels[9].

As the first centenary of the battle drew near, this began to arouse renewed interest in the conflict and, with it, a profusion of commemorative monuments.

In France, the rediscovery of the First Empire after 1871 was associated with the publication of numerous memoirs of former combatants and of the trilogy on 1815 by Henry Houssaye.

French feelings at the end of the nineteenth century were patriotic and held to the view that the heroism of its army on the plain of Waterloo could not remain unrecognised on the battlefield.

Before that time, in 1849, Hippolyte de Mauduit, author of *Histoire des derniers jours de la Grande Armée* (Paris, 1847-1848, 2 vols.) and former sergeant of the *1er Grenadiers de la Garde* at Waterloo, had floated the idea of the erection of a French monument on the battlefield. The magazine which he controlled, *La Sentinelle de l'Armée*, launched an appeal, but a few months later publication was banned by the Second Republic. The proposal was taken up again by Henry Houssaye who, at the beginning of the 1900s, acquired, with two friends, a plot of land along the side of the Charleroi road between La Belle Alliance and Rossomme, at the place thought to have been the scene of one of the last squares formed by the Guard, and offered it to the French review of military history and uniforms, *Les Carnets de la Sabretache*. The review then launched a public appeal to finance the construction of the monument.

The Brunswick monument

The architect Nenot designed a plinth in blue stone, on which was set a bronze replica of a stone statue of the Wounded Eagle, which had been exhibited at the Paris Salon in 1902 by Jean-Léon Gérôme (1824-1904). The monument was unveiled on 28 July 1904, in the presence of the French Ambassador in Brussels, of Henry Houssaye, the military painter Édouard Detaille and other public figures. According to the newspapers, nearly a hundred thousand people attended the ceremony[10].

Complementary to this project, a Belgian historian living in Paris, Hector Fleichmann (1882-1914), conceived the notion of erecting a monument to Victor Hugo, the chronicler of Waterloo. To this end, he formed a committee (yet another!) composed of figures from French and Belgian literary circles. In the first group were Sarah Bernhardt, the Comtesse de Noailles, Henry Bataille, Henri de Régnier and Auguste Rodin; in the second were Camille Lemonnier, Maurice Maeterlinck and Émile Verhaeren.

The French architect, A M Ley, and his Belgian colleague, J H Verhoeven, designed the monument, which was in the form

The monument at Evere by J de Lalaing

The Wounded Eagle monument (detail). Oil on canvas by Maurice Dubois (exhibited at the Paris Salon in 1902). The E Brassine Collection

of a column surmounted by a bronze cockerel. The first stone was laid on 22 September 1912, fifty years after the publication of *Les Misérables*, but the monument was not completed until 1955, after being left abandoned for forty years[11].

Hector Fleichmann was also the instigator of two other monuments, which were unveiled on 22 June 1913: a stele dedicated to the memory of the French soldiers killed at Goumont and placed in the orchard of the estate, and an ossuary located in the garden of Le Caillou farm. The purpose of the latter was as a repository for the bones still to be found here and there on the scene of the battle a century later, and was the result of collaboration between Fleichmann and a local scholar, Lucien Laudy, who had gathered together at Le Caillou a large collection of souvenirs of the fighting.

Belgian military circles, which had links with the political world through several influential persons, evinced great interest in the celebration of the hundredth anniversary of the battle. A Waterloo Centenary Committee was formed in 1911, under the chairmanship of General Baron de Heusch[12].

The aim was to commemorate 18 June 1815 with a grand ceremony, to be attended by representatives of the four countries (Germany, Great Britain, France and Holland) whose armies had taken part in the battle. The French authorities were approached, but refused to participate and the other governments also declined, not wishing, out of courtesy, to commemorate a centenary in which the vanquished did not wish to take part.

The committee then considered other schemes: the erection of a monument to the Belgian soldiers killed at Waterloo, a project which eventually came to fruition, though without its involvement; the preservation of the battlefield, achieved by means of the Act of 26 March 1914; and the construction of an international ossuary on the site of the battle. This last, financed by subscriptions, was due to be unveiled in June 1915. The outbreak of war in 1914 put an end to this project and the fate of the money which had been collected is unknown[13].

It seems that the idea of erecting a monument to the memory of the Belgian soldiers at Waterloo can be ascribed to Baron Lambermont, with the object ' … of correcting the myth maliciously accepted in England concerning the behaviour of the Belgians and Dutch at Mont-Saint-Jean[14].'

In 1908, a scheme for the erection of a common monument to the Belgian and Dutch officers and men who fell at Quatre-Bras was launched by the newspaper *La Métropole d'Anvers*. At the same time the work by Colonel de Bas, *La Campagne de 1815 en Belgique* appeared, which sought to repair the honour of the troops levied by the Kingdom of the Netherlands. The idea was well received in Holland, but subscriptions to the fund launched by the army did not come up to expectations and the project for a common monument at Quatre-Bras ground to a halt.

The magazine *La Belgique Militaire* now took up the cudgels and launched an appeal for the construction of a monument exclusively dedicated to the memory of the Belgian troops at Waterloo[15].

A committee of support was set up which was independent of that for the commemoration of the battle's centenary, although Baron de Heusch could be found occupying the

The sculptor Cain in his studio working on the cockerel which was intended to be placed on the Victor Hugo column. The piece was cast, but the founder, not having been paid, destroyed the work in order to recover the bronze.

vice-chairman's position. The success of the appeal was immediate and remarkable. Even if the cost of the monument was less than that estimated, there was enough left over to allow a monument to the Belgians to be erected at Quatre-Bras.

The one erected at Waterloo was designed by the architect Callewaerts. It consisted of a truncated pyramid in granite, decorated with a bronze flag torn by shrapnel and surmounted by a symbol of victory stamped with a shield bearing the Belgian lion decorated with laurels. It bore an inscription in French and Flemish: 'To the Belgians who died on XVIII June MDCCCXV fighting to defend the flag and the honour of their service.' It was raised on a plot of land on the north side of the Chemin de la Croix and east of the Brussels road.

The monument set up at Quatre-Bras, on the road to Houtain-le-Val, was simpler: a cenotaph in blue stone, bearing the same bilingual inscription.

The two monuments were made prior to August 1914, but their unveiling never took place on account of the war.

On the Allied side, no project emerged in Germany to celebrate the centenary. Clearly, memories of the war of liberation of 1813 took precedence over those of the Battle of La Belle Alliance, while the gigantic *Völkerschlachtdenkmal*, commemorating the Battle of Leipzig, had been unveiled in 1913. Activities went no further than to tidy up the surrounds of the Prussian Monument.

As regards the British, there was talk in 1907 of erecting a statue of the Duke of Wellington on the battlefield, but the idea got no further. That same year, at the instigation of the Brigade of Guards, a bronze plaque was mounted on the wall of the chapel at Goumont, in honour of the memory of the companies of the latter who had defended the château. In 1914, all British efforts were focussed on the appeal for the protection of the battle site.

After the bloody fighting of 1914-1918, public opinion turned its face away from military matters and pacifism became a popular theme; nothing more was erected on the battlefield until the fifties.

After the Second World War, the Belgian Society for Napoléonic Studies, which was founded by the journalist Théo Fleichmann (1893-1979), younger brother of Hector Fleichmann, purchased the farm at Le Caillou in 1954, after

the death of Lucien Laudy (1885-1948)[16], and established a museum there.

In a similar move, Comte Jacques-Henri Pirenne, with a few friends and the help of the *commune*, saved the British headquarters at Waterloo and installed there the collections maintained by *Les Amis du Musée Wellington*.

A Committee for the Historical Study of the Battle of Waterloo, an offshoot of the British Waterloo Committee, under the presidency of the Duke of Wellington, was set up in 1973, with the principal aim of safeguarding the battle site. It was responsible for the erection, by the side of the Chemin de la Croix, of a simple granite block to the memory of General Picton and, along the Chemin des Vertes Bornes, another recalling the role of Mercer's troop and that of the British horse artillery during the battle.

To counter what some consider to be the British takeover of Waterloo, a former Belgian politician, Jean-Émile Humblet, who is very francophile, founded in 1986 a Franco-European Waterloo Association. To him are owed several small, very simple monuments, which were erected in memory of French regiments at Waterloo.

In recent years there have been two more monuments built on the Quatre-Bras battlefield: one, decidedly modern, dedicated to the Dutch cavalry, and another, very classical, honouring the memory of the British regiments involved on 16 June 1815.

Thus, as the twenty-first century opens, the memory of Waterloo has remained very much alive, through associations of students passionately involved in military history, whose activities cause the thunder of 1815 still to echo today, though without bloodshed.

20. THE WATERLOO LION

The government of the Netherlands, aware of the symbolic value of the victory at Waterloo, could not fail to honour it and keep its memory alive[17]. By a decree of 11 December 1815, King William I directed that a commemorative monument be built on the plain of Waterloo and ordered the Commissioner-General for Education in the Arts and Sciences to organise an architectural competition.

On 21 July 1817, the Duc d'Ursel, Minister for Public Works, and Repelaer van Driel, Commissioner-General for Public Education, made the following report to the King: 'Nearly all the artists of any note in the country have already been approached to present their ideas; these schemes have been submitted to Your Majesty and the little success which has resulted must cast doubt on the results from any fresh attempt.' The ministers then proposed that the idea of a public competition be abandoned and submitted to the King the scheme produced by an engineer from Tournai named Vifquain. It consisted of a pyramid in dressed stone, simply bearing on each face the name of one of the Allied nations whose troops had fought in the battle, the expected cost being of the order of 500,000 florins. On 28 July, in a further decree, King William ordered the ministers concerned to carry out a more extensive study of the project and to include the cost in the 1818 budget.

In July 1818 Vifquain submitted a costed estimate which came to 644,000 florins and was thereupon asked to reduce it to 500,000 florins. For more than two years he laboured to produce his final project, the specification for which was not approved until 6 July 1819. Seized by last-minute doubts, the Minister for Public Works decided that, before presenting Vifquain's project for adjudication, he would ask the architect of the royal palaces, Charles van der Straeten, for his opinion. On 13 August, he put to him three questions. Are you content with the shape of the proposed monument?

Taking our climate into account, will it be durable? Is there no way of constructing the monument for a lower cost?

Charles van der Straeten pointed out that a pyramid was a burial monument and not a triumphal one and also referred to the vulnerability with this type of building to the risk of frost damage to its stone facing.

Before giving his view on the possibility of constructing a less costly monument, van der Straeten asked in his turn for a few clarifications: was it the purpose to erect a monument which celebrated the valour of the Belgian troops, or was it in honour of the nations which had won at Waterloo, or was it again of a more European character, given the political results of the day?

On 7 October 1819, the Minister for Public Works replied that the monument must be solid and free from any ornamentation likely to be a temptation to the covetous, such that no caretaker would be needed for its preservation, and that the cost of construction should not exceed 300,000 florins. Charles van der Straeten was requested to submit his proposals before the end of November, accompanied by an estimate.

In December 1819, the architect presented his scheme and explained the concept of a monument, the originality of which remains intriguing still today. He found himself 'needing to seek for a monument of a new kind which would at the same time be most suitable for a battlefield'. He had considered it necessary 'to make the soil itself contribute to his composition and to draw up his plan from nature, whose models are of a grandeur which the creations of man imitate with difficulty, and traces of which are to be found in Cyclopean architecture and in our ancient burial places, described somewhat incorrectly as Celtic. This circular-shaped artificial mountain would rise alone from the plain, without competition from any other nearby eminence

HRH the Prince of Orange in the glorious Battle of Waterloo, 18 June 1815, wounded at the instant of victory.
Coloured etching by W Van Senus, after T Odevaere. Musée Wellington, Waterloo.

[…] and would be surmounted by the monument proper, composed of a colossal lion set upon a marble pedestal. The lion is the symbol of victory; by resting on the globe, it proclaims the tranquillity which Europe has won on the plains of Waterloo. This monument, standing 43 metres above ground level, would stand out majestically on the horizon, producing the greatest effect. No maintenance or surveillance would be needed for its conservation'.

On 12 January 1820, the Minister for Public Works reported to the King, submitting the schemes of both van der Straeten and Vifquain.

On 19 January, influenced by his wife, Queen Frederica-Louise, William I chose van der Straeten's proposal, with simply the date, 18 June 1815, inscribed on the pedestal. He suggested that the lion should be cast at Liège, either in the State foundry or the workshops of John Cockerill, and that the sculptor Van Geel of Brussels should be asked to produce the model. The monument would be erected at the spot where the Prince of Orange, the heir to the throne, had been wounded as the battle was coming to an end.

The negotiations for the acquisition of the necessary land for the erection of the mound went on for a year. In July

1821, the owner of the farm at La Haie-Sainte, the Comte de Velthem, finally agreed to provide about seven *bonniers* of land, situated between the road and the location of the proposed monument, to accommodate it. The government promised that the arable soil on the surface of the earthwork would firstly be removed and then put back once the work had been completed.

These earthworks would have the effect of removing the southern embankment of the Chemin de la Croix, notably along the sunken stretch from the Brussels road, and of considerably lowering the bank which overlooked the buildings of La Haie-Sainte to the north-west.

The specification for the work contains interesting details about the design of the monument. It consisted of 'a truncated cone whose centreline will measure 160 m across the base and 16 m at the top, the perpendicular centre-line being 43.1 m. The mound will be made of soil, at the top of which will be set a large pedestal of blue stone, known as Arquennes granite (instead of the red marble originally proposed). The pedestal will be in the shape of a regular polyhedron, whose lower surface measures 10.2 m long and 7.2 m wide, while the upper surface will be 6 m long and 3 m wide. The total height, including plinths and cornices, will be 7.4 m. This pedestal is to be supported on the top of a brick masonry-work (fired on site and laid using lime mortar) 48.1 m high, foundations included, the latter being 12m long, 9 m wide, 5 m high and made of quarry-stone from Braine-l'Alleud'.

The architect estimated the quantity of soil needed to be 290,205 cubic ells (a Dutch ell was very roughly 60 cm, though a French ell, or *aune*, was about 1.2 m, so there is some difficulty here). He calculated the approximate cost price of one cubic ell of embankment at 0.50 cents, based on a wage of one florin per ten-hour working day for a workman digging 1 cu. m.

A carrier with his cart was to be paid three florins a day and the labourer employed in levelling the ground was to receive 0.80 florins. The banking was to be built up in layers 30 cm deep, duly levelled and rammed around the masonry support. The carts were to ascend the cone on a spiral ramp, which rose as the mound grew higher.

The total cost of the monument was estimated to be 291,412.76 florins.

It was not until 5 June 1823 that invitations to tender for the embankment and the masonry were issued. The work was awarded to the firm of Chapel et Cie of Charleroi, for a price of 129,000 florins, while the architect's estimate for this work came to 176,654 florins.

The work began in 1824. By the end of 1825 the embankment and masonry work was complete, except that the mound was still surrounded by scaffolding, necessary for hoisting the stones required for building the pedestal. Invitations to tender for the supply and laying of the stones of the pedestal were not issued until the end of January 1826.

The order for this work was awarded to a certain J A Drapier of Charleroi, a former associate of the general contractor Chapel, for a price of 30,000 florins. It included the raising to the top of the mound of the parts which would form the Lion. The pedestal was not completed until October 1826 when, at the end of the month, the colossal cast-iron Lion could be placed on its base. This had been ordered from the sculptor Van Geel at the beginning of 1820, as soon as the project had been approved. He travelled first to Holland and then to London, in search of a living lion as a model.

On his return, the artist made a plaster model and then a full-size one in clay. From this were made the plaster moulds used by the foundrymen in the Cockerill workshops in Liège, where the work was completed in seven months.

The statue was cast in nine pieces 'namely each leg with a part of the body, the head with a part of the mane, the globe, the tail and the plinth' in cast iron, an inch and a half thick and weighing 27,000 Dutch pounds. Its price, fixed by the tender, was 19,035 florins. After removal from the moulds, the statue was assembled and trued up in the workshops at Seraing, where it was inspected and accepted by the architect Suys, who had succeeded van der Straeten as architect for the royal palaces.

The means used to transport the pieces of the statue to Waterloo is not known. They were probably taken by water barge, via Dordrecht, the Scheldt estuary and the Willebroek canal to Brussels, and from there by road to the foot of the mound.

Once it had been hoisted to the top of its artificial hill, the Lion was permanently assembled, the joints hermetically sealed and bolted together, while forged iron bars slotted in the animal's paws were fixed in place with lead, in both paws and pedestal, to a depth of one metre. This was done on 4 November 1826.

The embankment of the mound was completed and it was sown with grass seed in the spring of 1827, together with the placing of 140 boundary-markers in blue stone and a hawthorn hedge surrounding it. In 1828, the Lion was painted with two coats of red lead and two coats of bronze paint, as well as the gilding of the inscription '18 juin 1815'.

Looking at the details reveals the absurdity of the legends which have been constantly peddled concerning the Lion: the mound is not a cenotaph beneath which the Waterloo dead have been buried; the Lion was not cast from the bronze of French cannon captured by the Allies on the evening of 18 June 1815; the Waterloo Lion is not an anti-French monument – it faces south as a symbol of the peace secured, for several decades at least, by the victory of the Allies over Napoléonic France.

Another persistent legend has it that '*boteresses*' hailing from Liège took part in the embankment work on the mound. The word '*boteresse*' comes from a Walloon dialect term from the Liège area, '*bot*', and simply means hod carriers (female), in other words women carrying a hod on their backs to transport not only building materials or coal, but also foodstuffs[18]. There is nothing to suggest that female workers were not involved in the construction of the monument and it is possible, even probable, that the contractor Chapel did use them, since their wages would have been lower. In that case, they would have been recruited locally; why should he go to Liège to find women capable of carrying panniers when he could have found them nearby[19]?

The evidence advanced in support of this tradition of the *boteresses Liègeoises* is scarce and unconvincing. No trace of these *boteresses* has been found, either in the civil registers or in the legal archives or those of the notaries.

We remain convinced that the tale derives from a blending of two traditions: in the nineteenth century, the *boteresses*

Machinery used for raising the Waterloo Lion. Lithograph by Jobard, after Bertrand.

Plaster model of the *Lion* installed on the top of the Waterloo Monument, by J-L Van Geel. Musée d'Art Ancien, Brussels.

Liègeoises were well-known, on account of their work in the coal-mining industry. In the popular mind an image was formed which combined the local women, who could have been employed to carry the soil, and the corresponding workers from Liège, especially since the statue of the Lion had been cast in Liège and some people thought that it was Cockerill who had constructed the mound.

21. THE PRESERVATION OF THE BATTLEFIELD

The opening in 1884 of the Brussels-Nivelles-Charleroi railway line, with stations at Waterloo and Braine-l'Alleud, followed by the laying of a local line from Brussels, firstly to La Grande Espinette (Rhode-Saint-Genèse) and then its extension to Braine-l'Alleud (1899) and Wavre, made visits to the battlefield much easier.

During the 1890s and the early years of the new century, hotel-restaurants sprang up around the foot of the mound and along the Chemin de la Croix. Country houses were built along the Nivelles road, as well as dwellings for agricultural workers on the La Haie-Sainte farm along the Charleroi road, in the direction of La Belle Alliance.

In about 1910, Louis Navez counted nearly fifty new houses which had been built on the battlefield in the course of the previous years and stressed that: 'It is above all the progressive invasion of the battlefield by country houses which seems to be the greatest fear in the future[20].'

According to the English journalist Demetrius Boulger, who placed his pen at the service of Léopold II's colonial policy and who met him frequently, the King began to be concerned about the preservation of the battlefield in 1898, at the same time taking the view that it was not for Belgium to take the lead[21].

In 1907, a patron of the arts, the somewhat eccentric Louis Cavens (1850-1940), who falsely claimed to be a Roman count, launched a campaign for the preservation of the battlefield in the international press[22]. His efforts found support in parliament, where questions were put to the government[23]. The Minister for Public Works, Auguste Delbeke, replied: 'For a long time my department has been looking for practical ways of protecting the battlefield of Waterloo from the changes resulting from building, new plantations or excavations. M. Cavens has not been content

to await the outcome of the current investigations. He has been seized by the idea and has made it the subject of a strident outburst[24].'

The Minister's proposal, as submitted to the government, was to get an international committee to purchase the battlefield and then reassign it to the Belgian State. Alternatively, he suggested that the State should buy it directly, while acknowledging that 'the state of the public finances would not allow this scheme to be realised, due to the exorbitant claims that the owners insist upon putting forward[25].'

The Belgian authorities were aware that the task of a committee would be a difficult one. One could not count on the participation of the French, for whom 'the very name of Waterloo spelt a veritable disaster, comparable to that of Sedan'. For the Russians and the Austrians, the fate of the battlefield was of no concern; in the end, the committee could count only on Great Britain, expected to be very generous, Germany and, to a lesser extent, the Netherlands.[26].

Conscious of these difficulties, the government chose a middle course, a solution typical of Belgian political practice. Rather than purchasing or expropriating the battlefield, it preferred to impose an obligation of *non aedificandi* (no construction allowed) on the areas it wished to safeguard, while granting an indemnity to the owners.

The matter passed through the parliamentary process with exceptional speed. The bill introduced by the new Minister for Public Works, Georges Helleputte, was presented to the Chamber of Representatives on 25 March 1914 and passed that same day, by 95 votes to 5, with 3 abstentions. The next day it was also adopted by the Senate, by 58 votes to 20, with 2 abstentions. The Act was sanctioned by the King and enacted on 27 March. Such headlong haste is perplexing, but is an explanation for the inaccuracies and obscurities in the legal text.

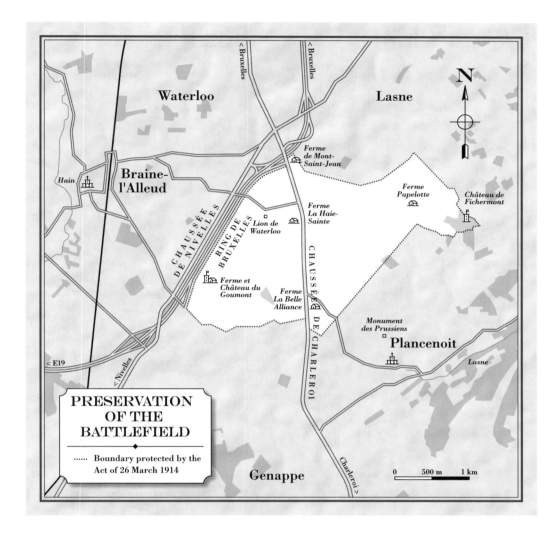

PRESERVATION
OF THE
BATTLEFIELD

······ Boundary protected by the
Act of 26 March 1914

Within a poorly-defined area of approximately 500 hectares, essentially covering that portion of the battlefield which saw the confrontation between the French troops and those commanded by the Duke of Wellington, but neglecting almost completely the Franco-Prussian battle zone[27], were prohibited henceforth, without prior authorisation, the planting of any trees that would grow to normal size, the erection or conversion of edifices or buildings, the opening of quarries and the making of excavations[28]. The government was also given the right to carry out expropriations within the protected area.

In return for this legally-imposed obligation, the proprietors and occupiers were accorded the right to an indemnity. In the absence of agreement between the parties, this was to be determined by the legal authorities, within a period of two years. No indication was given as to the procedure to be followed in order to obtain the indemnity. No overall figure was suggested.

With regard to the financial implications of the project, the Senate spokesman for legal affairs, Baron de Kerchove d'Exaerde, gave the Upper House this reassurance: 'A foreign party has made available the necessary funds for the payment of the indemnities. There will thus be no pecuniary sacrifice to be made by the Belgian Government[29].'

This was a case of counting chickens, for the British committee, which would be collecting the necessary funds, met for the first time only on 24 March, and that at the instigation of the Duke of Wellington, at his London home, Apsley House. The objective was to collect the sum of 10,000 pounds, or 250,000 francs, an amount which was considered to be adequate for the indemnification; but on what basis?

Several months later, Lieutenant-General the Baron de Heusch, chairman of the Belgian committee for the Waterloo centenary, was able to write: 'The British will contribute 10,000 pounds, their appeal having already got up to 8,000. What about us, though? I put this to the King (Albert I), who felt that Belgium could not allow Great Britain alone to bear the cost of the indemnities to be paid to the proprietors. The King has contributed 3,000 francs; I, 500; de Grunne, 500; Snoy, 500; Cavens, 500, and a list is being circulated in the Court for the military and civilian households. In short, we already have 9,000 to 10,000 francs. We need 25,000 to be able to say to the British: in proportion to our population and our wealth, we are contributing as much as you, since we have already collected 40,000 francs for the Waterloo and Quatre-Bras monuments. Then they will be satisfied and we shall be happy[30].'

The German invasion of Belgium on 4 August 1914 thrust the problem into the background. When or how the proprietors were indemnified is unknown.

The passing of the Act into law on 26 March 1914 brought no relief from the pressures of the financial interests which sought to build on the battlefield. On 23 March 1933, Jules Mathieu, the socialist deputy burgomaster of Nivelles, brought in a bill aimed at the repeal of the Act, justified in particular by the fact that: '... the population explosion demands the development of the region concerned, which is unjustly impeded by the obligations with which it is saddled.' Although this proposal received the support of the council of Braine-l'Alleud, which deplored the fact that expansion eastwards of the little housing estate was blocked by the protected zone, as well as the encouragement of the landowners and the hoteliers established on the battlefield, the idea got no further[31].

Fifty years later, a new proposal for the abrogation of the 1914 Act appeared in a decree laid before the Council of the Francophone Community (Belgium having become a federal state in the intervening period). Brought in by the deputy for the region, André Jandrain, but instigated by the senator Jean-Émile Humblet, it was driven by the concern to 'avoid unwanted foreign interference' or, in plain language, British interference in safeguarding the battlefield. It suggested that this should henceforth be covered by the common law concerning the protection of monuments and sites; but the proposal met with no greater success than that of Jules Mathieu.

France and Germany never enacted any specific laws directly creating a defined protection zone comparable to the Belgian legislation on Waterloo. In Italy, on the other hand, the order in council of 29 October 1922 nominated as 'monumental zones' four sites which were the scenes of fighting against the Austrian army in 1917. In the United States, there was no protection of historic sites until the National Historic Preservation Act was passed by Congress on 15 October 1966.

Thus, despite its imperfections, the Act of 26 March 1914 makes Belgium a leader in the protection of battlefields and it is easy to imagine what would have become of the location of the struggle of 1815 without it, given the urban expansion of Brussels.

22. WATERLOO AS POLITICAL SYMBOL

Studies concerning the political significance of Waterloo in the collective memories of Great Britain, Holland and Germany are hard to find. Though it can be said that the memory of Waterloo is overshadowed by that of the victory at Leipzig, considered to mark the dawn of German revival.

In France, the memory of Waterloo fluctuates between concealment, resurgence and shifting stance, to adopt the phraseology of Jean-Marc Largeaud[32].

Defeat, the return of the king, the White Terror and the occupation of a part of France by the Allies were all facets of the disarray in which those who had arisen to acclaim the return of the Emperor now found themselves. The memory which formed itself at that time was that of a national trauma, without precedent in the nation's history, not excluding 1814. Although the rejection of the treaties of 1815 was the basis of that memory, Waterloo was its central theme.

The revolution in July when it came appeared as a revenge for 1815. For those on the left of the political spectrum, Waterloo during those years remained an idea or symbol in the imagination. For the July monarchy, the scope for manoeuvre was limited, given the king's aim of avoiding all military adventures in Europe. The martial episode of the Hundred Days was approached with great caution, as was shown by the absence of any illustrations of the 1815 conflict in the gallery of battles at Versailles.

With the Second Empire, the Napoléonic legend began to blossom, as did that of Waterloo, combined with severe criticisms of the actions of liberal politicians after 18 June.

The autopsy of the defeat performed by the exiles Charras and Quinet found, however, a certain echo with the generation of younger republicans who were at odds with authority.

Under the Third Republic and up to 1914, more and more recollections and memories began to make their appearance, as part of the rediscovery of the First Empire. It wasn't until 1895, with the publication of Henri Houssaye's trilogy, that the Battle of Waterloo was examined with, on the whole, an opinion in favour of the Emperor. It was the exaltation of a glorious defeat. However, a more republican vision was to be found in the school textbooks, summed up in these words from an inspector of primary education: 'What is the point of deluding pupils with retrospective expectations, of leading them on to the battlefield of Waterloo with the illusion of a possible victory, if then they are to wonder superstitiously whether the disaster and its consequences should not be attributed to some misunderstanding, some chance [...] In Waterloo is revealed the final expiation, the abyss into which we must be fatally cast by the Empire, which we have submitted to and accepted.'

In Belgium, the bravery which the heir to the throne, the young Prince of Orange, had demonstrated during the battles at Quatre-Bras and Waterloo created an immediate popular consensus in favour of the new monarchy. In a way, the victory at Waterloo became the symbol of the new regime[33].

Throughout the existence of the Kingdom of the Netherlands, the anniversary of the victory of Waterloo was commemorated as an official holiday. Across the country, the anniversary of 18 June was a day of prayer and thanksgiving. Each year, the officials responsible for religious affairs, both the protestant and the catholic churches, used the occasion to issue homilies repeating that the independence of the kingdom had been won on the field of Waterloo and thanking the Almighty for the blessing that He had bestowed.

It is not difficult to understand how, in the context of the revolution of 1830, the Waterloo monument, symbolising and commemorating as it did the battle that for fifteen years had bound Belgium and Holland together, should have aroused the anger of dedicated patriots; particularly those who constituted what was referred to as the French Party. In the course of several days in September, volunteers who left Braine-l'Alleud and Waterloo to march on Brussels paused to plant a Tricolor on the summit of the mound.

In June 1831, the political situation in Belgium was particularly tense; opinion, rejecting the abandonment of Limburg and the purchase of Luxembourg, swung towards the republican camp, while the francophiles declared themselves openly.

On 18 June, demonstrators made their way towards Waterloo, with the intention of attacking the monument. On the following day, Sol, the Secretary of the French Legation in Brussels, went to see the Regent, Surlet de Chokier, who gave him a report of the incident and of the measures taken: 'The business yesterday at Waterloo could have turned serious had I not taken the precaution of dispatching a squadron of *chasseurs* and the *gendarmerie* to the spot. Two to three hundred inhabitants of the surrounding *communes*, all armed, were determined to defend the monument with firearms. For them it is a gold-mine, topped up every day by visitors to the site of the battle on that fatal day. One local man alone has made a fortune of more than 40,000 francs by selling the remains of weapons and decorations, purported to have been picked up off the battlefield, and often bought by dealers from Brussels.'

After the Treaty of the XXIV Articles had been imposed on Belgium on 15 November 1832, a French corps under the command of Marshal Gérard entered Belgium and laid siege to Antwerp, which William I refused to evacuate. According to legend, as they passed the foot of the Lion mound the soldiers assailed the Lion with several rifle shots and cut off a piece of its tail. The incident, if it took place, must have amounted to very little, for the statue remained unmutilated, its component parts being still joined together in their original state.

In that same year of 1832, the Waterloo Lion was threatened by a new danger which, being politically inspired, was more serious. On 23 December the Antwerp garrison surrendered. On the 28th, Alexandre Gendebien, leader of the French Party, submitted to the office of the Chamber a bill drafted in the following terms:

'Art. 1. The Belgian nation expresses its gratitude to the French army and its worthy commanders.

Art. 2. The Lion of Waterloo is to be converted into bombs and bullets to defend the liberty and the independence of the two peoples. It is to be replaced by a memorial on which is to be flown in perpetuity the colours of Belgium and France.'

Article 1 was accepted unanimously, but the second article met with widespread opposition, both in the Chamber and in the Press. It was pointed out that, had Waterloo not taken place, Brussels would still be the chief town of a French *département* and that it would be imprudent to irritate the rest of Europe. The second Article was not taken into consideration and the act, reduced to its single Article, was passed on 31 December 1832. Gendebien's proposition had embarrassed the government and had ruffled the feelings of both the French and the British.

The celebration of the fiftieth anniversary of the battle brought new problems for the Belgian government. Since 1863, Napoléon III had no longer hidden his 'revisionist' views, with their tendency to redraw the map of Europe. In his view, Belgium ought to be shared out between Great Britain and France. At the beginning of 1865, conflict was stirring between the Austrians and the Prussians and, in the struggle for hegemony in Germany, Belgium feared the possibility of being traded against French neutrality.

In order not to provoke Napoléon III, the Belgian authorities therefore proposed that the fiftieth anniversary of the battle should not be the subject of any demonstrations about which its French neighbour might take umbrage. However, a Flemish lawyer in Brussels conceived the idea of organising a grand demonstration on the battlefield, the object of which would be a celebration of the brotherhood of the nations, and this demonstration was allowed to go ahead. In a report to his government (20 June 1865), the Austrian ambassador described it in these terms: 'The three or four thousand individuals who formed the gathering were for the most part sightseers from the surrounding villages, who came partly to pass their Sunday leisure time, drawn by the grandiose announcements of the festivities which were due to take place. After luncheon, toasts were offered and speeches delivered. As the present government had refused to associate itself with the demonstration, the full-blooded democrats had the place to themselves and toasts in Flemish were proposed to the brotherhood of the nations. One orator prophesied that henceforth no war would be possible except one – that of the people against their sovereigns.'

The commemoration had assumed a character which was both pacifist and pan-German. The organising committee's manifesto left no doubt on the subject: 'In the name of the Flemish Movement, we appeal to the English, Germans, Dutch and Belgians, on this fiftieth anniversary of the Battle of Waterloo, to make a solemn visit to the battlefield and thus exalt the principles of political life. The alliance of the people, in freedom, peace and love, against violence and hegemonies.'

In 1890, during the celebration of the 75th anniversary of the battle, Waterloo was once more the scene of demonstrations organised by the Flemish Movement in Brussels. On 22 June, some 500 people, with banners, flags and fanfares, travelled by special train as far as Braine-l'Alleud and from there proceeded to the base of the Lion. The lawyer and historian, Maurits Josson, addressed them, praising peace between nations and the brotherhood of the Germanic peoples. His oration was followed by others from a German and a Dutch speaker. The ceremony ended with the performance of *Vlaamse Leeuw*, *Der Wacht am Rhein*, *Wien Neerlandsch Bloed* and *God Save the Queen*.

In parallel with the emergence of the Flemish Movement, there also arose, at the end of the nineteenth century, a movement to assert the rights of the Walloons. In the eyes of its adherents, the Lion was the symbol of a defeat which was odious to the irredentist and francophile sympathies of some.

During the First World War, Raymond Colleye, while a refugee in London and later Paris, suggested in *L'Opinion Wallonne* that, when victory was won, the monument should be blown up, as a sign of Franco-Walloon solidarity. After the armistice, the deputy Pépin asked the government to have the Lion turned round, so that its mouth was facing north. In 1925, another Walloon deputy, Victor Ernest, proposed that the monument should simply be demolished. In 1928, the Walloon *Avant-Garde* organised a first pilgrimage to Waterloo. Fourteen people took part, but in subsequent years the numbers regularly increased, reaching ten thousand on the eve of the Second World War.

The topics addressed at the foot of the Wounded Eagle dwelt on the loyalty of Walloons to the Napoléonic colours during the 1815 campaign, Wallonia's preference for and inclusion in French culture and its desire to resist the increasing influence of the Flemish provinces in Belgian political life.

After 1945, until the beginning of the seventies, pilgrims nostalgically remembering the French era returned to Waterloo in considerable numbers.

In another way, the memory of the battle encapsulated a nationalistic and proud vision of the military past of the new Belgium.

The question of the behaviour of the Dutch-Belgian troops on 18 June 1815 gave rise to impassioned discussions which would eventually insinuate themselves into the world of international politics.

Thus, the debate at Westminster in 1854 on the adoption of the Foreign Enlistment Bill, authorising the British government to recruit foreigners to meet the needs of the Crimean War, gave rise to less than flattering remarks on the behaviour of the Belgian troops at Waterloo, which were reported in the Belgian press. The criticisms were derived from the book by Captain Siborne on the 1815 campaign, which had appeared ten years earlier.

At the time, an atmosphere of veiled tension hung over the relationship between Napoléon III and Belgium and, rightly or wrongly, Brussels felt itself vaguely threatened by its powerful neighbour to the south. For several years the possibility of a war with the Second Empire could not be excluded. In addition, in 1848 the idea of making Antwerp the seat of the government in the event of war was adopted and work to construct a fortified camp was started there in 1852. In the following year, the strength of the army was increased from 80,000 to 100,000 men. In this situation, attacks on Belgian military valour provoked vehement reactions.

Major-General Renard, chief of the general staff and ADC to King Léopold I, took it upon himself to refute the British allegations and to this end wrote three letters to the newspapers *Indépendence belge* and *Émancipation*. As a result of their favourable reception by the public, they were then, with the addition of notes, collected up in a brochure entitled: *Replies by a general officer to English allegations on the conduct of Belgian troops in 1815*[34].

The incident was the subject of debates in both houses of the Belgian parliament, which paid tribute to the patriotism of General Renard. In the Senate, the intervention of the liberal Joseph Van Schoor, chairman of the Commission for War, with an order motion, demonstrated that, apart from their defence of the national honour, the reactions to the British allegations were born of a desire to defend the country's independence: 'Let the foreigner be under no illusions about us; let him be certain that, were our frontiers to be once more violated […], the Belgian army would fight with vigour and the courage of an army of robust constitution, whose ranks are completely organised; of an army composed of men jealous of their independence, who above all hold to the view that we have made treaties as a result of which we have been solemnly admitted as a free and neutral nation into the great European family[35].'

The international strains at the end of the nineteenth century would ensure that the question of the bravery and the cowardice of Belgian troops at Waterloo would reappear on the agenda. The dangers facing Belgium were bound up with the rise of Franco-German antagonism with, in the background, the risk of a war in which the country would be involved, despite its neutrality.

It was in this context that in 1899 the Minister for Foreign Affairs concluded an agreement with the British publicist Demetrius Boulger for the financing of a brochure whose aim was the rehabilitation of Belgian conduct at Waterloo. Three thousand copies of this work, *The Belgians at Waterloo*, were printed, 500 of which were presented to the principal libraries in Great Britain. Boulger's fee was 3,375 francs.

At the same time, pressure was exerted on the publishers of Baedeker's Guide to Belgium to have the malicious assertions concerning the national troops at Quatre-Bras and Waterloo corrected. The contents of the 1901 edition found favour in Belgian official quarters.

An article by the German historian, Julius von Pflugk-Harttung, *Die Verrat im Kriege 1815*, which appeared in the *Jahrbücher für die deutsche Armee und Marine* in July 1903, rekindled the controversy; this time, it was from the German side that the Belgians were presented as traitors and cowards.

Once more, it became necessary to mount a defence of national honour, to which was added an underlying warning against any violation of Belgian neutrality, which would be vigorously opposed by a nation both courageous and determined.

Offers of assistance from Colonel J de Bas, Director of Archives at the Netherlands War Department, who had already had some contact with Baron Lambermont on the subject in 1900, were accepted. For his services, the historian received a fee of 8,000 francs, part of which was carefully hidden behind some inoffensive items in the budget of the Ministry for Foreign Affairs, while the rest was paid out of secret funds, as the Belgian government did not wish to be seen as the instigator of the work.

General the Count T'Serclaes de Wommersom, Inspector-General of Infantry, patriotically agreed to be its co-signatory, since it was necessary for the work to appear as a joint Belgian-Dutch effort, and he bore the costs of publication.

The book was published in 1909, in three volumes. It was widely distributed in Germany, through the good offices of the Belgian Minister in Berlin, who sent copies to most of the major newspapers. The purpose behind it was to persuade German opinion that, in the event of aggression, the Belgians would defend themselves with vigour.

23. WATERLOO HISTORIOGRAPHY

This chapter takes the place of the usual bibliography, since the majority of the works referenced in this book have been cited in the footnotes.

Is this a historiography or a mythology of Waterloo? The question arises because it indicates at what point the desire to emphasise the decisive role of this or that participant appears like a watermark in the writings of Waterloo's historians.

The main body of the historical studies of the 1815 campaign was produced in the nineteenth century and it was during those years that the controversies about the causes of the French defeat and the respective roles of the British and Prussian armies first saw the light of day.

In France, the first works, essentially documentary or narrative, were those of A de Beauchamp: *Histoire des campagnes de 1814 et de 1815* (Paris, 1816, 4 volumes; J B Berton: *Précis historique, militaire et critique des batailles de Fleurus et de Waterloo en 1815* (Paris, 1818); and General de Vaudoncourt: *Histoire des campagnes de 1814 et de 1815 en France* (Paris, 1826, Brussels 1827, 5 volumes).

The controversy, still alive today, concerning responsibility for the defeat, was begun by the counsel for the defence – directly inspired by Napoléon – his companion in exile, Gourgaud, in *La campagne de 1815 ou relation des opérations qui ont eu lieu en France et en Belgique pendant les Cent-Jours* (Paris, 1818). The Emperor's allegations against his lieutenants were repeated in *Les Mémoires historiques de Napoléon. 1815* (London, 1820).

Marshal Grouchy, one of those accused, replied to the allegations against him from his own exile in America in *Observations sur la campagne de 1815 publiées par le général Gourgaud* (Philadelphia, 1818).

The controversy was further nourished by General Gérard, who published his own reply: *Quelques documents sur la bataille de Waterloo propres à éclairer la question portée devant le public par Monsieur le marquis de Grouchy* (Paris-Brussels, 1829).

The final shot in the quarrel between the two men was fired by Marshal Grouchy's son: *Campagne de 1815. Fragments historiques* (Paris, 1840).

In his major work, *Histoire du Consulat et de l'Empire*, Adolphe Thiers devoted the last volume to Waterloo, endorsing the Napoléonic version of the campaign (Paris, 1855).

In *Histoire de la campagne de 1815 – Waterloo*, published in Brussels in 1857 by Lieutenant-Colonel Charras, a republican officer exiled by Napoléon III, the events were treated in a totally different manner. In this work, the Napoléonic version was for the first time subjected to minute scrutiny.

The philosopher Edgard Quinet, one of the leading moral authorities of the republican party and also exiled by the Second Empire, took up the baton with his *Histoire de la campagne de 1815* (Paris, 1862), in which he rationalised the analyses of Charras and reopened the debate on the Bonapartist legend.

The study of the history of the campaign was resumed at the end of the nineteenth century by the Academician Henry Houssaye. Literary and art critic, classical scholar and eclectic spirit, he published, beginning in 1895, a three-volume work, *1815*, which met with enormous success. The second volume, devoted to Waterloo, had in 1903 reached its 41st edition and his disciple, Louis Madelin, estimated its total print-run to be 70,000 copies, exceptional for those days[36]. Very well documented, with the text supported by numerous footnotes, it presented an inspirational description of the battle which was both nationalist and favourable to Napoléon. Its conclusions contain the following illuminating assertion: 'When a country [France] withstands such catastrophes on so many occasions, when it triumphs over such crises, it shows that it possesses a miraculous vitality and unbelievable reserves of strength and energy […] How can the destiny of a people be doubted who, for ten centuries, have experienced one revival after another?' Such expression of nationalistic faith was probably born of the trauma from which French public opinion was still suffering after Sedan and Fashoda.

In Great Britain, Wellington's decisive victory engendered the publication of many works which, from the beginning, included a number of descriptions of visits to the battlefield.

In 1817, the first historical accounts of the battle appeared in London. Amongst these should be cited the work of W Mudford, *An historical account of the Campaign in the Netherlands. 1815*, interesting above all for its illustration, made on the spot by J Rouse on the day after the battle, and that of J Booth, *Additional particulars to the battle of Waterloo*, which is more of a compilation of documents than a structured history of the battle.

The outstanding work of all the British historical records is that by Captain William Siborne. On 18 May 1830, he was given the task by the British government of carrying out a survey of the Waterloo battlefield. Having completed his official assignment, he used the topographical data which he had collected to produce a model of the battlefield in relief, to a scale of 1/600. The model is 6.4 m long and 5.5 m wide and it covers an area of approximately 35 sq m. It represents the positions of the armies at 7.45 pm, at the moment when the Imperial Guard was being thrown back.

In order to gather all his information, Siborne was authorised to send to all the surviving officers a questionnaire from which he could discover the positions of their units at that time. The model was constructed several years later. This drawing in relief – diorama it would be called today, populated with nearly 150,000 tiny figures 3 mm high, was exhibited in London and in all the large towns in Britain. In 1851, it was purchased from Siborne for 40,000 francs collected by public subscription and presented to the Royal United Service Institution. For a long time it was on show in Whitehall and then at Woolwich. It is now in the National Army Museum in London.

Several years later Siborne made a second model along the same lines, this one being of the start of the battle, at the moment when the British heavy cavalry charged the columns of Drouet d'Erlon. This latter model is preserved in Dover Castle.

The documentation collected by Siborne was extensive, for many officers had not restricted themselves to answering his questionnaire, but described at length the roles and the movements of their units since 15 June. He had received 499 replies, representing 2,502 folios of letters, reports and cards, which are currently preserved in the British Museum[37]. From all these items he was able to publish *A History of the War in France & Belgium in 1815* (London, 1851, 2 volumes), which of all the British historical records remains essential reading.

The son of William Siborne, Major-General H T Siborne, published in 1891 a selection of 180 letters, the most interesting of the replies, under the title of *Waterloo Letters*. Today this book still remains a first-class research source. The same may be said of the publishing by John Gurwood of the *Dispatches of Field Marshal the Duke of Wellington*, (12 volumes, London, 1837-1839).

Among the copious literature which appeared in Great Britain in the nineteenth century, mention must also be made of the essay by General Sir James Shaw Kennedy, *Notes on the Battle of Waterloo* (London, 1865), both analysis and testimony, since the author held the post of chief of staff in Alten's division on 18 June 1815.

The Waterloo Lectures, by Lieutenant-Colonel Charles C Chesney (London, 1868), take the form of a critical study of the campaign, challenging the arguments upheld by the principal British and French historians.

Also to be mentioned is the book by George Hooper, *Waterloo. The Downfall of the First Napoleon* (London, 1861), and that of the American, John Codman Ropes, *The Campaign of Waterloo* (New York, 1891).

It was in Brussels, in 1815, that the first serious work dealing with the battle appeared. In July, Guillaume-Benjamin Craan, the engineer responsible for checking the cadastral survey of South Brabant, drew up a precise plan of the battlefield and then carried out an inquiry among the Allied officers or those French who were prisoners, to discover the positions and the movements of their units in the course of 18 June. The result was a magnificent map[38], accompanied by a *Notice historique sur la bataille de Waterloo dite de la Belle Alliance*, which remains a document of fundamental importance for historians. It was also translated into English by Captain Arthur Gore, under the title *An Account of the Battle of Waterloo* (London, 1817).

In the following year, 1816, Jacobus Scheltema published in Amsterdam *The Laatste Veldtogt van Napoleon Bonaparte*, which was to a large extent written from information supplied by Lieutenant-Colonel P van Hooff, who had taken part in the campaign as adjutant to the Prince of Orange.

In 1842, a Dutch officer, Emmanuel van Löben Sels, ADC to Prince Frederick of the Netherlands, published at The Hague *Bijdragen tot de Krijgsgeschiedenis van Napoleon Bonaparte. Vierde deel. Veldtogten van 1814 in Frankrijk en van 1815 in de Nederlanden*, a French translation of which, *Précis de la campagne de 1815 dans les Pays-Bas*, also appeared in The Hague in 1849. It contains the account of Baron de Constant de Rebecque, chief of staff of the Dutch army.

The criticisms expressed by Siborne concerning the courage of the Dutch troops succeeded in arousing the same strong reactions in Holland as they did in Belgium. To restore their reputation, W J Knoop published *Krijgsgeschiedkundige geschriften. Beschouwingen over Sibornes geschiedenis van der Oorlog van 1815 in Frankrijk en de Nederlanden* (Breda, 1846), followed by *Quatre-Bras en Waterloo* ('S Hertogenbosch, 1855).

From the Belgian side, General Renard, with his *Réponse aux allégations anglaises sur la conduite des troupes belges en 1815* (Brussels, 1855) and Lieutenant-General A Eenens, in his *Dissertation sur la participation des troupes des Pays-Bas à la campagne de 1815 en Belgique* (Ghent, 1879), defended vigorously, though without great objectivity, the conduct of their compatriots at Waterloo.

Also part of this nationalistic and chauvinist flood was a book by Louis Navez, *Les Belges à Waterloo* (Brussels, 1900). This prolific writer published several other works concerning the events of 1815, their recurrent themes leaving an impression of constant repetition. The mindset of Navez, conservative and patriot, is illustrated by the sentence: 'Our country has existed for eighty years solely because it possesses first-class fortresses and a good army, Belgium having always been a breeding ground of distinguished officers and excellent soldiers[39].' As a declared militarist, Louis Navez also wrote: 'It would be wrong to hide battles behind a cloak of silence. On the contrary, war must be treated with respect and we must glorify those great and decisive days, because war is a source of the highest virtues and, in present circumstances, provides the best possible sanction of justice[40].'

The work by J de Bas and J de T'Serclaes Wommerson, *La campagne de 1815 aux Pays-Bas* has already been mentioned.

The writings by Winand Aerts represent the best of the Belgian historical records during this era. *Waterloo. Opérations de l'armée prussienne du Bas-Rhin pendant la campagne de 1815 en Belgique* (Brussels, 1908) and *Études relatives à la campagne de 1815 en Belgique*, with co-author Jules Delhaize (Tome I only published, Brussels, 1915), are remarkable books, for which a very extensive range of documents was consulted.

With regard to the Prussians, the first work to appear was that of Carl von Plotho, *Der Krieg der Verbundeten Europas gegen Frankreich im Jahre 1815* (Berlin, 1818). This consisted of a description and a general study of the campaign which also covered the march on Paris.

The work by Johan Wagner, who had been attached to Gneisenau's general headquarters, *Recueil des plans de combats et de batailles livrés par l'armée prussienne pendant les campagnes des années 1813, 1814 et 1815 avec des éclaircissements historiques*, also contains first-hand information, thanks to the post held by the author. The fourth part, covering 1815, was published simultaneously in French and German (Berlin, 1825).

The interest of the work by Carl von Damitz, *Geschichte des Feldzuges von 1815 in dern Niederlanden und Frankreich, als Beitrag zur Kriegsgeschichte der neuen Kriege* (Berlin, 1837-1838, 2 volumes), with a French translation (Paris, 1840-1842), lies in his collaboration with Major-General von Grolman, Gneisenau's deputy.

The memoirs of Friedrich-Carl von Müffling, who was attached to Wellington's headquarters as the Prussian liaison officer, *Aus meinem Leben* (Berlin, 1842), supplement the officer's first publication, which appeared simultaneously in French and German under the title *Histoire de la campagne des armées anglo-batave et prussienne en 1815* (Stuttgart, 1817).

The following works fall within the German tradition of historical records based on precise information drawn from Prussian military archives:

– Karl Rudolf von Ollech: *Geschichte des Feldzuges von 1815 nach archivalischen Quellen* (Berlin, 1876).

– Julius von Pflugk-Harttung: *Vorgeschichte der Schlacht bei Belle-Alliance-Wellington* (Berlin, 1903) and *Von Wavre bis Belle-Alliance* (18 Juni 1815) (Berlin, 1908).

– Oskar von Lettow Vorbeck: *Napoleons Untergang 1815* (Berlin, 1904-1906, 2 volumes).

These authors draw attention to Wellington's slowness to react on 15 June and his ambiguous promises to Blücher before the Battle of Ligny.

While the inter-war period did not see the emergence of works of any significance, after the Second World War, a quickening of interest is in evidence. A number of works made their appearance after 1945. Of these, we need only be concerned with the most noteworthy publications, on account of either the quality of their prose or their understanding of the events and the range of their references. As with any selection, the following choice, being subjective, is not invulnerable to criticism. Of the works in French, the following make the list:

Commandant Henry Lachouque: *Le Secret de Waterloo* (Paris, 1952), well-written, but self-indulgently picturesque and sometimes containing information of doubtful reliability.

Robert Marguerit: *Waterloo. 18 juin 1815* (Paris, 1964), very well documented and discusses the role played in the Emperor's mind by the erroneous analysis of the victory at Ligny and of the quality of the British troops.

The English writer of German extraction, Peter Hofschröer, in his 2-volume work, *1815. The Waterloo Campaign* (London, 1998-1999), has assembled a considerable mass of documentation, including not only published sources, but unpublished archives as well, both English and Prussian. His criticism of Wellington's stance, drawn from Prussian historical records, found little approval on the British side[41].

The American Jac Weller, with his *Wellington at Waterloo* (London, 1967), reveals a critical view of the conduct of the three armies, without neglecting the technical aspects of war in 1815.

The book by David Howarth, *A Near Run Thing* (London, 1968 and published in New York the same year with the title *Waterloo. The Day of Battle*), gives the traditional British view of the battle, in which Wellington plays the essential role.

The publication edited by Lord Chalfont, *Waterloo. Battle of Three Armies* (London, 1979), is written by three historians: William Seymour (English), Jacques Champagne (French) and Colonel E Kaulbach (German). It offers the original aspect of an exposition by the three nationalities.

Waterloo: The Hundred Days (London, 1980), from the pen of David Chandler, gives a standard, though very comprehensive description of the Hundred Days and the 1815 campaign, placed in a European perspective.

The book by David Hamilton Williams, *Waterloo – New Perspectiv:. The Great Battle Reappraised* (London, 1993), represents a discordant voice in British historical records, by its criticism of the work and objectivity of William Siborne. The attitudes assumed by this author carry little conviction.

24. WATERLOO IN LITERATURE

Naturally enough, it was in the victors' camp that the Battle of Waterloo was first celebrated[42].

The first British writer to focus his attention on the subject was Sir Walter Scott (1771-1832), who visited the battlefield in the course of a journey through Belgium in the autumn of 1815. In epistolary form, as *Paul's Letters to his Kinsfolk*, the author describes a long tour which he took to Brussels and Paris. The work appeared anonymously in 1816 and was not published under Scott's name until 1822.

The use of letters to give an account of a journey was a device much favoured at that time. Of the sixteen letters composing the book, six are devoted to a description of the campaign and to the visit to the battlefield. The account is interesting, very lively and reliable. Scott reports that an English tourist in his party has purchased the gate to La Belle Alliance for twenty francs. The author is well-informed and undoubtedly interrogated officers who took part in the fighting. The book is documentary, rather than a poetic or romantic work. It should also be mentioned that Scott wrote *The Battle of Waterloo*, a grandiloquent and turgid ode, dedicated to the Duchess of Wellington. It was not a success and has rightly been forgotten.

The dramatist, poet and traveller, Robert Southey (1774-1843), whose talents had been marked in 1812 by his appointment as Poet Laureate, also came to Waterloo in 1815 and, the following year, published *The Poet's Pilgrimage to Waterloo*. The first part of this work describes a visit to the battlefield; the second, in allegorical form, describes the philosophical principles which the author had found in French political life, from Mirabeau to Bonaparte. This book, which Southey himself in his introduction described as an occasional work, is of only minor literary interest.

The poet, George Gordon, Lord Byron (1788-1824), in his famous work *Childe Harold's Pilgrimage*, also evoked Waterloo. The publication in February 1812 of the first two cantos of this classic work of English literature made him famous overnight. Four years later, following the failure of his marriage to Anne Milbanke, Byron left England for good. In May 1816, during a stay in Belgium, he visited the battlefield. According to some accounts, canto III of *Childe Harold* was written in Brussels, whilst he was lodging at the house of a compatriot on the rue Ducale. It is more likely that he composed it in Switzerland a few months later. It made its appearance in November 1816.

Verses XXI to XXXV are devoted to the Duchess of Richmond's ball, Quatre-Bras and Waterloo. In them, Byron, who had Scottish roots, evokes the part played by the Cameron Highlanders and the memory of Major Howard who was killed at Waterloo, the son of his tutor Lord Carlisle. It includes the celebrated image of the Duke of Brunswick, raised to the status of romantic hero as, at the Duchess of Richmond's ball, he foresees his own death:

> 'Within a window'd niche of that high hall
> Sate Brunswick's fated chieftain ; he did hear
> That sound the first amidst the festival,
> And caught its tone with Death's prophetic ear ;
> And when they smiled because he deem'd it near,
> His heart more truly knew that peal too well
> Which stretched his father on a bloody bier,
> And roused the vengeance blood alone could quell ;
> He rushed into the field and, foremost fighting, fell.

In verses XXVI to XLI, Napoléon takes the stage, presented by Byron in a light very different from that adopted by his contemporaries. Bonaparte is not described as the *Ogre of Corsica* and the implacable enemy of the human race. Rather is it a portrait of light and shade:

There sunk the greatest, nor the worst of men,
Whose spirit, antithetically mixt,
One moment of the mightiest, and again
On little objects with like firmness fixt ;
Extreme in all things! hadst thou been betwixt,
Thy throne had still been thine, or never been;
For daring made thee rise as fall: thou seekst
Even now to re-assume the imperial mien,
And shake again the world, the Thunderer of the scene !

Vanity Fair, published in 1847 by William Makepeace Thackeray (1811-1863), is the author's masterpiece and one of the greatest of English novels. It is a social satire and a panorama of English society at the time of the Napoléonic Wars. It is also the story of two women, Rebecca Sharp and Amelia Sedley, whose husbands, Rawdon Crawley and George Osborne, fight in the Waterloo campaign, the latter being killed. More than an account of the conflicts at Quatre-Bras and Waterloo, the book takes time to describe the Belgium of 1815 and the reactions of its people towards the wounded.

Thackeray was writing several years after the publication, in 1844, of William Siborne's monumental work, *History of the War in France and Belgium in 1815*. This echoed the accusations of cowardice levelled against the Dutch-Belgian regiments by certain British officers. Thackeray passed on these criticisms by creating the character of a Belgian hussar, Regulus Van Cutsem, who lost no time in deserting the moment his regiment found itself in action at Quatre-Bras: 'The young man knew his duty as a soldier too well not to obey immediately the order "every man for himself" given by his colonel.'

Vanity Fair remains a great work and the account is factually well founded, although Thackeray did not visit the battlefield until the year after the book appeared. It is certainly authentic in its descriptions of Brussels and Belgium, with the military point of view assuming only secondary importance.

In 1903 Thomas Hardy published the verse drama *The Dynasts: An Epic Drama of the War with Napoleon*. With its vast field of reference and cast of 'supernatural spectators', it is as well that Hardy confesses in the preface that it was never meant to be performed, only read. Some of the stage directions would have been challenging: 'Thereupon a vision passes before Napoléon as he lies, [at Charleroi] comprising hundreds of thousands of skeletons and corpses in various stages of decay. They rise from his various battlefields, the flesh dropping from them, and gaze reproachfully at him. His intimate officers who have been slain he recognizes among the crowd. In front is the Duke of Enghien as showman.' (Act Six, scene III.)

Another great name in English literature who dramatised the men of Waterloo was Sir Arthur Conan Doyle (1859-1930). In *The Great Shadow* (1892), two Scottish volunteers take part in the battle in the ranks of Adams' brigade. The plot is based on the rivalry in love between one of the heroes, Jim Horscroft, and a colonel of the Guard, de Lissac. The latter had seduced and married Horscroft's fiancée, while he was taking refuge in England after the fall of the Empire. The descriptions of the events preceding the campaign and of the fighting on 18 June are vivid, colourful and authentic. This agreeably written little book is still worth reading.

In 1896, Doyle published *The Exploits of Brigadier Gerard*, followed by *The Adventures of Gerard*. Étienne Gérard, the hero chosen by Doyle, had taken part in nearly all the Empire's campaigns. At Waterloo, as a colonel, he is one of Napoléon's ADCs. The latter dispatches him to Grouchy to ask him to bring his troops, but Gérard's mission is rendered impossible when he runs into the Prussian columns marching from Saint-Lambert to Plancenoit. Gérard intercepts some secret instructions given by Gneisenau to a Prussian officer to capture Napoléon. Doyle's hero moves to frustrate this plan, passing through the Prussian columns and the retreating French army in order to warn the Emperor. By a subterfuge, he manages to snuff out the danger and save Napoléon. In this account, there is little or no description of the battle, the main outlines of which are taken from Thiers and Houssaye. The adventures of Gérard are simply an adventure story placed in an historical context.

In France, the first author to be inspired by the battle of 18 June 1815 was Casimir Delavigne (1793-1843), who in 1816 published a poem of two hundred and fifty verses with the title *Waterloo*. Hopefully this work is not the most outstanding of the writer's output, judging by its bellicose and nationalist tone:

'France, réveille-toi, qu'un courroux unanime
Enfante des guerriers autour du souverain.
Divisés, désarmés, le vainqueur nous opprime.
Présentons-lui la paix, les armes à la main…'

In 1825, the song-writer Pierre-Jean de Béranger (1780-1857), prosecuted and convicted for his hostility to the Restoration, readily harked back to the glorious days of the

Unsigned lithograph. Musée Wellington, Waterloo

Hôtel des Colonnes
à Mont-Saint-Jean

With Les Misérables *and* Les Châtiments, *Victor Hugo devoted a significant part of his writing to the battle on 18 June, playing an important role in the creation of the myths of Waterloo, even though, during his first stay in Belgium in 1837, he declined to visit the battlefield.*

'I considered it pointless to pay this visit to Lord Wellington,' he wrote to his wife, 'Waterloo is more abhorrent to me than Crécy. It was not only the victory of Europe over France, it was the triumph – complete, absolute, brilliant, indisputable, definitive and sovereign – of mediocrity over genius'.

In 1861, while he was completing Les Misérables, *he stayed at the Hôtel des Colonnes, on the Mont-Saint-Jean crossroads. He resided there from 7 May until 14 July and with unwearying devotion crisscrossed what he would call the "dismal plain". 'I spent two months at Waterloo,' he wrote. 'It was there that I carried out my autopsy on the catastrophe, spending two months bent over the corpse'. The Hôtel des Colonnes was compulsorily purchased in 1954 and, despite protests from intellectual circles, pulled down to make way for highway improvements.*

Revolution and, above all, the Empire, comparing them with the regime of the Bourbons. He remembered Napoléon's last campaign in *Couplets sur la bataille de Waterloo*. These lines define the mood:

'Le géant tombe et ces nains sans mémoire
À l'esclavage ont voué l'univers.'

In 1829, Auguste-Marseille Barthélemy (1796-1867) and Joseph Méry (1798-1866) published *Waterloo, au général Bourmont*, a poem both epic and satirical, exalting the Emperor, ridiculing his enemies, glorifying the dead and lashing traitors such as Bourmont:

'Quatorze ans ne font point oublier ces forfaits
La peine se prescrit, et la honte jamais.'

Of a quite different stature was the first major work of fiction to have Waterloo for its background, *La chartreuse de Parme* (1839). In this great novel, Henri-Marie Beyle, better known as Stendhal (1783-1842), combined his love of Italy, his admiration for Napoléon and his nostalgia for the Empire, the fall of which had constituted an obstacle to his career.

Stendhal had not visited Waterloo and never did. Clearly, through his whimsical but famous description of the fighting, he wanted to point up the artificiality and inaccuracy of the usual descriptions of the battle. He showed that the development of the fighting is practically incomprehensible for those taking part. The writer therefore drew on his own memories of the Battle of Bautzen, at which he had been present without taking part. He noted in his diary: 'We see very well everything that can be seen of a battle, in other words nothing.' His hero, Fabrice del Dongo, was present at Waterloo, as an onlooker, lost in the smoke, deafened by the firing and caught up in the total confusion. There was no question of historical or topographical veracity, Stendhal described not Waterloo but a battle, and on that basis it mattered little to him whether or not there was a canal running across the battlefield, provided that his hero's horse could splash around in it.

Very different was the approach taken by Victor Hugo (1802-1885). At Brussels, where he had taken refuge after the *coup d'état* of 2 December 1851, he wrote *Histoire d'un crime* and *Napoléon-le-Petit*. Contrary to a persistent myth, during this first stay he did not visit the battlefield[43].

At the end of 1852 he wrote the celebrated and marvellous *Waterloo, morne plaine*, which was published several months later in *Les Châtiments*, a collection of poems attacking the grandeur of Napoléon III's Second Empire.

He returned to Belgium in March 1861 from Guernsey, where most of *Les Misérables* had been written; however, in order to write the long chapter devoted to Waterloo, from May to July Hugo took up residence at the Hôtel des Colonnes at Mont-Saint-Jean. 'I spent two months at Waterloo. It was there that I carried out my autopsy on the catastrophe, spending two months bent over the corpse'. From this intimate and prolonged contact with the 'dismal plain' a masterpiece was born.

The main plot is merely a pretext to allow a description of the fighting to be introduced. The battle itself is the principal subject and from the pen of the great poet it becomes an epic, a *chanson de geste*. Certainly, poetic licence prevails over historical accuracy, but the events are described with scrupulous care and in chronological order, without loitering at a hero's pace, unless it is Napoléon's.

The fabulous imagination of Victor Hugo has given rise to persistent myths which for many have, through the magic of his pen, become the truth: the sunken road, grave of the French cavalry; the well at Goumont, that improbable ossuary; etc.

Nearly twenty years later, while the Prussians were besieging Paris, he dedicated to the Waterloo Lion his poem *L'avenir*, which ended with a message of peace:

'De sentir un esprit profonde me visiter
Et peuples, je compris que j'entendais chanter
L'espoir dans ce qui fut le désespoir naguère
Et la paix dans la gueule horrible de la guerre.'

When Victor Hugo laments the defeat of Waterloo, he seeks, while magnifying the memory of the uncle, to humiliate the nephew, while also expressing his nostalgia for a time when the writ of Paris ran throughout Europe. A verse from the poem *Au moment de rentrer en France (31 août 1870)* captures some of this dichotomy:

'Je vois en même temps le meilleur et le pire;
Noir tableau!
Car La France mérite Austerlitz, et l'Empire
Waterloo.'

This train of thought also found its expression in two authors whose collaboration made them seem as one, Émile Erckmann

(1822-1899) and Alexandre Chatrian (1826-1890). Their series of so-called 'national' novels, *Le fou Yégof* (1862), *Madame Thérèse ou les Voluntaires de 1792* (1863) and *Histoire d'un conscrit de 1813* (1864), drew their inspiration from the years of Revolution and the Empire and were marked by the most fervent seal of patriotism. *Waterloo* (1866) is the sequel to *Histoire d'un conscrit de 1813* and tells of the last campaign of a soldier from Lorraine, Joseph Bertha. These novels enjoyed very great popularity. Writing simply, very far from the lyrical flights of Victor Hugo, Erckmann and Chatrian bring alive the skirmishes and perils just as they were experienced by the fighting men. The research is correct and the descriptions true to life. From the pen of these authors, it is a Napoléon who defends the Republic's achievements, the national soil and the honour of France, who appears in their pages.

In the nineteenth century, many other French writers demonstrated their interest in Waterloo by exploring the battle site: Joseph Proudhon (1858), Charles Baudelaire (1864), Verlaine and Rimbaud (1872). Some left accounts of their visits: Alexandre Dumas (1838), Edgard Quinet (1852) and Jules Vallès (1869)[44].

In the twentieth century, few French writers chose the Battle of Waterloo for a subject. In 1937, Robert Aron, who was to write the history of France during the Second World War, imagined in *Victoire à Waterloo* that Grouchy arrived on the battlefield to join Napoléon, enabling him to win, though without changing the course of history, since the Emperor nevertheless chose to abdicate.

In 1956 René de Obaldia published *Une Fugue à Waterloo*, a short burlesque which contains only a brief glance at the battle.

Robert Marguerit, in his novel *La Terre aux Loups* (1958), which opens at the start of the nineteenth century, has his hero, Lucien de Montalbert, participating in the battle. His descriptions of the fighting are similar to those by Stendhal.

In the case of Belgian writers, there was no likelihood that they would refrain from invoking memories of 1815.

Joseph Lemayeur, with his *Ode sur la bataille de Waterloo* (1816), composed a work suited to the event, celebrating the Allied victory in grandiloquent and laudatory verse. In the same vein and appearing in the same year is *La Belle Alliance, ode dédiée à S.A.R. la Princesse d'Orange*, by Cocquebeau, alias Bouqueau, one of the sons of the farmer who owned Le Caillou Farm. Only their historical notes, which contain various details of a first-hand nature, are now of any interest.

In 1903, the diplomat, later turned militant Walloon, Albert du Bois (1872-1940) published *Waterloo: Belge ou Français*. This novel features a native of Nivelles, Louis Hévellard, a former officer in the Imperial Guard, who rejoins Napoléon's troops as a volunteer during their incursion into Belgium and takes part in the fighting. Hévellard has a counterpart in the form of an NCO from Brussels in the Dutch army, Van Cutsem (a clear reference to Thackeray's work), who suffers a thousand insults in his unit, because he is not Flemish. In a book that is more political than romantic, the author deplores the subservience of the Walloons to the Flemings and does not hide his belief that Wallonia should be part of France[45].

Albert Bailly (1866-1978) is the author of a novel, *Au service de la France* (1921), which also portrays Belgians who joined Napoléon's army during the 1815 campaign. While the author's sympathies are firmly with the Belgians who chose to serve France, the book's tone is much less polemical than that of Albert du Bois and the writing is more accomplished.

Other Belgian writers have tackled the Waterloo theme, but in the form of historical fiction.

With Marcel Thiry (1897-1977) and his *Échec au temps*, the battle becomes the theme of a science fiction novel. The author imagines that Napoléon has won, Wellington having retired before Blücher's arrival. A young British doctor conceives the notion of rehabilitating his great-grandfather, an aide-de-camp to the Duke, who had omitted to report the timely approach of the Prussian troops. He invents a kind of television which, under the control of its viewers, can capture the past, enabling his ancestor to rectify his error and notify Wellington. The latter calls off the retreat, leading to the French defeat as a result.

The play by Robert Merget (1907-1974), *La prise de Bruxelles, 19 juin 1815* (1970) imagines that Grouchy has won the fight at Wavre and occupies Brussels, where he frees the prisoners captured at Waterloo.

In *La Mort de Napoléon* (1986), Pierre Ryckmans, alias Simon Leys and a Chinese scholar of distinction, imagines that the Emperor escapes from Saint Helena and visits the battlefield incognito.

So far as Germany is concerned, to our knowledge no romantic or poetic work, directly inspired by the Battle of Waterloo, has appeared in that country.

25. WATERLOO IN THE CINEMA

Of the many films featuring Napoléon, several have depicted the Battle of Waterloo[46]. From the days of the silent screen, there are four films which merit our attention.

Two of them, *Un épisode de Waterloo* and *Le Baiser de l'Empereur*, were both shot in 1913, partly in the studio and partly in the historic locations, by the Belgian film-maker Alfred Machin. Among the cast were Fernand Cromelynck and Cécile May. An article in the newspaper *L'Étoile belge* of 9 August 1912 describes amusing incidents during the shooting of *Un épisode de Waterloo* at Goumont farm[47].

The Battle of Waterloo (1913), by Charles Weston, was a prestigious re-creation which was the first British film spectacular. It was shot in the studio at East Finchley and on location in the flat country of Northamptonshire and drew large audiences. Ernest G Batley played Napoléon, George Folet was Marshal Blücher and Vivian Ross was Marshal Ney.

The film of Karl Grune, *Waterloo. Eine Zeitbild*, was shot in 1928-1929 in Munich and in the Isar valley. Grune, a left-winger and a pacifist, took care not to make it a nationalistic hagiography, but its perspective is German and the role of Wellington is more or less evaded. Charles Vanel took the part of Napoléon and Otto Bebuhr was Marshal Blücher. In Germany the film was a failure; the version distributed in Switzerland was considerably longer and dwelt more on the battle scenes than the one seen in France[48].

Campo di Maggio, made in 1935 by Giovacchino Forzano and the first talking film on Waterloo, was an Italo-German co-production produced by Vittorio Mussolini, a son of *Il Duce*, and was shot by the Pisorno studios in Tirrenia and on the island of Elba. Forzano and Mussolini propagated the myth of the Titan betrayed, victim of the narrow-minded-ness and pettiness of his contemporaries, particularly when he attempted to organise the defence of the sacred soil of *La Patrie* following the defeat in Belgium – an expression of Fascist scorn for parliamentary rule.

Contrary to Karl Grune's work, the film sticks closely to the vicissitudes of the fateful 18 June. Corrado Rocca played Napoléon, with Werner Krauss in the part for the slightly shortened German version. It was extracts from this film which were shown for many years after 1945, in the small specially-equipped cinemas at the foot of the Lion mound.

Waterloo, shot in 1970 by Sergei Bondarchuk and co-produced by Dino De Laurentis, is the most spectacular example of all the films of the battle. The battle scenes were shot in the Ukraine, employing considerable resources – 16,000 soldiers of the Red Army and 3,000 Russian and Yugoslav horsemen – and completed in the studio at Cinecitta. The official cost of the production was $25 million.

Anxious to avoid historical errors, Bondarchuk staged the fighting on an extravagant scale. Christopher Plummer personified a Wellington who was elegant, haughty and phlegmatic, on watch for the errors of Napoléon, played by Rod Steiger. The latter had chosen to imbue his part with an interpretation that was perhaps eccentric and somewhat over-acted. Indecisive, choleric, turgid, perspiring, bespectacled and badly shaven – this is far from the traditional image of the Emperor. The film itself, despite its undeniable qualities, such as the remarkable depiction of the British squares surrounded by a whirlpool of French cavalry, filmed from a helicopter, was a resounding failure, earning scarcely one million four hundred thousand dollars.

More documentary and scientific in nature were *Waterloo: 1815* by Jacques Dupont (1977), in the Great Battles of the

The advance of the Old Guard, a scene from the film *Waterloo* by Sergei Bondarchuk (1970)

Past series by Henri de Turenne and Daniel Costelle, with interviews, documents and film clips; and the video *Les Cent Jours et Waterloo* by Jean-Paul Sfey (1995), produced to coincide with the one hundred and eightieth anniversary of the battle and employing 3,000 extras to re-enact some of its scenes.

26. ENGLISH AND FRENCH PAINTERS OF WATERLOO

Before Waterloo, few English artists had devoted themselves to the painting of military subjects[49], whereas French painters had been frequently employed by monarchs and by Napoléon to embellish their image[50]. The unpopularity of the genre was a result of the low esteem in which the Royal Academy held this kind of painting.

It was pressure from the British Institution for the Promotion of the Fine Arts, founded in 1805, that brought pictures celebrating doughty deeds and military glory out of the shadows. At the exhibition organised by that body in 1815, fourteen of the fifteen painters represented devoted their work to the Waterloo campaign.

The first prize went to John Ward, Member of the Royal Academy, for an allegorical work representing the Genius of Wellington. The works of the other painters, however, showed a more realistic tendency, with depictions of the battle that would prove more popular in the decades to come.

George Jones was one of the most prolific military painters of his era. Profiting from considerable personal experience, having, as a captain in the South Devon militia, been a member of the occupying troops in Paris in 1815, he produced the *Battle of Waterloo*, which he sold for 500 pounds[51].

Among the exhibitors were Luke Clennell, a painter of animals and engraver, who painted *Sauve qui peut*, depicting the charge of the Life Guards at the start of the battle; and Abraham Cooper, who painted *The Battle of Ligny*, purchased by the Duke of Marlborough for hanging at Blenheim.

Denis Dighton was a protégé of the Prince Regent, who sent him to Belgium during the summer of 1815, where he drew the inspiration for his own *Battle of Waterloo*, exhibited in 1816 and depicting the charge of the Marquis of Anglesey.

In 1818, William Turner, who had visited the battlefield the previous year, painted *The fields of Waterloo*, directly inspired by Byron's romantic verses[52].

The picture by David Wilkie, *Chelsea Pensioners reading the Waterloo Despatch*, commissioned by the Duke of Wellington, met with great success in 1822. (Wilkie had originally been asked by the Duke simply for a painting of old soldiers outside a public house; his interpretation of the commission was therefore extremely clever.)

However, during the three decades after Waterloo, military painting did not succeed in crossing the threshold of the Royal Academy – with the sole exception of George Jones, who remains the great artist of Waterloo. His works not only betray a propagandist aspect – in which he resembles Gros, the painter of Napoléon's battles – but also a topographical fidelity which gives an illusion of reality.

The restoration and embellishment of the Palace of Westminster, destroyed by a fire in 1834, offered a new opportunity for British military painting devoted to the subject of Waterloo. A great contest was held, ending in 1847, which produced a number of important pictures.

Although the work by Maclise showing *The meeting of Wellington and Blücher at La Belle Alliance* was the only one to be hung in the Palace, the occasion gave rise to the painting of two major pictures.

William Allen painted *The Battle of Waterloo, 18 June 1815, from the French side* (1843) and Thomas Sidney Cooper offered *The defeat of Kellermann's cuirassiers and carabiniers* (1847), which he took from Siborne's model[53]. These two high-quality works were not chosen for hanging at Westminster.

Chelsea Pensioners reading the Waterloo Despatch. Oil on canvas by Sir David Wilkie. The Wellington Museum, Apsley House, London.

The period from 1874 to 1914 witnessed a fascination with battle scenes. The painter who was most representative of the era was Elizabeth Thomson, Lady Butler, who was the artist of the age of British imperialism *par excellence* and may be considered as the founder of the modern English school of military painting.

Those were the days when the army, the regiment and the flag were embedded in the mythology of the ruling classes; and they could use these concepts either to deify or dehumanise men. The place occupied by Lady Butler is all the more surprising in such a masculine culture and age. Her vision of war conformed to that of her era and her background: 'My own notion of war', she wrote, 'is that it calls upon the highest and the most profound impulses in human nature.'

The vitality of *The charge of the Scots Greys* and the energy of *The 69th Regiment at Quatre-Bras* are balanced by the melancholy of *The Dawn at Waterloo*.

The battles of the Waterloo campaign are central to the nostalgia about military history pertaining at the end of the nineteenth century. At the 1897 Salon of the Royal Academy, no less than eleven pictures found their inspiration there. Amongst the most well-known painters of that time were Stanley Berkeley and Ernest Crofts – considered as the imitators of Lady Butler – William Wollen, Robert Hillingford and Richard Caton Woodville.

There were few French paintings depicting Waterloo until the end of the nineteenth century. However, the first to appear was in 1817, the lithograph by Charlet, *The grenadier of Waterloo*, after which one had to wait for the July monarchy before compositions in a similar vein appeared.

The first were in 1835: the celebrated lithograph of Auguste Raffet, *The retreat of the sacred battalion at Waterloo, 18 June 1815* and, at the Salon the same year, the first picture by Charles Steuben entitled *The Battle of Waterloo*.

Yet the subject remained absent from the Gallery of Battles at Versailles[54]. During the same period, Charles Langlois, a former officer who had served with the Guard at Waterloo, painted *Gravel pit at La Haie-Sainte* and *The Battle of Plancenoit*, while Hippolyte Bellangé produced a picture also called *The Battle of Waterloo*.

The military painters of the Second Empire, bent on extolling the glory of Napoléon III, held themselves aloof from the subject of Waterloo and it needed the advent of the Third Republic to once more set the paint brushes to work, particularly from 1889 onwards.

A count of the pictures to be found in the Salons from 1872 to 1914 reveals that Waterloo headed the list of subjects from the Napoléonic era, with some forty pictures[55]. Amongst them was another *Battle of Waterloo*, by Félix Philippoteaux (1874).

One of the most popular subjects were the great cavalry charges, echoing Hugo's vision and invoking more recent memories of the Battles of Reichshoffen and Rezonville, fought during the war of 1870. Another was the Last Square.

The Battle of Waterloo was also the subject of a number of panoramas, a genre much in vogue in the nineteenth century. The first to be produced was set up in London, in Leicester Square, by Henry Aston Baker in 1815. Its success was such that it made its owner's fortune, enabling him to retire in 1826.

A second panorama, by the Dutch painters Maaskamp, Moritz, Kamphuisen, Hansens and de Kruyf, was exhibited in the place Saint Michel, Brussels, in 1818.

At the end of the nineteenth century, the French painter, Charles Castellani, put a panorama representing the battle on show in premises in the Place Fontainas in Brussels, while another one was set up in Antwerp by the Belgian Charles Verlat. The vogue for these attractions lasted as late as the painting of the Panorama of Waterloo by the French artists Dumoulin, Robiquet, Malespina and Desvarreux in 1912.

27. WATERLOO'S PLACE IN EUROPEAN HISTORY

The adventure of the Hundred Days cost France very dearly. In July 1815, she was under the occupation of the coalition armies. This meant that nearly one million two hundred thousand men made regular demands on the nation in the form of requisitions[56].

In the second Treaty of Paris, signed on 20 November 1815, the Allies, driven by Prussia, imposed draconian conditions on France. The frontiers, which in 1814 had been left untouched, were brought back inside those of 1790. In the north, Philippeville and Mariembourg were transferred to the Netherlands; in the east, Sarrelouis and Sarrebruck went to Prussia; Savoy was taken by Piedmont, which also replaced France in the protectorate of Monaco.

By a military convention signed earlier, on 22 October, eighteen fortresses in the northern frontier *départements* were to be occupied by 150,000 men for at least three years; the cost of this occupation, 450 million francs per year, was to be met by France. In addition, she was required to pay the victors a war indemnity of 700 million, of which 175 million was to be devoted to the construction of a fortress barrier, notably in the Netherlands.

Another treaty was signed in Paris, also on 20 November, between Great Britain, Austria, Prussia and Russia, creating the Quadruple Alliance. It was in the nature of a defensive alliance against France, which was excluded from the treaty. It was expressly stated that any return to power by Napoléon or a member of his family would be considered a *casus belli*.

Article 6 of the treaty concerned the security of the European continent as a whole and gave rise to a new concept: the maintenance of peace by the collective action of the Great Powers. Its text is worth quoting: 'The […] contracting parties agree to hold, at specific periods […] meetings devoted to their common major interests and to the examination of measures which will be judged beneficial for the harmony and prosperity of the peoples and for the maintenance of peace.'

Various congresses were held to put this policy into effect. The congress of Aix-la-Chapelle in 1818 decided upon an end to the occupation of France, as well as its admission to the Quadruple Alliance. This congress was followed by those of Troppau (1820), Laybach (1821) and Verona (December 1822), at which authorisation was given for French intervention in Spain.

Just prior to Waterloo, on 9 June, the final transaction of the Congress of Vienna had been signed by the Powers who had signed the first Treaty of Paris in May 1814, and the other members of the Congress were invited to give their assent on 19 June 1815.

Europe, after twenty years of uninterrupted war, now found itself completely remodelled.

Out of its ashes, the kingdom of Poland was reborn, under the rule of Tsar Alexander I; Hanover, enlarged by the addition of eastern Friesland, became a kingdom under the British crown; Prussia, as well as recovering the lands to the west of the Elbe, Swedish Pomerania and Westphalia, planted its feet on the left bank of the Rhine; Sweden gained Norway; lastly, Denmark, in a territorial exchange with Prussia, combined with the duchy of Holstein.

The Confederation of the Rhine was replaced by the German Confederation, composed of independent States, joined together by a fairly loose federal relationship and with a Diet sitting in Frankfurt. Prussia and Austria each had their spheres of influence, one to the north, the other in the south. The kingdoms of Saxony and Bavaria paid for their alliance with Napoléon with the loss of parts of their territories.

The kingdom of the Netherlands saw the union of the former United Provinces with the territory of the future Belgium, under the rule of William I.

Although, in Germany, Austria recovered only the Tyrol, Voralberg and Salzburg, she reoccupied strong positions in Italy. Piedmont was returned to the King of Sardinia, who was also given Genoa, but the Venetian lands on the Po and the Adige reverted to Austria.

After the failure of Murat's attempt at Tolentino on 20 May 1815, the kingdom of Naples was returned to its old masters, the Bourbons. The Papal States were re-established in their entirety and the Duchies of Tuscany, Modena and Reggio were assigned to a Habsburg; Parma was left to the ex-Empress Marie-Louise during her lifetime, but was to be returned to Austria after her death. Switzerland, endowed with a federal pact, had its neutrality guaranteed by the Powers.

The great loser from the adventure which had begun at Valmy in 1792 was France. She found herself once more confined within the frontiers from which she had set out, notwithstanding the sacrifice of nearly a million and a half of her young men. Her status as a great European power, which had been confirmed by the Treaties of Westphalia (1648), was shattered by the rising strength of Prussia.

Half a century later, with the war of the duchies between her and Denmark in 1864, the Austro-Prussian conflict, with the Battle of Sadowa (1866), and the confrontation with France (Sedan 1870), the pre-eminence of Prussia in Europe was confirmed.

In that respect, the proclamation of the German Empire in the Hall of Mirrors at Versailles on 18 January 1871 was symbolic, for at its head was the Emperor Wilhelm I, none other than that Prince Wilhelm of Prussia who had commanded Bülow's reserve cavalry corps at Waterloo.

Nevertheless, the balance sheet of the Revolutionary years was not completely devoid of a credit side. In France, absolute monarchy belonged finally to the past, the powers of Louis XVIII, restored to the throne, remained limited by the Charter which he had granted to the French nation in 1814 and which the Allies ensured would be maintained, by the second Treaty of Paris.

It was a return to the ideals of 1789 and the time when the National Assembly had attempted to conciliate the monarchical principle with that of representation, such as to guarantee the rights and liberty of the people, 'As much against the tyranny of the mob as against that of a single man[57]'.

In Europe also, the receding tide of the French armies had left behind a profound impression of liberal ideas, the inheritance of the Revolution.

The principle of the limitation of the sovereign's powers by a constitutional charter spread to some extent everywhere. On 12 November 1815, the Tsar granted a constitution to Poland; in the following year, the Duke of Saxe-Weimar did the same for his own subjects. In 1818, the Grand Duke of Baden granted to his domains a constitutionally based representative system, as did Bavaria, based on a charter. Finally, in 1819, the King of Wurtemburg granted his people a constitutional representative system which was liberal in its nature.

However, that same year, reactionary forces led by Metternich began to gain the upper hand in the German Confederation and, the following year, right across European politics[58].

With regard to national laws, the French model of justice, based on the positive codification of laws and the setting up of a unified and rational judicial system, left indelible and lasting traces nearly everywhere in Europe[59].

NOTES

PART ONE

1. Diplomatic Note handed to the French Ambassador in London on 31 December 1793.
2. H HOUSSAYE, *1815 – Première Restauration*, Paris, 1902, 40th Edn., p.296.
3. Gunther E ROTHENBURG, *The Art of Warfare in the age of Napoleon*, Padstow, 1997, p.69.
4. *Gazette des Armes*, October 1977, n° 53, p.13-19. The French army had perfected an equivalent weapon called a *'carabine de Versailles'* since Year XII, but although its use had been mandatory since 1806, it had incurred the dislike of the line regiments, who considered it to be no more than a club once it had been discharged. It was not available to the French troops at Waterloo.
5. B P HUGHES, *La puissance de feu. L'efficacité des armes sur le champ de bataille de 1630 à 1850*. Lausanne, 1976, p.13.
6. J NAYLOR, *Waterloo*, London, 1960, p.38.
7. The expression 'oblong formation' simply means a rectangular-shaped formation with bayonets fixed.
8. The lance, as defined by the French army regulation of 5 February 1811, was 2.76 m long and weighed 1.96 kg, *Traditions*, n° 60, January 1992, p.10.
9. A BRIALMONT, *Précis d'Art Militaire*, Brussels, s.d., t.., *p.87.*
10. John KEEGAN, *Anatomie de la bataille*, Paris, 1993, p.123.
11. Alain PIGEARD, 'La garde du drapeau sous le Premier Empire', in *Traditions*, n°. 59, December 1991, p.34.
12. John KEEGAN, *op. cit.*, p.161.
13. Philip HAYTHORNTHWAITE, *Weapons & Equipment of the Napoleonic Wars*, Poole, 1979, p.141.
14. C H SCHELTENS, *Souvenirs d'un vieux soldat belge de la Garde impériale*, Brussels, 1880, p.58.
15. J B LEMONIER-DELAFOSSE, *Campagnes de 1810 à 1815*, Avray, 1850, p.386.
16. *Relation de la bataille de Mont-Saint-Jean par un témoin oculaire*, Paris, 1815, p.25.
17. WELLINGTON, *Supplementary Despatches*, Vol. XII, p.514.
18. A PIGEARD, *L'armée de Napoléon*, Paris, 2000, p.288-291.
19. WELLINGTON, *Supplementary Despatches*, Vol. X, London, 1863, p.365.
20. L STOUFF, *Le général Delort d'après ses archives et les archives du ministère de la Guerre 1792-1815*, Paris, Nancy, 1906, p.139.
21. H HOUSSAYE, *1815 – Waterloo*, Paris, 1903, 41st Edn., p.301-305.
22. *Ibidem*, p.271.
23. NAPOLÉON, *Correspondance générale*, n°. 22.042.
24. WELLINGTON, *Despatches*, Vol. VI, p.576, letter to Lord Bathurst, 2 July 1813. For the British army, see also E HALEVY, *Histoire du peuple anglais au XIXᵉ siècle*, s. l., 1973, t. I, p.63-89.
25. WELLINGTON, *Despatches*, Vol. VI, p.201, letter to Colonel Torrens, 6 December 1812.
26. Of the units recruited in Belgium, the following were present at Waterloo: n°ˢ 3 and 7 infantry battalions; n°ˢ 35 and 36 light infantry battalions; the cavalry regiments – n° 5 light dragoons, n° 2 *carabiniers* and n° 8 hussars; the Stevenart foot artillery battery and the Krahmer de Bichin horse artillery battery, making a total of 4,000 men. In the French army, the officers and men who were natives of the Belgian provinces were unequally distributed among the various units. Their precise number is unknown, but it might be imagined that it would not be greater than that of the Belgians who fought under the flag of the Netherlands. A BIKAR, 'Les Belges à Waterloo', *Revue internationale d'Histoire militaire*, n° 24, 1965, p.365-392; H J COUVREUR, *Le drame belge de Waterloo*, Brussels, 1959.
27. E OWEN, *The Waterloo Papers. 1815 and beyond*, Tavistock, 1998, p.32.
28. W AERTS, *Waterloo. Opérations de l'armée prussienne du Bas-Rhin*, Brussels, 1908, p.71.
29. P HOFSCHRÖER, *The Waterloo Campaign, Wellington, his German Allies and the Battles of Ligny au Quatre-Bras*, London, 1998, p.116.
30. H HOUSSAYE, *1815 – Waterloo*, Paris, 1903, 41st Edn., p.107.
31. WELLINGTON, *Dispatches*, Vol. XII, p.462, letter to Lord Lynedoch, 13 June 1815.
32. The details of the information gathered by the Allies between 31 May and 14 June can be found in appendix 6 of the work by Major-General VON LETTOW-VORBECK, *Napoleon's Untergang*, p.513-518.
33. The time at which Wellington was informed of the French attack is still a subject of controversy. Recently, P HOFSCHRÖER, *op. cit.*, p.192-199, has reiterated – with reasons – the thesis formulated in 1847 by Major Gerwien, keeper of the archives of the Prussian general staff, according to which Wellington received the news at 9 o'clock in the morning. This chronology, which has been accepted by the majority of German historians, convinced Siborne, who adopted it in the third edition of his work on the 1815 campaign. Hofschröer's views have been refuted by John HUSSEY, in 'At What Time on 15 June 1815 did Wellington learn of Napoleon's Attack on the Prussians?', in *War in History*, 1999, 6, p.88-116.
34. A report by General Dörnberg on 6 June had induced Wellington to presume that, if there were to be a French attack, it would be accompanied by a diversion. Dörnberg wrote: 'It is supposed he [Napoleon] would make a false attack on the Prussians, and a real

one on the English army.' On the same day, the Prince of Orange had sent the Duke a report by one of Louis XVIII's envoys in France who returned from Paris with information according to which '… the Emperor will have taken himself to Avesnes to carry out a sham attack on the Allies in the area of Maubeuge, while the main attack should take place in the Flanders region between Lille and Tournay and towards Mons.', WELLINGTON, *Supplementary Dispatches*, Vol. X, 1863, p.423-424.

35. Col. HEYMES, *Relation de la Campagne de 1815*, Paris, 1829, p.6.

36. E DE GROUCHY, *Relation succincte de la campagne de 1815 en Belgique*, Paris, 1843, p.13.

37. C VON MÜFFLING, *Aus meinem Leben*, Berlin, 1855, p.198.

38. E LONGFORD, *The Years of the Sword*, London, 1971, p.502.

39. J DE BAS & J DE T'SERCLAES DE WOMMERSOM, *La campagne de 1815 aux Pays-Bas*, Brussels, 1908, t. l., p.427.

40. E LONGFORD, *op. cit.*, p.508.

41. 'Reminiscences of William Verner, 1782-1871, 7th Hussars' in *Army Historical Research*, London, 1965, p.40.

42. E LONGFORD, *op. cit.*, p.508.

43. The conversation took place in French between Wellington and the officers of the Prussian general staff, for the Duke did not speak German and Blücher spoke only his own tongue. P HOFSCHRÖER, *op. cit.*, p.233-242, quotes and analyses all the accounts by those present at the meeting. The version by A UFFINDELL, *The Eagle's Last Triumph*, London, 1994, p.73-76, based mainly on Wellington's later words (between 1836 and 1840), does not seem very likely, given that the Duke allows himself to openly criticise the tactical assets of his Prussian ally.

44. E LONGFORD, *op. cit.*, p.513.

45. *Documents inédits sur la campagne de 1815*, published by the Duc D'ELCHINGEN, Paris, 1840, p.42.

46. J LOGIE, Ph DE MEULENAERE, 'Le témoignage inédit de Fr. E Kellermann', in *Société Belge d'Études napoléoniennes*, 2001, n° 38, p.19.

47. BAUDUS, *Études sur Napoléon*, t. I, Paris, 1841, p.210-211.

48. Duc D'ELCHINGEN, *Documents inédits, op. cit.*, p.64-65; see the detailed study by Fr. T'SAS, 'Les mouvements du Ier corps de Drouet d'Erlon au cours des batailles de Ligny et des Quatre-Bras, le 16 juin 1815', in *Revue Belge d'Histoire Militaire*, XVII, 1967, p.268-300.

49. H HOUSSAYE, *op. cit.*, p.166.

50. W AERTS, *1815 – Waterloo*, p.125.

51. E LEFOL, *Souvenirs sur le Prytanée et l'Empereur Napoléon pendant les Cent-Jours*, Versailles, 1854, p.63.

52. H HOUSSAYE, *1815 - Waterloo*, p.176.

53. *Ibidem*, p.220.

54. E DE GROUCHY, *op. cit.*, p.18.

55. *Ibidem*, p.19-20.

56. *Idem*.

57. R MARGERIT, *18 juin 1815, Waterloo*, Paris, 1964, p.306.

58. E DE GROUCHY, *op. cit.*, p.23.

59. R MARGERIT, *op. cit.*, p.322-323.

60. E OWEN, *The Waterloo Papers*, p.10.

61. Lord MALMESBURY, *A series of Letters of the First Earl of Malmesbury to his Family and Friends from 1745 to 1820*, s.l., 2 vol., 1870, t. II, p.447.

62. C VON MÜFFLING, *op. cit.*, p.208.

63. E OWEN, *op. cit.*, p.10.

64. General CAVALIÉ MERCER, *Journal of the Waterloo Campaign*, London, 1927, p.147.

65. *Ibidem*, p.148.

66. H HOUSSAYE, *1815 - Waterloo*, p.264.

67. Jean-François LEMAIRE, *Les blessés dans les armées napoléoniennes*, Paris, 2002, p.72-73, shows that, contrary to legend, Sourd was not sent back to command his regiment after his amputation.

68. CAVALIÉ MERCER, *op. cit.*, p.152-154.

69. Baron PETIET, *Souvenirs militaires de l'Époque contemporaine*, Paris, 1844, p.204.

70. E OWEN, *op. cit.*, p.11.

71. NAPOLÉON, *Mémoires historiques de Napoléon. 1815*, London, 1820, p.123-124.

72. This assertion has been repeated by all the historians of Waterloo, from Thiers to Margerit. The error is partly excusable in the case of those who were writing in the nineteenth century and who had no other accounts but those which Napoléon himself had given in his *Mémoires*, even though they ought to have been alerted by the singular nature of a tour of the outposts by a commanding general on an ink-black and stormy night. Since the publication in 1921 of the *Souvenirs du Mameluk Ali sur l'Empereur Napoléon* and, even more so after the appearance in 1952 of Marchand's *Mémoires*, there can be no further doubt concerning Napoléon's presence at Le Caillou for the entire night – see J LOGIE, 'Napoléon à Waterloo', *Revue Belge d'Histoire Militaire*, XXI, 1976, p.586.

73. E OWEN, *op. cit.*, p.11. According to Fitzroy Somerset, the position originally chosen by the British staff would have been based around La Belle Alliance farm, but the Quartermaster-General, William de Lancey, considered that this gave too extended a front and had a position adopted 1,300 metres to the rear, along the Chemin de la Croix.

74. Marquess of ANGLESEY, *One Leg*, London, 1961, p.132-133.

75. Elizabeth LONGFORD, *Wellington. The Years of the Sword*, p.535-536. from H Houssaye onward, the majority of historians have alleged that Wellington received Blücher's dispatch, sent from Wavre at eleven in the evening, at two o'clock in the morning. There is no proof to support this assertion. On the contrary, the testimonies of witnesses in Wellington's entourage indicate that the Prussian courier did not arrive at Waterloo until the morning – at six o'clock according to Lord Fitzroy Somerset, the Duke's military secretary, or at nine o'clock according to General Müffling, the Prussian liaison officer wirh Wellington. These testimonies are of the highest value and are consistent with the difficulties encountered by the courier, who had to cover nearly twenty kilometres, at night, in the rain, through unfamiliar country and along bad roads.

76. A BRETT-JAMES, *The Hundred Days*, London, 1964, p.95-96.

77. J CARMICHAEL-SMYTH, *Histoire abrégée des guerres…*, Liège, 1843, p.324. The officer commanding the engineers in Wellington's army considered it to be '… passable for cavalry, infantry and artillery in nearly all directions'.

78. J SHAW-KENNEDY, *Notes on the Battle of Waterloo*, London, 1865, p.133.

79. WELLINGTON, *Supplementary Despatches*, Vol. IX, p.494, Memorandum of 23 December 1814.

80. NAPOLÉON, *Mémoires historiques de Napoléon. 1815*, p.127-128.

81. H HOUSSAYE, *1815 – Waterloo*, p.311.

82. R MARGERIT, *op. cit.*, p.335-336 and ref. quoted. The words reported by Jérôme were imagined, since Wellington's decision to retreat on Mont-Saint-Jean was not taken until the morning of the 17th at Quatre-Bras.

83. H HOUSSAYE, *op. cit.*, p.311-312.

84. COUCQUEBEAU, *La Belle Alliance. Ode dédiée à S.A.R. le prince d'Orange...*, Brussels, 1816, p.17.

85. J B DROUET D'ERLON, *Vie militaire écrite par lui-même et dédiée à ses amis*, Paris, 1844, p.97.

86. H HOUSSAYE, *op. cit.*, p.323-324.

87. J B LEMONIER-DELAFOSSE, *Souvenirs militaires*, Le Havre, 1850, p.406.

88. J LOGIE, 'Napoléon à Waterloo', in *Revue Belge d'Histoire militaire*, XXI-6, 1976, p.589.

89. *Souvenirs et correspondances sur la bataille de Waterloo*, Paris, 2000, p.52-54. According to the account by General Albert de Salle, who was in command of this battery, it actually had only 54 guns, of which 24 were twelve-pounders. General Ruty, commander-in-chief of the artillery, having observed that this battery was not near enough to the British line, gave instructions for the guns to be moved forward, but this was frustrated by the charge of Uxbridge's cavalry.

90. E OWEN, *The Waterloo Papers*, p.56. Colonel Augustus Frazer, who commanded the British horse artillery at Waterloo, confirmed that the British artillery had been given strict orders to fire only on attacking troops, disregarding the enemy cannon.

91. At about half-past four, Durutte's skirmishers took possession of several houses in La Marache, but they were driven out again by a counter-attack by two companies of Nassauers.

92. L STOUFF, *op. cit.*, p.156, note 1.

93. H HOUSSAYE, *op. cit.*, p.356.

94. J SHAW-KENNEDY, *op. cit.*, p.98-101. The author, who filled the post of chief of staff in Alten's division, had assembled his battalions in oblong formation, composed of four companies in the front face, four in the rear and one on each side, which allowed for a rapid deployment in line if necessary. Alten's division was drawn up with a first echelon of five oblongs and a second of four.

95. CAVALIÉ MERCER, *op. cit.*, p.171-172.

96. R H GRONOW, *The Reminiscences and Recollections of Captain Gronow*, London, 1862, t. I., p.190-191.

97. General G GOURGAUD, *Campagne de 1815*, Brussels, 1818, p.86.

98. NAPOLÉON, *Mémoires historiques de Napoléon. 1815*, p.165.

99. In his account, Kellermann strongly criticised the engagement of his cavalry corps and that of General Guyot. He attempted to hold back a last reserve by ordering the brigade of *carabiniers* not to take part in the charges, but his orders were ignored. As a consequence, at the end of the battle the French no longer had any cavalry with which to oppose the Allied efforts.

100. Archives historiques de l'Armée de Terre, Vincennes, *Inventaire Tuetey*, n° 717 to 729.

101. J LOGIE, Ph DE MEULENAERE, 'Le témoignage inédit de Fr. E Kellermann...', p.26.

102. J B LEMONIER-DELAFOSSE, *op. cit.*, p.384.

103. E LONGFORD, *op. cit.*, p.569.

104. M GIROD DE L'AIN, *Vie militaire du général Foy*, Paris, s.d., p.282.

105. BAUDUS, *op. cit.*, p.227.

106. H T SIBORNE, *Waterloo Letters*, London, 1861, letter 96 from Captain Pringle.

107. E LONGFORD, *op. cit.*, p.574.

108. The first battalion of this regiment defended the gravel pit opposite La Haie-Sainte for a long time.

109. Marquess of ANGLESEY, *op. cit.*, p.148.

110. E LONGFORD, *op. cit.*, p.576.

111. A BRETT-JAMES, *op. cit.*, p.166-167.

112. *Journal de route du capitaine Robinaux*, Paris, 1908, p.210.

113. Vicomte A D'AVOUT, 'L'infanterie de la Garde à Waterloo', in *Carnets de la Sabretache*, 1905, p.29.

114. H T SIBORNE, *op. cit.*, p.366.

115. *Ibidem*, p.340.

116. LARREGUY DE CIVRIEUX, *Souvenirs d'un cadet 1812-1823*, Paris, 1912, p.170-171.

117. H HOUSSAYE, *op. cit.*, p.403.

118. Vicomte A D'AVOUT, *op. cit.*, p.20.

119. *Ibidem*, p.34.

120. W AERTS, *op. cit.*, p.192.

121. *Ibidem*, p.193.

122. *Idem.*

123. Major VON DAMITZ, *Histoire de la campagne de 1815*, t.I., p.245.

124. NAPOLÉON, *Mémoires historiques de Napoléon. 1815*, p.143.

125. *Ibidem*, p.148.

126. *Ibidem*, p.146.

127. P HOFSCHRÖER, *1815, The Waterloo Campaign. The German Victory*, p.97.

128. W AERTS, *op. cit.*, p.196. The Prussian chief of staff had in fact dictated a postscript to the letter that Blücher had sent to Müffling at half-past nine, which showed that his mistrust of Wellington's intentions was still aroused: 'General Gneisenau has the honour of requesting you to make a careful assessment of whether the Duke really intends to fight where he now stands or whether it is simply a demonstration, which could become very dangerous for our army.'

129. *Ibidem*, p.211.

130. E DE GROUCHY, *op. cit.*, 8th series, p.51. The allegations made by Colonel Marbot in a letter to Marshal Grouchy in May 1830, to the effect that his hussars would have attacked the heads of the Prussian columns as they crossed the Lasne, are contradicted by all the accounts from the Prussian side.

131. P HOFSCHRÖER, *op. cit.*, p.116.

132. Vicomte A D'AVOUT, *op. cit.*, p.7.

133. *Ibidem*, p.9-11. General Pelet's version is confirmed by the account of a Prussian officer, J L LOWE, *Mit der Schlesischen Landwehr nach Paris-Erlebnisse aus den Befreiungskriegen 1813, 1814, 1815*, Berlin, 1996, p. 75-79.

134. J DE BAS & J DE T'SERCLAES, *op. cit.*, t. III, p.509.

135. Vicomte A D'AVOUT, *op. cit.*, p.19.

136. C VON MÜFFLING, *op. cit.*, p.215, and L VON REICHE, *Memorien des königlich preussischen General der Infanterie Ludwig von Reiche*, Leipzig, 1857, 2 vol., t. II, p.209-213.

137. H HOUSSAYE, *op. cit.*, p.403.

138. Major von Keller sold one of the Emperor's carriages to the Prince Regent. It was then rapidly sold on to a certain Bullock, who placed it on show in the Egyptian Hall in London. The coach subsequently passed to Madame Tussaud's and became one of that museum's attractions. It was destroyed in a fire in 1925. Some of the diamonds were presented to the King of Prussia. The Emperor's sword and hat remained in the Blücher family. In 1973, one of its descendants presented one of the carriages captured at Genappe to the Malmaison museum.

139. J LOGIE, 'La rencontre de Wellington et de Blücher au soir de Waterloo', in *Revue Belge d'Histoire militaire*, XVIII-3, 1969, p.161-184.

140. Lt. Col. Basil Jackson, *Notes and Reminiscences of a Staff Officer*,

London, 1903, p. 57-58.

141. 5th Earl STANHOPE, *Notes of Conversations with the Duke of Wellington*, London, 1888, p.245; J LOGIE, 'La rencontre de Wellington et de Blücher au soir de Waterloo', in *Revue Belge d'Histoire militaire*, XVIII-3, 1969, p.161-184.

142. This officer, born in 1786 of a very old Scottish family, was the brother of Lord Aberdeen (1784-1860), who was several times Prime Minister. Alexander Gordon entered the army in 1803 and took part in the campaigns in Portugal and Spain. Promoted lieutenant-colonel in 1813 and made a Knight Commander of the Bath in 1814, he was noticed by Wellington and joined his personal circle in 1810. In 1815 he was his aide-de-camp, enjoying his friendship and his confidence.

143. E LONGFORD, *op. cit*, p.583.

144. A. BRETT-JAMES, *The Hundred days, Napoleon's Last Campaign from eye-witness accounts*, London, 1964, p. 182.

145. H HOUSSAYE, *op. cit.*, p.421.

146. John KEEGAN, *Anatomie de la bataille*, Paris, 1993, p.175.

147. G R GLEIG, *The Story of the Battle of Waterloo*, London, 1847, p.255.

148. A SOUBIRAN, *Le baron Larrey, chirurgien de Napoléon*, Paris, 1966, p.346. Intercepted and captured by the Prussians during the retreat, Larrey, bearing two sabre wounds, was taken for Napoléon and almost shot. He was saved by another surgeon, who recognised him and conducted him to Blücher, whose son he had cared for in the past. He was treated with the greatest consideration and later taken first to Louvain and then to Brussels, where he immediately lent his services to the hospitals.

149. R L BIANCO, *Wellington's Surgeon. General Sir James McGrigor*, Durham, 1974, p.159.

150. CAVALIÉ MERCER, *op. cit.*, p.182-183.

151. L LAUDY, *Les lendemains de Waterloo*, Braine-l'Alleud, 1921, p.25.

152. B JACKSON, *op. cit.*, p.91-92.

153. R L BIANCO, *op. cit.*, p.153.

154. A BRETT-JAMES, *The Hundred Days, Napoleon's last Campaign from eye witness accounts*, p. 201.

155. J KEEGAN, *op. cit.*, p.157-158.

156. Sgt.-Major E. COTTON, *A Voice from Waterloo*, Bruxelles, 1913, p. 289-290.

157. J B JOLYET, 'Souvenirs de 1815', in *Revue de Paris*, 1903, p.547.

158. A BIKAR, 'Les pertes à la bataille de Waterloo, Légende et réalité', *Bulletin de la Société Belge d'Études napoléoniennes*, 1990, nº 11, p.5-11.

159. W SIBORNE, *op. cit.*, p.252.

160. Every indication suggests that the Belgian-Dutch casualties given by F de Bas, in *Prins Frederik der Nederlanden en zijn tijd*, Schiedam, 1902, t. III 2, p.1228, were greatly over-estimated; A BIKAR, *op. cit.*, p.10, has compared the official casualty figures for hussar regiment nº 8 – 11 killed, 151 wounded and 112 missing, for a total strength of 439 officers and other ranks – with the numbers in the regimental roll. These are very different: 6 killed, 10 wounded and 33 deserters on the day of the battle, to which should be added another 54 between 1 and 17 June.

161. J Fr LEMAIRE, *Les blessés dans les armées napoléoniennes*, Paris, 2002, p.31-96. The wounded in the Napoleonic Wars pose a difficult problem. Jean-François Lemaire's thesis has revealed the relative severity of many of the wounds recorded in the official returns, but which did not prevent those affected from distinguishing themselves several days or several weeks later. Thus, General de Bonnemains, who fought in the 1815 campaign,

received a sabre wound in the left shoulder on 3 November 1806, but was observed at the capture of Lübeck, three days later!

162. J KEEGAN, *op. cit.*, p.175-181.

163. L CAPDEVILLA, D VOLDMAN, *Nos morts. Les sociétés occidentales face aux tués de la guerre*, Paris, 2002, p.65.

164. G BRAIVE, *Duhesme*, Cercle d'histoire et d'archéologie du pays de Genappe, Cahier nº 12, 2001, p.536-537.

165. A PIGEARD, *L'armée de Napoléon. Organisation et vie quotidienne*, Paris, 2000, p.226-227. One of the most enduring traditions of the French army of that time was the sale by auction of the effects and belongings of officers and men who had been killed. If possible, the money from the sale was sent to the family, if not, it was added to the unofficial regimental funds.

166. L LAUDY, *op. cit.*, p.35.

167. Archives générales de la Royaume, Brussels, miscellaneous manuscripts, Dansaert Papers, nº 21.

168. L LAUDY, *op. cit.*, p.35.

169. Archives générales de la Royaume, Brussels, Provincial Government of Brabant, Series A, nº 18.

170. W AERTS, *op. cit.*, p.199.

171. *Ibidem*, p.203-204.

172. M LEFOL, *Souvenirs sur le Prytanée militaire de Saint-Cyr...*, Versailles, 1854, p.76-77. Some historians have seen in Grouchy's meal of strawberries a symbol of his indolence and indecision. The aide-de-camp of General the Baron Lefol, who related the anecdote, commented on it in these terms: 'In the field, the officer, like the soldier, lives on whatever comes to hand – too often he has no choice. At Walhain he [Grouchy] ate strawberries, probably because he had not been able to find any more substantial food, which would undoubtedly have been better for his stomach.'

173. E DE GROUCHY, *op. cit.*, p.33-34.

174. W AERTS, *op. cit.*, p.227-228.

175. E DE GROUCHY, *op. cit.*, Appendix IV, p.49.

176. *Journal du général Fantin des Odoards*, Paris, 1895, p.433-434.

177. W AERTS, *op. cit.*, p.233-234.

178. E DE GROUCHY, *op. cit.*, p.41.

179. *Ibidem*, p.43.

180. *Ibidem*, p.42.

181. E DE GROUCHY, *op. cit.*, Appendix IV, p.47.

182. General C VON CLAUSEWITZ, *Geschichte des Feldzuges von 1815 in Frankreich*, Berlin, 1835; General Antoine DE JOMINI, *Précis politique et militaire de la campagne de 1815*, Brussels, 1846.

183. The criticisms expressed with regard to Soult come principally from the works of Henry Houssaye. Napoléon, in his writings on Saint Helena, made no accusations against the major-general.

184. J DE BAS and J DE T'SERCLAES, *op. cit.*, t. II, p.61.

185. H HOUSSAYE, *op. cit.*, p.357.

186. NAPOLÉON, *Mémoires historiques de Napoléon. 1815*, p.19-130.

187. R MARGERIT, *op. cit.*, p.334.

188. Napoléon had at his disposal 266 artillery pieces, while Wellington could put no more than 174 into the field.

PART TWO

1. R CHALON, 'Numismatique de Waterloo', in *Revue Belge de Numismatique*, Brussels, 1878, p.421-443; Major L L GORDON, *British Battles & Medals*, London, 1971, p.48-55.
2. J KEEGAN, *op. cit.*, p.181.
3. P ERRERA, 'La dotation du Prince de Waterloo', in *Revue de l'Université de Bruxelles*, December 1911, p.225-242; the woods of Bossut, Petit-Bossut and Pierrepont, in particular, which covered a part of the Quatre-Bras battlefield, formed part of the inheritance.
4. The fate of the entailed property had been settled by the French parliamentary bills of 12 May 1835 and 7 May 1849. Amongst others may be cited the question directed to the Minister of Finances in the Second Section of the Chamber during the examination of the 1890 budget, and the questions posed by the parliamentarians Caluwaert (Chamber, 1911), Bary (Chamber, 1966), du Monceau de Bergendael (Senate, 1973) and Humblet (Senate, 1983).
5. Jean E HUMBLET, *Wellington et l'argent des Belges ou la seconde bataille de Waterloo*, Brussels, 2001.
6. In 1988, by joint agreement between the Duke and the Belgian Government, the pension, without the defined capital, was terminated, the Duke receiving 25 hectares of land in exchange.
7. J R LECONTE, 'Notes sur le fonds dit "Pour l'encouragement et le soutien du service militaire" ou "Fonds de Waterloo", créé en 1815 par Guillaume Ier, roi des Pays-Bas', in *Revue Belge d'Histoire militaire*, XVI-2, p.83-91.
8. Algemeen Rijksarchief, s'Gravenhage, Staatssecretarie, n° 6573.
9. Just BERLAND, *Les dommages de guerre après Valmy, département de la Marne*, Chalons-sur-Marne, 1931, p.365.
10. In 1815, the administrative organisation of the former Belgian *départements* of the Napoléonic Empire were in a state of transition. At the head of the *départements*, which with the implementation of the new Constitution would be called provinces, the *Intendant* had taken the place of the *Préfet*, the *Sous-Intendant* that of the *Sous-Préfet*, and the *Conseil de Préfecture* would henceforth be called the *Conseil d'Intendance*.
11. Archives générales du Royaume, Provincial Government of Brabant, Series A, n° 18, letter from the duc d'Ursel, Commissioner-General of the Interior to the *Intendant* of South Brabant, 3 December 1815.
12. *Ibidem*, letter of 23 August 1817.
13. *Idem*.
14. Algemeen Rijksarchief, s'Gravenhage, Staatssecretarie Kabinet, n° 6506.
15. A debate in the municipal council of Jamioulx (Charleroi district) on 7 July 1815 reveals the same desire to bring aid to those most in need. A provisional aid had been granted to the *commune* by the Minister of the Interior. 'After a debate, the Council had decided to distribute this sum to the heads of family with children to support, who were in dire want, owing to complete lack of work, on top of the great destruction suffered by the village, who have been supported by the better-off of the village, there being none of the latter who can be deemed to be ruined', Musée du Caillou, Libioulle Papers.
16. Algemeen Rijksarchief, s'Gravenhage, Staatssecretarie Kabinet, n° 6506.
17. Archives générales du Royaume, Provincial Government of Brabant, Series A, n° 19. According to the table, the damage in the Brussels district, of which in those days the *commune* of Chapelle-Saint-Lambert was a part, the losses of standing crops had been assessed at 8,456 francs and those of livestock at 5,071 francs.
18. *Ibidem*, letter from the governor to the Wavre Regency on 10 April 1818: 'The distribution must not be made on a pro rata basis of the losses suffered, since both humanity and justice demand that it be based on needs and on the greater or lesser effect that the misfortunes to which they have been subjected has had on their lives and on their means of livelihood.'

PART THREE

1. Archives générales du Royaume, Provincial Government of Brabant, Series A, n° 18, letter from the *sous-intendant* of the Nivelles district to the governor of South Brabant, 6 April 1816.
2. Alain REYNIERS, 'Waterloo ou la déroute de l'Aigle est gloire posthume du Lion', in *Recherche en communication*, n° 12, 1999, p.81-96.
3. There is no question here of an exhaustive inventory of all the monuments commemorating the 1815 campaign.
4. In 1890 the mortal remains of these officers were collected beneath the monument raised in Evere cemetery. The monuments to Holland and Stables can now be found in the gardens of the Musée Wellington.
5. J LOGIE, 'Le cent cinquantenaire du Lion de Waterloo', *Revue belge d'histoire militaire*, XXI-8, December 1976, p.830-831.
6. Its appearance was altered at the beginning of 1914 by the construction of masonry buttresses and the installation of a grid, at the instigation of the Society of German Officers in Belgium (Ministry of Foreign Affairs, Brussels, B75).
7. See the chapter devoted to the Lion of Waterloo.
8. *Bulletin de la Société belge d'Études Napoléoniennes*, n° 31, September 1959, p.24-25.
9. In 1889, the last memorial to an individual was mounted on the walls of Goumont, in the form of a plaque commemorating the death of Thomas Crawford, an officer in the Guards, by one of his relatives.
10. *Carnet de la Sabretache*, 1904, p.67.
11. The cockerel originally proposed was in the end replaced at the base of the column by a bas-relief in bronze representing Victor Hugo, the work of the sculptor Demanet.
12. *La Belgique militaire*, 28 May and 25 June 1911.
13. Ministry of Foreign Affairs, B75, note from Comte de Hemricourt de Grunne to Baron Van der Elst (24 April 1914).
14. *Ibidem*, political departmental note for the Minister, 27 May 1913.
15. N° of 7 September 1913.
16. T F (Théo FLEISCHMANN), 'Le souvenir de Lucien Laudy', in *Bulletin de la Société belge d'Études Napoléoniennes*, n° 65,

December 1968, p.5-6.

17. The bibliography concerning the construction of the Waterloo monument is fairly limited: W AERTS, 'Les origines du Lion de Waterloo', in *Folklore brabançon*, 19th year, 1940, no 114, p.451-477; J PURAYE, 'Aux origines d'un monument célèbre. Le Lion de Waterloo relie des souvenirs historiques à l'industrie sidéurgique liégeoise', in *Cahiers léopoldiens*, new series, VI, February 1960, p.24-32; J LOGIE, 'Le cent cinquantenaire du Lion de Waterloo', *Revue belge d'histoire militaire*, XXI-8, December 1976, p.828-859; M WATHELET, 'Ériger la mémoire d'un lieu: le monument de Waterloo et le ministère du Waterstaat (1816-1830)', in *Waterloo, lieu de mémoire européenne (1815-2000). Histoires et controverses*, Louvain-La-Neuve, 2000, p.161-183.

18. Georges JACQUEMIN, *Les boteresses liégeoises à la butte du Lion de Waterloo*, (1826), Braine-l'Alleud, 2000, p.122-123.

19. Georges JACQUEMIN has also uncovered traces of traditions which corroborate this use of local workers, *op. cit.*, p.208-217.

20. L.V.A.N. (Louis NAVEZ), *À propos du champ de bataille de Waterloo. Ce qu'on en a fait; ce qu'on veut en faire*, Brussels, s.d., p.51.

21. Article in the *Morning Post*, 23 May 1913.

22. Jean COPIN, 'Délicieux Brabant, Waterloo, le folklore de la bataille', in *Folklore brabançon*, 1961, n° 151, p.438-442; Jean-Jacques PATTYN, 'En marge du 175e. Un projet de monument au Belges de 1815 du comte Louis Cavens', in *Bulletin de la Société belge d'Études Napoléoniennes*, 1960, n° 11, p.12-17.

23. L CAVENS, *Waterloo sera sauvé*, s.l., n.d., p.1-2.

24. Ministry of Foreign Affairs, Brussels, B75, letter to the Minister for Foreign Affairs, 17 May 1907.

25. *Ibidem*, undated note for the political department to the Minister.

26. In the *Morning Post* article previously quoted, D Boulger had made a suggestion which was completely impractical, given the French refusal to be associated in any way in the commemoration of the centenary of Waterloo. Great Britain had acquired Hougoumont (Goumont) and France La Belle Alliance and Le Caillou. Belgium had La Haie-Sainte and would have prevented any building work in the vicinity, which it was important to preserve.

27. L NAVEZ, *Quelques observations concernant la loi du 26 mars 1914 pour la préservation du champ de bataille de Waterloo*, Brussels, 1914, p.12-13. This author correctly observed that the protected area was defined only by a plan attached to the bill, which was not published along with the legal text in the Belgian *Moniteur*. The original of this plan is preserved in the Institut Géographique National. The thickness of the line enclosing the protected areas represents a full-scale width of 10 to 20 metres, the status of which is unknown. The lines of demarcation define registered plots, which are not listed in the bill.

28. Some fifteen years later, the prohibition on new building work was contravened by the government itself, when in 1929 it authorised the construction of the Fichermont Dominican convent along the Vieux Chemin de Wavre, in the middle of the position occupied by the British left wing.

29. *Annales parlementaires*, Senate, sitting on 26 March 1914, p.177.

30. Ministry of Foreign Affairs, Brussels, letter from Heusch to Bassompierre, 4 July 1914.

31. *Documents parlementaires*. Chamber of Representatives, session of 1932-1933, n° 98; *L'Étoile belge*, 23 December 1930; *Le Soir*, 22 January 1931.

32. The items concerning the French perception of Waterloo are due entirely to Jean-Marc LARGEAUD. Pending the publication of his thesis, one has to fall back on his article: 'Découvertes de Waterloo', In *Les cahiers de la vie urbaine et rurale. Lieux de mémoire de guerre*, n° 129, December 1995, p.34-47.

33. Jacques LOGIE, 'Le cent cinquantenaire du Lion de Waterloo', in *Revue belge d'Histoire militaire*, XXI-8, December 1976, p.828-859. All the quotations have been taken from this article.

34. J LORETTE, 'Problèms de politique étrangère sous Léopold Ier. À propos d'éventuelles participations belges à la guerre de Crimée, 1854-1856', in *Bulletin des séances de l'Académie royale des Sciences d'Outre-mer*, Brussels, 1965-2, p.235-236. This pamphlet was translated into English under the title '*Reply of a Belgian officer to the charges made in England against the character of the Belgian troops in the Campaign of 1815*' and sent to every member of the British Parliament.

35. *Annales parlementaires*, Senate, 1854-1855, sitting on 27 February.

36. L MADELIN, 'Henry Houssaye', in *Revue des Deux Mondes*, 1911, t. VI, p.666-696.

37. François T'SAS, 'Les Waterloo Letters', in *Bulletin de la Société belge d'Études napolèoniennes*, 1971, n° 77, p.12-23. The article by P HOFSCHRÖER, 'Peer Pressure: Siborne & The Waterloo Model', in *The Waterloo Journal*, Vol. 25, 1, 2003, p.19-27, reveals the difficult conditions under which Siborne worked.

38. This simplified map has been reproduced many times.

39. L NAVEZ, *La campagne de 1815 de Waterloo à Paris, Brussels, 1912, p.114*.

40. *Ibidem*, p.117.

41. See John HUSSEY, 'At What Time on 15 June 1815 Did Wellington Learn of Napoleon's Attack on the Prussians?', in *War in History*, 1999, 6 (1) 88-116.

42. For a certain number of writers, particularly those in the twentieth century, the reference to Waterloo, often in the title, is no more than a pretext and we have given our consideration only to those for whom the battle plays an important role in the plot or in the theme.

43. Jean LACROIX, *Victor Hugo: Mille jours en Belgique*, Waterloo, 2002, p.207.

44. Jean LACROIX, *Waterloo et les écrivains*, Waterloo, 2000, *passim*. Edgard Quinet, prior to his exile in Brussels, had written two poems about Waterloo, 'Les bergers' and 'L'orage', which figure in his anthology *Napoléon*, which appeared in Paris in 1836.

45. In 1907, A DU BOIS published an anthology of poems in the same vein, entitled *La destruction du Lion de Waterloo*, which he described as 'a sombre and menacing beast'.

46. J P MATTEI (director) *Napoléon et le cinéma*, Ajaccio, 1998, p.325-338. In this descriptive filmography, compiled by Hervé Dumont, we have chosen only those films which depict the battle, his appraisals of which we have been permitted to reproduce.

47. This text appears as an appendix to the pamphlet by Hector FLEISCHMANN, *La tragique histoire du château d'Hougoumont*, Paris, 1913.

48. Édouard ARNOULDY, 'Waterloo de Karl Grune ou deux visages de Napoléon au cinéma', in *Napoléon et la cinéma*, p.111-119.

49. J W M HICHBERGER, *Images of the Army. The Military in British Arts, 1815-1914*, Manchester, 1998.

50. Annie JOURDAN, *Napoléon, héros, imperator, mécène*, Paris, 1998, p.152-173.

51. The painting is in the Royal Hospital at Chelsea. In 1817 Jones published *The Battle of Waterloo, with those of Ligny and*

Quatre-Bras described by Eye-Witnesses, illustrated by numerous engravings of very great interest.

52. The painting is in the Tate Gallery, London.

53. This monumental work (3.24 m x 2.65 m) portrayed 800 figures and is currently to be found in the Williamson Art Gallery & Museum in Birkenhead.

54. François ROBICHON, 'Victor Hugo, "peintre" des guerres napoléoniennes', in *Hugo et la guerre*, Paris, 2003, p.87-102.

55. François ROBICHON, *La peinture militaire française de 1871 à 1914*, Paris, 1998. p.193.

56. J A DE SEDOUY, *Le Congrès de Vienne, L'Europe contre la France, 1812-1815*, Paris, 2002, p.262.

57. Jacques-Henri PIRENNE, 'Les conséquences de la bataille', in *Waterloo, 1815. L'Europe face à Napoléon*, Brussels, 1990, p.168.

58. *Ibidem*, p.169.

59. J LOGIE, 'Conclusions du colloque' in *Influence du modèle judicaire français en Europe sous la Révolution et l'Empire*, Lille, 1999. p.327-330.

Acknowledgements

Firstly, my thanks to my long-standing friends and leading authorities on the period, who have helped me with their advice and their erudition: Pierre d'Harville, curator of the Musée Napoléon at Ligny, Philippe de Callataÿ, curator of the Musée Wellington at Waterloo, Philippe de Meulenaere, bibliographical archivist of the campaign, Dorian Van Hoorde, specialist in weapons of the past, and Jacques Declercq, experienced collector and numismatist.

I should also like to thank Madame Françoise Dupriez and Monsieur Gilbert Menne, who allowed us full access to the treasures in the Musée Wellington and to those in the museum at Le Caillou.

However, as with all my other works, this one would never have seen the light of day without the assistance of my wife who, as usual, supplied constant encouragement and wise criticism.

INDEX

Page references in *italic* refer to captions.